The Multi-Asset Strategist

Stocks, Bonds, and Alternatives in Harmony

Noble Trex

Published by NobleTrex Press

For permissions and other inquiries, write to:
P.O. Box 3132, Framingham, MA 01701, USA

Contents

Introduction

In the grand orchestra of global finance, the role of the multi-asset strategist is akin to that of a conductor. Where a single-asset manager may master the violin or the percussion, perfecting the nuances of a specific instrument, the multi-asset allocator must understand how the entire ensemble resonates in unison. The objective is not merely to select individual securities that perform well in isolation, but to construct a symphony-a coherent portfolio-where the interaction of disparate asset classes creates a whole that is robust, efficient, and greater than the sum of its parts. *The Multi-Asset Strategist: Stocks, Bonds, and Alternatives in Harmony* is dedicated to the art and science of that composition.

The modern investment landscape has rendered the simplistic heuristics of the past obsolete. The traditional 60/40 portfolio, once the gold standard of diversification, faces existential challenges in an era of suppressed yields, shifting inflation regimes, and structurally higher correlations. To navigate this complexity, the contemporary allocator must evolve from a gatherer of assets into an architect of exposures. This text is designed to guide that evolution, moving systematically from the granular mathematics of return measurement to the high-level philosophy of risk governance.

We begin our journey by establishing the "Quantitative Foundations of Multi-Asset Investing." Finance is a language spoken in the dialect of probability and statistics. Before one can allocate capital effectively, one must master the tools of measurement. We strip away the marketing gloss of retail finance to reveal the rigorous standards required for professional management. This involves a deep examination of compounding mechanics, the non-normality of return distributions, and the critical distinction between arithmetic and geometric realities. We explore the dangers of estimation error-the risk that our maps do not reflect the territory-and the vital importance of data architecture. In a world awash with data, the ability to distinguish signal from noise, and to construct benchmarks that are free from look-ahead and survivorship biases, is the first line of defense against capital destruction.

With the mathematical scaffolding in place, we descend into "The Asset Class Ecosystem." A strategist must be intimately familiar with the building blocks at their disposal. We dissect equities not merely as tickers, but as engines of growth susceptible to factor decomposition. We analyze fixed income beyond simple yield, exploring the convexity and duration mechanics that allow bonds to serve as both a source of carry and a hedge against deflationary shock. Furthermore, we venture into the complex terrain of credit, commodities, and real assets, treating them as distinct sources of risk premia. The discussion extends to private markets, where the theoretical elegance of modern portfolio theory clashes with the practical frictions of illiquidity, forcing the allocator to grapple with the realities of commitment pacing and the J-curve.

However, a collection of assets does not constitute a strategy. "Portfolio Theory, Dynamics, and Regimes" bridges the gap between the components and the whole. Here, we delve into the physics of finance. We examine the nature of correlation-not as a static number, but as a dynamic, unstable force that shifts violently during market stress. We revisit the Mean-Variance framework, acknowledging its genius while ruthlessly exposing its sensitivity to input assumptions. Crucially, we introduce the concept of macro regimes. Assets do not move in a vacuum; they breathe the air of the macroeconomy. By mapping asset behavior to the four quadrants of growth and inflation, and understanding the transmission mechanisms of monetary policy, the strategist learns to position portfolios not for the past, but for the probable economic future.

Transitioning from theory to implementation, "Modern Portfolio Construction and Risk Budgeting" addresses the engineering challenge of allocation. The shift from capital allocation to risk allocation represents one of the most significant advancements in modern finance. We explore the philosophy of Risk Parity, where the goal is to balance risk contributions rather than capital weights, often utilizing leverage to equalize the playing field between low-volatility bonds and high-volatility equities. We discuss robust optimization techniques designed to immunize the portfolio against uncertainty, and the Black-Litterman model, which allows the systematic integration of subjective views into quantitative baselines.

Yet, even the most elegantly constructed portfolio is vulnerable to the "black swan." "Advanced Risk Management and Tail Control" deals with the dark side of distribution. Traditional risk metrics like Value-at-Risk (VaR) often fail precisely when they are needed most. We examine the limitations of these measures and explore the mechanics of correlation breakdown and contagion. The text provides a rigorous framework for stress testing and scenario analysis, ensuring that the portfolio is resilient not just to statistical noise, but to genuine regime shifts and liquidity crises. We also tackle the difficult calculus of tail risk hedging-weighing the bleeding cost of protection against the preservation of capital during market crashes.

To enhance the portfolio's efficiency and reach, we turn to "Derivatives, Overlays, and Alternative Strategies." The modern toolkit extends far beyond cash securities. We discuss how to utilize futures for capital-efficient beta management, allowing the strategist to gain exposure without fully funding the position, thereby freeing up capital for alpha generation. We explore the world of options, not as instruments of speculation, but as tools for shaping non-linear payoff profiles. Additionally, we analyze alternative risk premia and systematic trend following (CTAs), strategies that offer the holy grail of uncorrelated returns, particularly during periods of prolonged market distress.

Finally, we arrive at the operational reality of "Performance, Governance, and Lifecycle Management." A strategy is only as good as its execution and its governance. We analyze the frictions of the real world: transaction costs, taxes, and the implementation shortfall. We debate the merits of various rebalancing protocols, seeking the optimal trade-off between tracking error and turnover. Perhaps most importantly, we address the behavioral aspects of investing. The greatest enemy of the multi-asset portfolio is often the emotional reaction of its manager or stakeholders during periods of underperformance. We outline governance frameworks designed to enforce discipline, ensuring that the logic of the investment policy statement survives the volatility of the market.

This book is not a collection of trading tips; it is a comprehensive manual for the design and maintenance of wealth across generations and regimes. It assumes the reader is willing to engage with complexity, to challenge received wisdom, and to appreciate that in multi-asset investing, there are no silver bullets-only trade-offs. By harmonizing the mathematical rigor of quantitative finance with the economic intuition of the fundamentalist, *The Multi-Asset Strategist* aims to equip you with the clarity and confidence to conduct your own financial symphony amidst the noise of the global markets.

Chapter 1

Quantitative Foundations of Multi-Asset Investing

Before constructing the skyscraper of a multi-asset portfolio, we must stress-test the bedrock. This chapter bridges the gap between academic finance and the messy reality of trading desks, defining the specific mathematical language-and its crucial dialects-necessary to measure what we earn, quantify what we risk, and survive the frictions of the real market.

1.1 Return Measurement and Compounding Mechanics

Multi-asset portfolio construction begins with a deceptively simple question: *what do we mean by "return"*? The answer determines how we compare asset classes, how we forecast, and how we judge whether a strategy truly compounds wealth. This section builds the quantitative foundation for the rest of the book by separating three closely related concepts:

- **Single-period returns** (what happened over one period),
- **Arithmetic average return** (a statistical average across periods), and
- **Geometric (compound) return** (the long-run growth rate of wealth).

The key takeaway is that **volatility is not just "noise" around an average**. Volatility mechanically reduces compound growth for any asset that is allowed to fluctuate, even when the arithmetic average return is unchanged. This reduction is commonly called *volatility drag* or *variance drain*.

Single-period returns: simple vs. log

Let P_t be the price (or total-return index level) at time t. The **simple (arithmetic) return** from t to $t+1$ is

$$R_{t+1} = \frac{P_{t+1} - P_t}{P_t} = \frac{P_{t+1}}{P_t} - 1.$$

Wealth compounding under simple returns is multiplicative:

$$W_T = W_0 \prod_{t=1}^{T} (1 + R_t).$$

This multiplicative structure is the heart of why averaging returns is subtle: the *path* matters.

A second common definition is the **log return** (continuously compounded return),

$$r_{t+1} = \ln\left(\frac{P_{t+1}}{P_t}\right) = \ln(1 + R_{t+1}).$$

Log returns are additive through time:

$$\ln\left(\frac{W_T}{W_0}\right) = \sum_{t=1}^{T} r_t.$$

This additivity makes log returns convenient for aggregation and many statistical models. However, investors ultimately care about *wealth*, which compounds geometrically.

Arithmetic average return: a one-period expectation, not a growth rate

Given a time series of T simple returns $\{R_1, \ldots, R_T\}$, the **arithmetic average return** is

$$\bar{R}_A = \frac{1}{T}\sum_{t=1}^{T} R_t.$$

The arithmetic average is the natural estimator for the *expected return of a single period* if returns are independent and identically distributed. In other words, if you ask:

> "If I pick a random month from my sample, what return should I expect in that month?"

then the arithmetic average is aligned with that question.

But arithmetic averaging is **not** the same thing as compounding. Investors do not get to average returns; they must live through sequences of returns. And sequences of returns multiply, they do not add.

Geometric average return: the true long-run growth rate

The **geometric average return** (also called the **compound annual growth rate** when the period is annual) is defined as the constant per-period return that would produce the same final wealth:

$$\bar{R}_G = \left(\prod_{t=1}^{T}(1 + R_t)\right)^{1/T} - 1.$$

Equivalently, in log space:

$$\ln(1 + \bar{R}_G) = \frac{1}{T}\sum_{t=1}^{T} \ln(1 + R_t) = \bar{r}.$$

Thus, the average log return $\bar{r}$ corresponds exactly to the geometric mean of simple returns.

Why the geometric mean is always below the arithmetic mean (unless volatility is zero)

A foundational inequality explains much of the "variance drain" intuition:

$$\frac{1}{T}\sum_{t=1}^{T}\ln(1+R_t) \leq \ln\left(1+\frac{1}{T}\sum_{t=1}^{T}R_t\right),$$

because $\ln(\cdot)$ is concave (Jensen's inequality). Exponentiating both sides implies:

$$\bar{R}_G \leq \bar{R}_A,$$

with equality only when returns do not vary (i.e., no volatility). This is not an opinion about markets; it is a mathematical property of compounding.

Volatility drag: the intuitive "two-step" example

A short example makes the point more forcefully than any formula.

Suppose a portfolio goes up $+50\%$ one period and down -50% the next:

$$(1+R_1)(1+R_2) = 1.5 \times 0.5 = 0.75.$$

So wealth is down 25% after two periods. Yet the arithmetic average return is

$$\bar{R}_A = \frac{0.50+(-0.50)}{2} = 0.$$

A 0% arithmetic average sounds "flat," but the investor lost money. The reason is that losses compound on a smaller base. A subsequent gain must work harder to recover a prior loss.

This is the simplest expression of **path dependence**: in a multiplicative process, the order and dispersion of outcomes affect the final result, even when the arithmetic average does not change.

A useful approximation: geometric return $\approx$ arithmetic return minus half the variance

For relatively small per-period returns (a good approximation for monthly or daily data, and often acceptable for annual data in diversified portfolios), we can use a Taylor expansion:

$$\ln(1+R) \approx R - \frac{R^2}{2}.$$

Taking expectations (or sample averages) yields:

$$\mathbb{E}[\ln(1+R)] \approx \mathbb{E}[R] - \frac{1}{2}\mathbb{E}[R^2].$$

Using $\mathbb{E}[R^2] = \text{Var}(R) + (\mathbb{E}[R])^2$ gives:

$$\mathbb{E}[\ln(1+R)] \approx \mathbb{E}[R] - \frac{1}{2}\text{Var}(R) - \frac{1}{2}(\mathbb{E}[R])^2.$$

If $\mathbb{E}[R]$ is modest (so $(\mathbb{E}[R])^2$ is small relative to $\text{Var}(R)$), then a widely used rule of thumb emerges:

$$\underbrace{\text{Geometric growth (in log terms)}}_{\mathbb{E}[\ln(1+R)]} \approx \underbrace{\text{Arithmetic mean}}_{\mathbb{E}[R]} - \frac{1}{2}\underbrace{\text{Variance}}_{\text{Var}(R)}.$$

Interpretation. Holding the arithmetic mean fixed, a higher variance lowers compound growth approximately one-for-one with "half the variance." This is the mathematical meaning of **volatility drag**. It is not that volatility is always "bad" (many strategies intentionally take volatility risk); it is that volatility must be *paid for* with sufficiently high expected return, diversification benefits, or convex payoffs.

Why this matters more in multi-asset portfolios than in single-asset discussions

Multi-asset investors live at the intersection of three realities:

- **Different asset classes have different volatility levels.** Equity-like assets typically have higher volatility than high-quality bonds; many alternatives have non-linear or smoothed return patterns.
- **Diversification changes portfolio variance.** Even if each asset has the same arithmetic expected return as before, the portfolio's compound growth improves if correlations reduce variance.

- **Rebalancing interacts with compounding.** Rebalancing forces "sell some winners, buy some losers." That discipline can increase long-run growth *when it reduces variance without sacrificing too much mean*, but it can also hurt if trading costs or structural trends dominate. Trading frictions will be treated explicitly later; for now, we isolate pure compounding arithmetic.

The operational consequence is simple: **you should never evaluate a long-horizon strategy using arithmetic average returns alone**. Arithmetic averages are fine as intermediate inputs (e.g., estimating expected one-year return), but long-run wealth is governed by geometric compounding.

Volatility drag made visual: same arithmetic average, different ending wealth

The cleanest way to see volatility drag is to compare two portfolios engineered to have the *same* arithmetic average return but different volatility. The higher-volatility portfolio will almost always end with less wealth, because a wider dispersion of outcomes increases the compounding penalty described above.

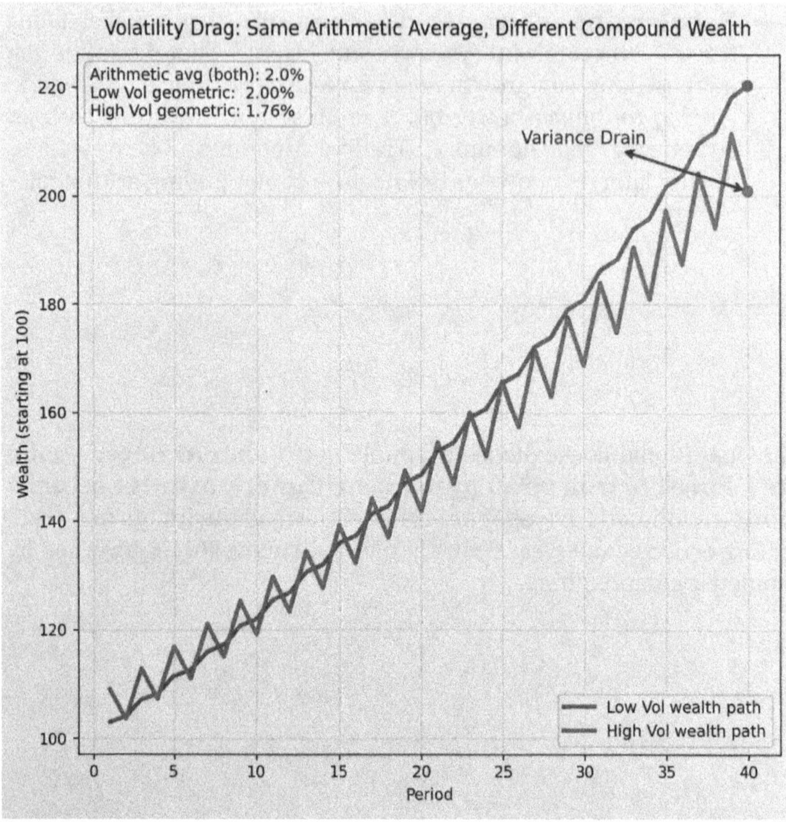

Practical guidance: which return should you use, and when?

To prevent costly misinterpretations, align the return measure with the decision you are making:

- **Use arithmetic average returns for one-period forecasting and mean-variance inputs.** If you are estimating next month's expected return or building an optimizer that expects single-period expected returns, arithmetic means are the natural estimator (subject to estimation error, discussed later).

- **Use geometric returns for statements about long-run wealth and "what you actually earned."** Client reporting, multi-year strategy evaluation, and retirement-like objectives should be framed in geometric (compound) terms.
- **Use log returns for aggregation, modeling, and attribution in continuous time.** If you need additivity across time or you are building models that assume approximate normality in log space, log returns are often the cleanest tool. But always convert back to wealth compounding when interpreting results.

A compounding lens you will use throughout the book

From this point forward, whenever we discuss the "return" of an asset class, a factor, or a strategy, you should ask two questions:

- **Is this a single-period expectation (arithmetic), or a long-run realized growth rate (geometric)?**
- **What is the volatility required to earn that return, and how much of it survives compounding after volatility drag?**

This is the first step toward a professional multi asset mindset: not merely chasing high average returns, but designing portfolios whose *risk, correlation structure, and compounding arithmetic* work together to produce robust long-horizon wealth growth.

1.2 Risk Measurement: Volatility and Beyond

The previous section established a central fact of compounding: *volatility is not just movement; it is a direct tax on long-run geometric growth.* That result immediately raises the next practical question for a portfolio manager:

> If volatility matters so much, is *standard deviation* the right way to define and manage risk?

Standard deviation is a useful starting point because it is mathematically tractable and fits naturally into mean–variance portfolio theory. But standard deviation also embeds an assumption about what "risk" means: it treats upside surprises and downside crashes as equally undesirable deviations from the mean. Real investors do not experience risk symmetrically. They experience risk as **pain**: losses, drawdowns, forced deleveraging, funding pressure, missed spending targets, and the behavioral and governance consequences of being "underwater."

The baseline: variance and volatility

Let R denote a single-period simple return and let $\mu = \mathbb{E}[R]$. The **variance** and **standard deviation** are

$$\begin{aligned} \mathrm{Var}(R) &= \mathbb{E}\big[(R-\mu)^2\big], \\ \sigma &= \sqrt{\mathrm{Var}(R)}. \end{aligned}$$

When we say an asset has "15% volatility," we typically mean an **annualized** standard deviation. If returns are measured monthly with standard deviation σ_m, a common approximation is

$$\sigma_{ann} \approx \sigma_m \sqrt{12},$$

and similarly for daily data $\sigma_{ann} \approx \sigma_d \sqrt{252}$. (These scalings are approximations; they implicitly assume weak serial dependence and stable distributional properties. We will revisit these assumptions when discussing estimation error and regime behavior.)

Why volatility is appealing

Volatility is popular because it is:

- **Simple to estimate** from return histories,
- **Additive in portfolio space** via covariances (risk can be decomposed and budgeted),

- **A first-order proxy** for many constraints (e.g., leverage limits and risk parity design often start from volatility).

Why volatility can be misleading

Volatility is also incomplete because:

- It **penalizes upside** and downside equally.
- It says nothing about **path dependence** (drawdowns and time-to-recover).
- It is easily distorted by **non-normality**, illiquidity smoothing, and option-like payoffs.

A portfolio manager should therefore treat volatility as *necessary but not sufficient*: it is a good **baseline risk unit**, but it is not the full risk story.

Downside-focused risk: semi-variance and semi-deviation

Many investment objectives are asymmetric. Consider a pension plan: returns above target are welcome but do not reduce the harm of returns far below target if contributions must rise or benefits must be cut. Similarly, an endowment cares far more about sustaining spending (avoiding shortfall) than about "excess" upside volatility.

To capture this asymmetry, we focus on **downside-only dispersion**. Choose a **minimum acceptable return** (MAR) τ (often 0, the risk-free rate, inflation, or a policy benchmark). Define the downside deviation from τ as

$$D = \min(0, R - \tau).$$

The **semi-variance** (downside variance) is

$$\mathrm{SemiVar}_\tau(R) = \mathbb{E}\big[D^2\big] = \mathbb{E}\Big[\min(0, R - \tau)^2\Big],$$

and the **semi-deviation** is

$$\mathrm{SemiDev}_\tau(R) = \sqrt{\mathrm{SemiVar}_\tau(R)}.$$

Intuition. Semi-deviation answers the question:

> "How variable are outcomes *when we are failing* relative to a threshold?"

Upside volatility is not counted as risk under this definition—which often matches investor utility more closely than standard deviation.

Sortino ratio (a Sharpe ratio with downside risk)

The **Sharpe ratio** uses total volatility:

$$\text{Sharpe} = \frac{\mathbb{E}[R] - R_f}{\sigma}.$$

The **Sortino ratio** replaces σ with downside semi-deviation (typically relative to $\tau = R_f$ or $\tau = 0$):

$$\text{Sortino}_\tau = \frac{\mathbb{E}[R] - \tau}{\text{SemiDev}_\tau(R)}.$$

Practical use. Sortino becomes especially informative when comparing strategies with asymmetric payoff profiles (e.g., trend following, option-based overlays, carry strategies). Two strategies can have the same Sharpe ratio but very different downside behavior. When the mandate is "avoid bad years" more than "avoid volatility," Sortino is usually closer to what stakeholders mean by risk-adjusted performance.

Tail risk in probability terms: VaR and Conditional VaR (Expected Shortfall)

Volatility and semi-deviation describe dispersion. Many risk decisions, however, are framed as: *What is my loss in a bad scenario?* That leads to tail risk measures.

Value at Risk (VaR)

Fix a confidence level $\alpha \in (0,1)$, such as $\alpha = 95\%$ or 99%. Define the loss as $L = -R$ (so positive values are losses). Then **Value at Risk** is the α-quantile of the loss distribution:

$$\mathrm{VaR}_\alpha = \inf\{\ell : \mathbb{P}(L \le \ell) \ge \alpha\}.$$

Equivalently, in return space, VaR_α corresponds to a threshold such that the probability of losing more than that amount is $1 - \alpha$.

Interpretation. A one-month 95% VaR of 4% means:

> "Based on the model, 95% of months should lose *no more than* 4%; 5% of months may be worse."

Limitations. VaR is widely used for reporting and limits, but it has a crucial weakness: it does **not** tell you how bad losses are *beyond* the VaR threshold. Two portfolios can share the same 95% VaR, yet one may occasionally suffer catastrophic tail losses.

Conditional VaR / Expected Shortfall (CVaR / ES)

To address that, define **Expected Shortfall** as the expected loss conditional on being in the tail:

$$\mathrm{ES}_\alpha = \mathbb{E}\left[L \,\middle|\, L \ge \mathrm{VaR}_\alpha\right].$$

In words, Expected Shortfall is the *average of the worst* $(1-\alpha)\%$ *outcomes.*

Why ES is often better aligned with investor pain. If VaR answers "how bad is a bad day likely to be," ES answers "how bad are the truly bad days on average." Portfolios that sell insurance (short-volatility profiles) often look acceptable under variance and even VaR, but are exposed under Expected Shortfall.

Model risk: historical vs parametric estimation

Both VaR and ES can be estimated in different ways:

- **Historical (empirical):** use the empirical quantile of realized returns.
- **Parametric:** assume a distribution (often Normal or t) and compute quantiles from fitted parameters.
- **Simulation-based:** generate scenarios from a model (e.g., GARCH, copulas, Monte Carlo with regime shifts).

The choice is not cosmetic. It determines whether your risk measure is sensitive to fat tails, serial dependence, and changing correlations—issues that will become central in the next section on distributions and estimation error.

Path-dependent risk: drawdowns, not just dispersion

Volatility and tail quantiles are *distributional* measures: they focus on what returns look like in the aggregate. Many real-world failures, however, are **path failures**. Investors are forced to sell because they are down too much for too long. Committees lose patience. Leverage covenants bind. Spending becomes unsustainable. These are drawdown problems.

Defining drawdown

Let W_t be the portfolio wealth (or index level) through time, and define the running peak

$$M_t = \max_{0 \le s \le t} W_s.$$

The **drawdown** at time t is

$$\mathrm{DD}_t = \frac{W_t}{M_t} - 1,$$

which is a non-positive number (e.g., -0.20 means down 20% from the previous peak). The **maximum drawdown** over a horizon is

$$\mathrm{MDD} = \min_{0 \le t \le T} \mathrm{DD}_t.$$

Why MDD resonates with stakeholders. Maximum drawdown measures the worst peak-to-trough experience. This is close to how clients narrate pain:

> "How far down were we at the worst point?"

This question matters even if average returns are strong, because deep drawdowns can trigger liquidation, mandate termination, or behavioral capitulation precisely at the wrong time.

Drawdown duration and time-under-water

Depth is only half the story. Two portfolios can share the same maximum drawdown and still feel radically different. The second dimension is **duration**: how long the portfolio stays below its prior peak.

A practical definition is **time under water** (TUW): the length of time between a peak and the subsequent recovery above that peak. Formally, define a peak time t_0 where $W_{t_0} = M_{t_0}$ and the next recovery time

$$t_1 = \inf\{t > t_0 : W_t \geq W_{t_0}\}.$$

Then the time-under-water for that drawdown episode is $t_1 - t_0$. Long durations create governance risk: even moderate drawdowns become intolerable if they persist.

Ulcer index (optional but useful)

Another path-sensitive measure is the **Ulcer Index**, which penalizes both depth and persistence by averaging squared drawdowns:

$$\mathrm{UI} = \sqrt{\frac{1}{T}\sum_{t=1}^{T} \mathrm{DD}_t^2}.$$

It is especially helpful for comparing strategies that have similar volatility but different recovery behavior.

Why Sharpe ratios can fail for skewed and nonlinear strategies

The Sharpe ratio is built on the idea that risk is fully described by standard deviation. This becomes fragile when return distributions are skewed or fat-tailed.

A common failure mode: "smooth" returns with hidden tail risk

Some strategies exhibit low reported volatility most of the time while being exposed to rare, severe losses (classic examples include certain option-selling profiles, leveraged carry, or illiquid assets with appraisal smoothing). Such strategies can look outstanding under volatility-based metrics:

- Small month-to-month variation (low σ),
- A steady positive drift (high $\mathbb{E}[R]$),
- Therefore a high Sharpe ratio.

Yet they may have poor Expected Shortfall and devastating drawdowns when the tail event arrives. This is not a philosophical objection; it is a direct consequence of using a symmetric dispersion statistic to judge an asymmetric payoff distribution.

Putting the toolkit together: mapping risk measures to decisions

A practical way to remember these measures is to map them to the decision they are meant to support.

Risk measure	Best used for
Volatility (σ)	Baseline risk budgeting; comparing "typical" variability; covariance-based diversification; leverage sizing under normal conditions
Semi-deviation / Sortino	Mandates with asymmetric objectives (capital preservation, target returns); comparing strategies where upside volatility should not be penalized
VaR	Simple limit frameworks; communicating threshold losses at a stated confidence; regulatory reporting (with strong caveats)
Expected Shortfall (ES/CVaR)	Tail-risk-aware limits; comparing strategies with crash exposure; stress-aware portfolio construction
Maximum drawdown (MDD)	Client experience; governance risk; evaluating whether a strategy is "survivable" through a cycle
Drawdown duration / TUW	Liquidity and patience constraints; mandate durability; assessing whether recovery dynamics fit the investor's horizon

The bridge to portfolio construction: risk is multi-dimensional

With the compounding lesson in mind (volatility reduces geometric growth), it is tempting to declare volatility the one true risk metric. The more accurate professional stance is:

> **Volatility is a risk unit; downside and path measures are risk realities.**

In multi-asset investing, you will routinely face trade-offs such as:

- Lower volatility versus worse tail risk,
- Better Sharpe versus deeper drawdowns,
- Higher expected return versus longer time-under-water,
- Diversification that looks strong in normal times versus correlations that rise in stress.

1.3 Probability, Distributions, and Estimation Error

The prior sections established two foundational ideas:

- **1. Compounding is geometric.** Volatility reduces long-run wealth growth even when arithmetic average returns look attractive.
- **2. Risk is multidimensional.** Standard deviation is a convenient baseline, but downside and path-dependent measures (semi-deviation, VaR/ES, drawdowns) often align better with investor pain.

This section explains why these lessons become *dangerously distorted* when we commit two common modeling errors:

- **1.** assuming returns are Normally distributed (the **Normality Fallacy**), and
- **2.** treating estimated inputs (means, volatilities, correlations) as if they were known constants rather than noisy estimates (the **Estimation Error Problem**).

Both errors push portfolio models toward false precision—and in multi-asset portfolios, false precision tends to produce concentrated, fragile allocations.

Probability as a portfolio-management tool (and a liability)

Probability is indispensable in investing because most decisions are made under uncertainty:

- how wide should risk limits be,
- how much capital can we allocate to volatile assets,

- what losses are plausible, and
- whether diversification is likely to hold in stress.

But probability models are only as reliable as the distributional assumptions behind them. In particular, many textbook results are built on an implicit template:

Returns are i.i.d. Normal with stable mean and covariance.

Real markets violate each clause:

- **Not Normal:** returns have fat tails and often skewness.
- **Not i.i.d.:** volatility clusters; correlations rise in stress; regimes change.
- **Not stable:** the "true" mean and covariance evolve with macro conditions, policy regimes, and market structure.

The practical implication is not that quantitative tools fail, but that they must be used with humility and defensive design.

The Normality Fallacy

A Normal distribution is fully characterized by its mean and variance. If returns were truly Normal, then:

- extreme events would be extraordinarily rare,
- standard deviation would be an unusually complete risk descriptor, and
- VaR/ES computed from μ and σ would be reasonably stable.

Markets, however, exhibit **tail risk**: extreme outcomes occur far more often than a Gaussian model predicts. This matters for multi-asset design because tails are where diversification often fails and where portfolio survival is decided.

Skewness and kurtosis: what "non-Normal" looks like

Let R denote (demeaned) returns. Two statistics help describe deviations from Gaussian behavior:

Skewness (asymmetry). Skewness measures whether extreme outcomes are more likely on one side:

$$\text{Skew}(R) = \frac{\mathbb{E}\left[(R-\mu)^3\right]}{\sigma^3}.$$

Negative skewness is common in strategies that earn small gains frequently but suffer occasional large losses (many carry and short-volatility profiles). For such strategies, volatility can appear modest while drawdowns and ES are severe.

Kurtosis (tail thickness). Kurtosis measures the heaviness of tails relative to the Normal:

$$\text{Kurt}(R) = \frac{\mathbb{E}\left[(R-\mu)^4\right]}{\sigma^4}.$$

A Normal distribution has Kurt $= 3$. Values materially above 3 correspond to **fat tails**: more probability mass in extreme outcomes.

Why kurtosis is a portfolio problem (not just a statistical curiosity)

Kurtosis directly undermines common risk reasoning. Under a Normal model:

- a $\pm 3\sigma$ daily move is extremely rare,
- a $\pm 5\sigma$ daily move is almost "impossible."

In real equity markets, moves in the "multiple sigma" range occur far more often than Gaussian logic suggests. That gap between predicted and realized extremes is exactly where VaR breaches, forced deleveraging, and drawdowns live.

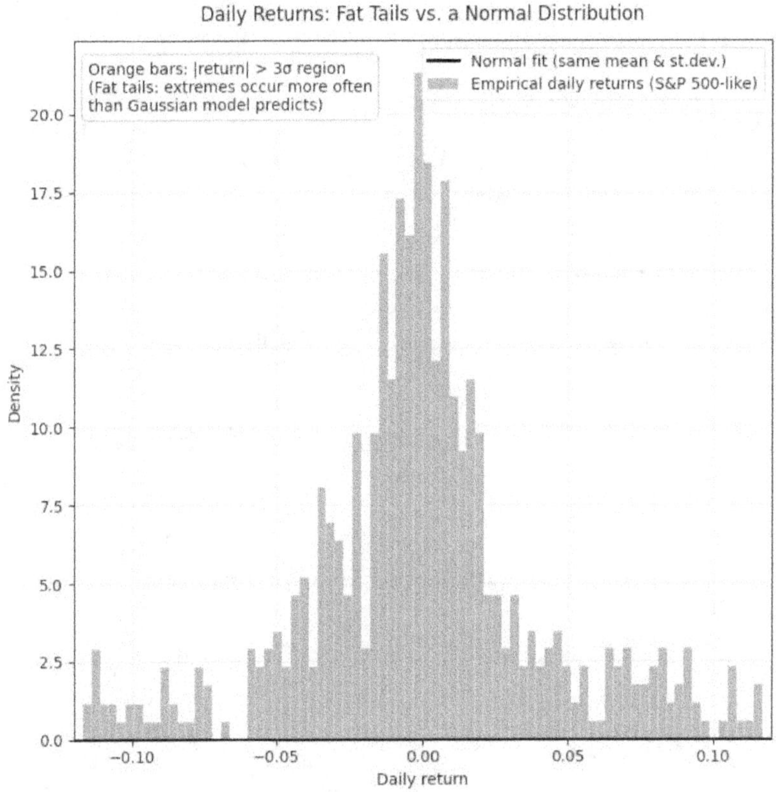

Tail risk: the practical meaning of "fat tails"

Fat tails are not merely "more outliers." They change the economics of risk taking:

- **Risk limits based on Gaussian VaR will be breached more often than expected.** If a portfolio is sized so that a "99% VaR" under Normal assumptions fits within a loss budget, realized losses can still exceed that budget with uncomfortable frequency when tails are fatter than Normal.
- **Diversification can be regime-dependent.** Correlations of-

ten rise during stress, effectively fattening the portfolio tail even if individual asset tails appear moderate in isolation.

- **Compounding interacts with tails.** A small number of large negative days can dominate long-run wealth outcomes because losses compound multiplicatively and recovery requires disproportionately large gains.

For multi-asset portfolios, this means that a risk process must explicitly consider **tail-aware measures** (e.g., Expected Shortfall, drawdowns) and **stress scenarios**, not just volatility.

Estimation error: the hidden risk in "optimal" portfolios

Even if the world were stable, we would still face a hard limitation: we never observe the true parameters (μ, Σ) of asset returns. We estimate them from finite samples.

Let $\mathbf{R}_t \in \mathbb{R}^N$ be the vector of returns for N assets at time t, for $t = 1, \ldots, T$.

Sample mean.

$$\hat{\mu} = \frac{1}{T}\sum_{t=1}^{T} \mathbf{R}_t.$$

Sample covariance.

$$\hat{\Sigma} = \frac{1}{T-1}\sum_{t=1}^{T} (\mathbf{R}_t - \hat{\mu})(\mathbf{R}_t - \hat{\mu})^\top.$$

These are reasonable estimators, but they are noisy—and critically, **mean estimates are far noisier than volatility estimates**. A useful mental model is:

Volatility is hard but measurable; expected return is harder and often dominated by noise at practical sample lengths.

Why mean estimates are especially fragile

Suppose (for intuition) a single asset has i.i.d. returns with standard deviation σ and true mean μ. The standard error of the sample mean is approximately

$$\mathrm{SE}(\hat{\mu}) \approx \frac{\sigma}{\sqrt{T}}.$$

Daily data does not magically solve this, because daily returns have small means and noisy dispersion. Annualizing does not remove uncertainty; it simply rescales it.

This is why optimizers that are highly sensitive to $\hat{\mu}$ (such as unconstrained mean–variance optimizers) often produce extreme allocations: the optimizer is "believing" noise.

The optimizer as an error amplifier

In classic mean–variance form, the tangency (maximum Sharpe) portfolio weights are proportional to

$$\mathbf{w} \propto \hat{\Sigma}^{-1}(\hat{\boldsymbol{\mu}} - R_f \mathbf{1}).$$

Two amplification mechanisms appear immediately:

- **Inverting covariance magnifies noise.** Small estimation errors in $\hat{\Sigma}$ can become large errors in $\hat{\Sigma}^{-1}$, especially when assets are highly correlated or when N is large relative to T.
- **Small differences in estimated means dominate weights.** If two assets have similar risk, a tiny difference in $\hat{\mu}$ can produce a large weight tilt, even if that difference is not statistically meaningful.

This is the practical meaning of the well-known critique: *the mean–variance optimizer is not a portfolio construction engine; it is an estimation error engine unless you constrain and regularize it.*

Correlation is not a constant: the multi-asset trap

Multi-asset portfolios are built on diversification, which mathematically depends on covariance and correlation. But correlations are:

- time-varying,
- regime-dependent (often rising in stress),
- sensitive to sampling window choice.

This creates a common trap: a backtest may show low correlations and excellent diversification *on average*, while real-time experience during drawdowns reveals that the portfolio was effectively long a single macro risk factor when it mattered most.

Practical defenses against non-Normality and estimation error

The goal is not to abandon quantitative modeling, but to **design models that degrade gracefully**. Common robust practices include:

Use tail-aware risk measures in parallel with volatility

Volatility remains useful, but it should be supplemented with:

- Expected Shortfall (not just VaR),
- drawdown depth and duration,
- stress tests (historical and hypothetical),
- scenario correlations ("correlation in crisis").

Shrinkage and regularization for covariance matrices

Rather than relying on the raw sample covariance $\hat{\Sigma}$, many practitioners use a **shrunk** estimator:

$$\tilde{\Sigma} = (1-\lambda)\hat{\Sigma} + \lambda F,$$

where F is a structured target (e.g., constant-correlation, factor model covariance, or diagonal matrix) and $\lambda \in [0,1]$ controls how aggressively we reduce estimation noise. The intuition is straightforward: *we trade a small amount of bias for a large reduction in variance.*

Penalize or constrain the mean

Because $\hat{\mu}$ is noisy, robust approaches often:

- shrink expected returns toward a common value or toward a benchmark,
- use wide confidence intervals and treat means as uncertain,
- impose constraints that prevent extreme tilts driven by tiny mean differences.

Favor designs that rely more on risk than on precise mean forecasts

Many resilient multi-asset frameworks (risk parity variants, volatility targeting, diversification-first allocations, and constrained optimizations) are popular in practice because they are less sensitive to mean estimation error. They are not "better" in theory for all cases; they are often **more stable** under uncertainty.

What to carry forward

This section's practical message is simple and consequential:

- **1. Returns are not Gaussian.** Fat tails and skewness mean that extreme losses occur more often than Normal-based intuition suggests, which affects VaR/ES, drawdowns, and diversification.
- **2. Your inputs are estimates.** Sample means, volatilities, and correlations are noisy; unconstrained optimization will overfit that noise.
- **3. Robustness beats precision.** Multi-asset portfolios should be built with risk measures that reflect tails and with estimation methods (shrinkage, constraints, stress testing) that prevent fragile concentration.

The next section turns these principles into a concrete operational discipline: how to construct datasets and benchmarks that do not accidentally bake bias into the parameters you estimate. In portfolio engineering, *data quality is a first-order risk control.*

1.4 Data Architecture and Benchmark Selection

The previous section showed why quantitative portfolio tools can fail even when the math is correct: returns are not reliably Normal, tail risk is real, and—most importantly for day-to-day portfolio work—the inputs to our models are estimated with error. That discussion naturally leads to a practical conclusion:

If estimates are fragile, then data quality and dataset design are not "back-office details." They are primary risk controls.

In multi-asset investing, this is doubly true. Different asset classes have different trading calendars, different index construction conventions, different liquidity profiles, and different data vendors. Without a disciplined data architecture, the portfolio manager can easily build a model that is internally inconsistent—and then spend months optimizing noise.

This section provides a framework for (i) building robust historical datasets, (ii) avoiding common backtest biases, and (iii) selecting benchmarks that genuinely measure skill rather than artifacts.

Start with the decision: what question is your dataset supposed to answer?

Before pulling any data, specify the **investment decision** the dataset is meant to inform. Common questions include:

- **Strategic allocation:** What long-run risk and diversification properties should we expect across asset classes?
- **Tactical overlay:** Do signals have predictive power net of trading frictions?
- **Risk budgeting:** How do covariances behave in normal times versus stress regimes?
- **Manager evaluation:** Did a portfolio add value beyond its benchmark exposures?

Each question implies different requirements:

- strategic allocation requires **long, regime-diverse** histories,
- tactical overlays require **high-frequency, trade-timestamp-consistent** data and costs,
- risk budgeting requires **clean covariance estimation** and calendar alignment,
- manager evaluation requires **benchmark integrity** and exposure controls.

When the question is unclear, practitioners often default to "get as much data as possible and run an optimizer." That is precisely how estimation error and bias enter the process.

A multi-asset data architecture: the minimum viable "data contract"

A robust dataset is less about the vendor and more about a **data contract**: explicit definitions that force internal consistency.

For each return series in your research universe, document:

- **Instrument definition:** what the series represents (index, ETF, futures continuous contract, swap index, fund NAV).
- **Return type:** price return vs total return (income reinvested).
- **Currency:** local vs base-currency hedged vs unhedged.
- **Calendar and timestamp:** close-to-close, 4pm ET, London close, end-of-month NAV, etc.
- **Corporate actions / contract rolls:** splits, dividends, futures roll rules, carry.
- **Availability lag:** when the data would have been known in real time (critical for backtests).
- **Liquidity proxy:** bid–ask, volume, or at least an estimate of implementation shortfall parameters.
- **Missing-data policy:** how gaps are treated (drop, forward-fill, interpolate—usually avoid the last two for returns).

Why this matters. Portfolio math (covariances, correlations, drawdowns) assumes that series are commensurate: the "same" dates, the same information set, and comparable economic meaning. A dataset without an explicit contract is almost guaranteed to violate those assumptions.

Return series choices: indices, ETFs, futures, and manager returns

Multi-asset research often mixes series types. Each has advantages and traps.

Index returns

Pros: long history, broad representation, often total-return variants.
Cons: may be theoretical (ignoring costs), may embed reconstitution rules, and may not be investable at low cost historically.

Index selection matters most in:

- credit (changes in rating composition and defaults),
- commodities (roll yield is part of the experience),
- alternatives (private markets use appraisals and smoothing).

ETF returns

Pros: investable, includes fees implicitly, real trading frictions are observable.
Cons: limited history; early-period liquidity can be poor; tracking difference and lending revenue vary over time.

A common best practice is to use indices for long-horizon calibration and ETFs for **implementation reality checks** in the overlapping window.

Futures-based series (continuous contracts)

Pros: clean implementation for many macro strategies; leverage and capital efficiency are realistic; long data history in major contracts.
Cons: the continuous return depends on roll methodology; margining and collateral returns must be handled; some contracts have structural regime changes.

Total futures experience $\approx$ spot/price move $+$ roll yield $+$ collateral return $-$ costs. Ignoring collateral return (or double-counting it) is a classic multi-asset modeling error when comparing futures to cash indices.

Manager or fund returns

Pros: reflect real frictions and constraints.
Cons: survivorship and backfill biases can be severe; valuations can be smoothed; exposures can drift.

If you include manager returns in allocation studies, treat them as **imperfect measurements of underlying risks** rather than clean asset class proxies.

Frequency, alignment, and aggregation: the calendar is part of the model

A multi-asset dataset usually combines assets trading on different schedules (e.g., US equities, global bonds, commodities, crypto, private assets). Misalignment creates artificial correlation and misleading risk.

Choose a research frequency that matches your decision horizon

- **Strategic allocation:** monthly is often appropriate, reducing microstructure noise and focusing on regime risk.
- **Risk monitoring and leverage sizing:** daily or higher may be needed, but beware of noise, stale pricing, and asynchronous closes.
- **Signals and execution research:** daily/intraday is required, with strict timestamp discipline.

Non-synchronous trading bias

If one market closes earlier than another, same-day returns may not reflect the same information. This can:

- dampen measured correlation (making diversification look better than it is),

- distort lead–lag relationships (creating false predictability).

Practical fixes include using common close conventions (where possible), lagging one series for correlation estimation, or estimating covariance at a lower frequency where the effect is reduced.

Aggregation must preserve compounding

From Section 1, we know compounding is multiplicative. Therefore:

- aggregate simple returns by compounding: $(1 + R_{month}) = \prod_{d \in month}(1 + R_d)$,
- aggregate log returns by summation: $r_{month} = \sum_{d \in month} r_d$.

Mixing arithmetic averages into multi-period aggregation is a subtle but common error that overstates performance and misstates drawdowns.

The big three backtest biases (and how to prevent them)

Backtest bias is not academic; it is the main reason live performance disappoints. Three biases are so common that any serious research process must explicitly defend against them.

Survivorship bias

Definition. Survivorship bias occurs when the dataset includes only assets that exist today (survivors) and excludes those that disappeared (bankrupt companies, delisted stocks, closed funds).

Why it matters. Excluding failures systematically inflates historical returns and understates risk. The bias is severe in:

- single stocks and equity factors using modern constituents,
- mutual funds and hedge funds (dead funds are missing),

- credit and EM where default and restructuring are part of reality.

Controls.

- Use **point-in-time constituent data** for equity universes.
- Use **dead fund** databases (or at minimum acknowledge the limitation).
- Prefer **index series designed to incorporate defaults** for credit where possible.

Look-ahead bias

Definition. Look-ahead bias occurs when a backtest uses information that would not have been available at the decision time:

- using revised macro data instead of first releases,
- using end-of-day prices to trade at that same close without modeling execution,
- using index constituent changes before they were announced/implemented,
- using accounting data before reporting dates.

Controls.

- Enforce an **information timestamp**: signals at t may only use data known by t.
- Apply **publication lags** for macro and fundamentals.
- Separate **signal time** (decision) from **trade time** (execution), even in a simple model.

Selection and backfill bias

Definition. Selection bias occurs when we choose a universe because it performed well. Backfill bias occurs when databases include a manager only after it has a good track record, retroactively filling earlier returns.

Why it matters. These biases can create "too good to be true" Sharpe ratios, especially in alternatives.

Controls.

- Pre-register universe inclusion rules (what qualifies and when).
- Use inception-to-date returns starting from the time the series becomes investable/observable.
- Treat alternative manager indices cautiously; corroborate with multiple sources when possible.

Handling missing data, illiquidity, and stale pricing

Missingness is not random in finance. Assets are often missing precisely when they are distressed, suspended, or illiquid.

Principles

- **Do not forward-fill returns.** Forward-filling prices creates artificial low volatility and inflated Sharpe ratios.
- **Prefer dropping periods to inventing data,** but understand the induced sample selection.
- **Flag illiquid series explicitly.** Illiquidity can smooth reported returns, understate covariance, and mask tail risk.

Volatility and correlation under smoothing

Smoothing lowers measured volatility and correlation, which can make an illiquid asset look like a perfect diversifier. A robust process therefore:

- runs analysis both on reported returns and on **de-smoothed** proxies when appropriate,
- stress-tests correlation assumptions (e.g., impose higher crisis correlations),
- uses drawdown and liquidity-aware measures, not just variance.

Benchmark selection: measuring skill requires the right yardstick

Benchmarks are not ornaments. They define what counts as "alpha" and what counts as compensated beta risk.

The benchmark must match the economic exposure

A benchmark should be:

- **Investable in spirit** (replicable at reasonable cost),
- **Consistent with the mandate** (risk profile, region, duration, credit quality),
- **Total return when appropriate** (include coupons/dividends if the portfolio earns them),
- **Currency-consistent** (hedged vs unhedged should match the portfolio policy).

A common error is to benchmark a multi-asset or alternative strategy against a single broad equity index. This confuses diversification benefits (a structural allocation choice) with skill (security selection, timing, execution).

Benchmark mismatch creates false alpha

Suppose a portfolio holds a meaningful allocation to duration (bonds). If it is benchmarked to equities only, it can appear to have alpha in equity drawdowns simply because bonds rallied. That is not alpha; it is **beta to duration**. Proper benchmarking decomposes performance into systematic exposures and residual skill.

Custom benchmarks for complex strategies

Many multi-asset strategies require **policy benchmarks** rather than off-the-shelf indices.

Policy benchmark (strategic allocation benchmark)

A policy benchmark is typically a fixed-weight blend of asset class indices (or a rules-based rebalanced blend) that reflects the intended strategic mix:

$$R_t^{policy} = \sum_{i=1}^{N} w_i R_{i,t},$$

with weights w_i chosen by mandate.

Best practice. Make the policy benchmark **rebalanced** at a clear frequency (e.g., monthly or quarterly). Otherwise, benchmark drift turns into an unintended bet on past winners.

Alternative risk premia and factor-aware benchmarks

For strategies that explicitly harvest carry, value, momentum, quality, trend, volatility, or liquidity premia, a single asset-class benchmark is insufficient. Factor-aware benchmarking seeks to answer:

Did we outperform because we had exposure to known premia, or because we executed that exposure better than a simple replication?

This is especially important for evaluating "liquid alternatives" and systematic macro strategies.

Private assets and appraisal-based indices

Private equity and private real estate indices often reflect appraisal smoothing and lagged valuation updates. When benchmarking liquid portfolios to private indices (or vice versa), you must:

- acknowledge that reported volatility and correlation are not apples-to-apples,
- incorporate liquidity and gating risk into the interpretation,
- consider public-market equivalents (PME) where appropriate for private equity evaluation.

A practical workflow: from raw data to research-ready panel

A disciplined workflow reduces accidental bias:

- **Define the universe** and document the data contract for each series.
- **Choose a base currency** and specify hedging policy for each asset class.
- **Select frequency** consistent with the decision (monthly for strategic; daily for risk/execution).
- **Align calendars** and enforce timestamps to prevent non-synchronous and look-ahead errors.
- **Compute returns consistently** (total return where relevant; correct aggregation).
- **Audit for biases** (survivorship, look-ahead, selection/backfill).
- **Validate economically** (do returns and volatilities look plausible across regimes? do drawdowns match known history?).

- **Define benchmarks** (policy and factor-aware as needed) before testing for alpha.

What to carry forward

The central message of this section is that **data is part of the model**. Poorly designed datasets create:

- overstated geometric performance (through aggregation mistakes and biases),
- understated risk (through smoothing, missing failures, and misaligned calendars),
- false diversification (through stale pricing and non-synchronous closes),
- false alpha (through benchmark mismatch).

With a research-ready dataset and honest benchmarks, we can finally confront the next real-world wedge between theory and practice: even if a strategy works on paper, **trading frictions**—spreads, slippage, and market impact—can consume its edge. The next section quantifies that implementation gap.

1.5 Market Microstructure and Trading Frictions

This section addresses the final wedge between a clean backtest and live results: **A model is not a market.** Trading is an engineering problem with costs, frictions, and capacity limits.

Even a modest friction can dominate long-run outcomes because it compounds *negatively* every time you trade. In multi-asset portfolios—especially those that rebalance frequently, trade less liquid instruments, or use leverage—implementation can be the difference between a robust strategy and an elegant spreadsheet fantasy.

From paper returns to realized returns: the implementation gap

A backtest often assumes fills at mid prices, instantaneous execution, and no market impact. Live trading rarely provides any of these. The practical objective is to translate a *theoretical return* into a *net realized return*:

$$R^{net} = R^{gross} - \text{Trading Costs} - \text{Financing/Carry Costs} - \text{Fees}.$$

This section focuses on **trading costs** as they arise from market microstructure: bid–ask spreads, slippage, and price impact.

Market microstructure in one page: what you trade against

At the moment you trade, the market offers two primary prices:

- the **bid** b: the highest price someone is willing to pay you (if you sell),
- the **ask** a: the lowest price someone is willing to sell to you (if you buy).

The **midprice** is

$$m = \frac{a+b}{2},$$

and the **bid–ask spread** is

$$s = a - b.$$

Immediate implication. If you buy at the ask and could immediately sell at the bid, you would lose approximately the spread. This is not a 'bad fill'; it is the market's fundamental toll.

Why spreads exist. Spreads compensate liquidity providers for:

- **order processing** and exchange fees,
- **inventory risk** (holding position while waiting to unwind),

- **adverse selection** (trading against informed flow),
- **volatility** (risk that price moves before they can hedge).

Because these drivers vary across assets, microstructure costs are **asset-class dependent**. A highly liquid equity ETF may have a 1–2 bps effective spread, while high-yield bonds, EM rates, small-cap equities, and many commodities can be orders of magnitude more expensive in stressed conditions.

The three components of trading cost

For most portfolio applications, it is helpful to separate trading cost into:

- **Explicit costs:** commissions, exchange fees, ticket charges, taxes (where applicable).
- **Implicit costs (spread):** paying the bid–ask spread when crossing the market.
- **Execution costs (slippage and impact):** getting worse prices because the market moves while you trade or because your own order moves the price.

This decomposition matters because each component scales differently with turnover, order size, and liquidity.

Implementation shortfall: a professional definition of execution quality

Institutional trading often measures cost via **Implementation Shortfall** (IS), introduced by Perold. The idea is simple: compare the value you would have achieved if you could execute instantly at the **decision price** to what you actually achieved.

Let p^* be the **decision price** (the price when the decision to trade was made). Suppose you trade Q shares (or units). Let p_i be the execution price of the i-th fill for quantity q_i, with $\sum_i q_i = Q$. The **average execution price** is

$$\bar{p} = \frac{\sum_i q_i p_i}{Q}.$$

For a **buy** order, implementation shortfall in dollars is

$$\text{IS}_{\$} = Q(\bar{p} - p^*) + \text{Fees},$$

and for a **sell** order,

$$\text{IS}_{\$} = Q(p^* - \bar{p}) + \text{Fees}.$$

Expressing in **basis points** (bps) is common:

$$\text{IS}_{bps} \approx 10{,}000 \times \frac{\text{IS}_{\$}}{Qp^*}.$$

Why IS is the right mental model. Implementation shortfall naturally captures the full cost of real trading:

- spread crossing (implicit cost),
- adverse movement during execution (slippage),
- market impact (your order moves price),
- explicit fees.

It also aligns with the portfolio manager's real objective: maximizing *realized* portfolio value, not theoretical fill quality at mid.

Spread cost: the quiet compounding leak

If you cross the spread, a common approximation for the expected spread cost is half the spread per trade:

$$\text{Spread cost (per trade)} \approx \frac{s}{2}.$$

In relative terms (bps), use the **relative spread** s/m:

$$\text{Spread cost (bps)} \approx 10{,}000 \times \frac{s}{2m}.$$

Turnover makes it compound. If a strategy has annual turnover TO (dollar traded per year divided by average portfolio value), then a simple first-order estimate of annual spread drag is:

$$\text{Annual spread drag} \approx TO \times \left(\frac{s}{2m}\right).$$

This relationship is why high-turnover strategies can be fragile: even tiny per-trade costs become large when multiplied by frequent trading.

Slippage: when the market moves while you execute

Slippage is the gap between an expected execution price and the realized execution price due to price movement during the execution window. It can be decomposed into:

- **Delay cost:** price move between signal time and order arrival.
- **Trading cost:** price move during execution (which can be market-driven or impact-driven).

Slippage tends to increase with:

- higher volatility,
- wider spreads,
- lower depth (thin order books),
- longer execution times,
- stressed market conditions.

Portfolio relevance. Even if your long-run expected return is correct in a statistical sense, slippage can reduce realized return *and* add noise, making the strategy harder to manage and harder to stick with.

Market impact: trading as a price-moving force

Market impact is the portion of slippage attributable to your own order. Impact is central to institutional sizing because it creates capacity constraints: as you scale a strategy, impact rises and eventually consumes the edge.

A widely used empirical model is that impact increases with trade size relative to daily volume:

$$\text{Impact (bps)} \approx k \left(\frac{Q}{ADV} \right)^{\alpha},$$

where:

- Q is the order size (shares or dollars),
- ADV is average daily volume,
- $k > 0$ is a liquidity parameter,
- $\alpha \in [0.3, 0.8]$ is often near 0.5 (a square-root-like scaling in many markets).

Key intuition. Impact is nonlinear. Doubling order size generally *more than* doubles impact if you are already a meaningful fraction of liquidity. This is why portfolio design and execution design are inseparable.

Why frictions are different across asset classes

Microstructure is not uniform. Multi-asset portfolios should assume heterogeneous implementation costs:

Equities

- Deep order books in large caps; tight spreads.
- Fragmented venues; execution quality depends on smart routing.
- Shorting introduces borrow costs and recall risk.

Government bonds (cash vs futures)

- Cash bonds can be OTC with episodic liquidity.
- Futures are often more liquid for macro positioning; but require collateral and rolling.
- "On-the-run" vs "off-the-run" liquidity differences can dominate costs.

Credit

- High transaction costs, often wide bid–ask spreads.
- Mark-to-model pricing can mask true execution cost.
- Liquidity can vanish in stress, making impact and delay costs spike.

Commodities

- Futures-based exposure includes roll mechanics.
- Liquidity varies massively by contract and maturity.
- Stress regimes can widen spreads and increase gap risk.

FX

- Typically tight spreads in major pairs, but costs can rise around fixings and events.
- Execution depends on venue, time-of-day liquidity, and order type.

Alternatives and private assets

- "Trading cost" may appear low because transactions are infrequent, but liquidity is an embedded option granted to the manager (gates, lockups).

- Measured volatility can be artificially low due to smoothing, but liquidation cost can be enormous.

Rebalancing is trading: the hidden cost of "simple" portfolio maintenance

Strategic multi-asset portfolios rebalance to maintain risk budgets and prevent drift. Rebalancing is often presented as "free discipline," but it has a cost that should be explicitly budgeted.

Turnover from drift

Even a buy-and-hold portfolio generates turnover when you rebalance because weights drift with relative performance. Higher cross-asset volatility and lower correlations tend to increase drift and thus turnover.

Bandwidth and threshold rebalancing

A practical compromise is to rebalance only when weights breach a band:

$$\text{Rebalance if } |w_i - w_i^{target}| > \delta_i.$$

Wider bands reduce turnover and cost but allow more deviation from the intended risk profile. The correct setting depends on:

- transaction cost level,
- risk tolerance for drift,
- whether the asset has convex crash exposure (where drift can be dangerous),
- governance constraints (how much tracking error is acceptable).

Cost-aware performance measurement: why gross Sharpe is not net Sharpe

A strategy with high gross Sharpe can be mediocre net if it relies on frequent trading in costly markets. When evaluating a backtest, always separate:

- **gross return and gross Sharpe** (before trading frictions),
- **net return and net Sharpe** (after realistic spreads, slippage, fees),
- **capacity** (how performance changes as AUM scales).

Because costs reduce returns but often do not reduce volatility proportionally, costs can sharply reduce Sharpe:

$$\text{Sharpe}^{net} = \frac{\mathbb{E}[R^{gross}] - \mathbb{E}[\text{cost}] - R_f}{\sigma_{net}}.$$

In many strategies, $\sigma_{net} \approx \sigma_{gross}$ while expected return drops, so Sharpe falls almost one-for-one with cost drag.

A practical cost model for portfolio research

For research and portfolio design, you need a cost model that is:

- simple enough to apply across assets,
- conservative enough to avoid overfitting,
- explicit about what it includes and excludes.

A common structure is:

$$\text{Cost} = c_{fixed} + c_{spread} + c_{impact},$$

where:

- c_{fixed} includes commissions/fees (often small in liquid markets),

- c_{spread} is approximated by half-spread times turnover,
- c_{impact} scales with size versus liquidity (e.g., square-root form).

Conservative research practice. If the strategy still looks attractive under conservative costs (and under stressed-liquidity assumptions), it is more likely to survive live trading. If it only works with optimistic mid-price fills, it is not a strategy; it is an accounting identity.

Microstructure risk as portfolio risk

Trading frictions are not merely "return drag." They also create **risk**:

- **Liquidity risk:** the inability to exit without large concessions.
- **Gap risk:** discontinuous price jumps that defeat stop-loss logic.
- **Correlation-in-stress:** liquidity evaporates simultaneously across assets.
- **Operational risk:** execution errors, venue failures, and limit breaks.

These risks interact with the earlier sections: fat tails and drawdowns are often *amplified* by microstructure during stress.

What to carry forward

Three principles should guide every multi-asset strategy design:

- **Every rebalance is a trade, and every trade is a cost.** Costs compound negatively with turnover.
- **Liquidity is state-dependent.** The cost you pay in calm markets is not the cost you pay when you most need to transact.
- **Capacity is part of the strategy.** Market impact makes returns scale nonlinearly; a strategy that works at small size can fail at large size.

1.6 Defining Objectives and Constraints

The previous sections built the quantitative foundations required to make portfolio choices that survive contact with reality:

- **Returns compound geometrically**, so volatility and path matter.
- **Risk is multidimensional**, so downside and drawdown-aware measures belong alongside standard deviation.
- **Distributions are not reliably Normal** and inputs are estimated with error, so models must be robust.
- **Data and benchmarks** must be engineered to avoid bias.
- **Trading frictions are real** and can erase theoretical edges.

Translate an investor's qualitative goals into a mathematical problem that can be analyzed, stress-tested, and implemented.

That translation is the job of an **Investment Policy Statement (IPS)**. In this book, we treat the IPS not as prose, but as an *optimization specification*: an objective function plus a set of constraints reflecting real-world limits.

The IPS as a mathematical specification

In institutional practice, an IPS typically describes:

- the investment objective (growth, capital preservation, income, liability hedging),
- the investment horizon and liquidity needs,
- risk tolerance (drawdown limits, volatility targets, shortfall constraints),
- allowable asset classes and instruments,
- governance and operational constraints (leverage rules, concentration limits, rebalancing policy).

To make the IPS operational, we express it in two layers:

- an **objective function** (what we are trying to maximize or minimize),
- **constraints** (what is forbidden or limited).

Mathematically, for portfolio weights $\mathbf{w} \in \mathbb{R}^N$, we write

$$\max_{\mathbf{w}} \ f(\mathbf{w})$$

subject to

$$g_j(\mathbf{w}) \leq 0, \quad j = 1, \dots, J,$$

and

$$h_k(\mathbf{w}) = 0, \quad k = 1, \dots, K.$$

This is not merely notation. It forces clarity:

- What exactly is "risk" for this investor?
- What is the performance metric (arithmetic expectation, geometric growth, utility)?
- Which limits are non-negotiable, and which are preferences?

Step 1: define the portfolio and the investable set

Before specifying objectives, define the **decision variables** precisely.

Weights and the budget constraint

Let $\mathbf{w} = (w_1, \dots, w_N)^\top$ be portfolio weights. A standard fully-invested long-only portfolio imposes

$$\sum_{i=1}^{N} w_i = 1, \qquad w_i \geq 0.$$

If leverage is allowed, the budget constraint can take different forms depending on the instrument set:

- **Cash securities:** weights may still sum to 1, but borrowing and margin appear through explicit leverage constraints.
- **Futures/derivatives:** weights are often better modeled in risk units (e.g., notional or DV01), with collateral and margin constraints handled separately.

Return model and risk model inputs

An IPS-ready specification must also commit (explicitly) to the modeling inputs it will use: $\hat{\mu}$ (expected returns), $\hat{\Sigma}$ (covariance matrix), and, when relevant:

- downside parameters (semi-deviation, ES),
- drawdown statistics,
- stress scenarios and regime assumptions,
- trading cost models (turnover penalties, market impact functions).

From earlier sections, the key discipline is: **treat these as estimates, not truths**. That reality should influence objective choice and constraint tightness.

Step 2: choose an objective that matches the investor's real goal

Objectives are often stated loosely ("maximize return with prudent risk"). In quantitative form, we must choose *what* we optimize and *how* risk is priced.

Below are objective functions commonly used in multi-asset portfolios, along with when they are appropriate.

Maximize expected return for a given risk budget (mean–variance form)

A classical formulation is

$$\max_{\mathbf{w}} \ \mathbf{w}^\top \hat{\mu}$$

subject to

$$\sqrt{\mathbf{w}^\top \hat{\Sigma} \mathbf{w}} \leq \sigma^{\max}.$$

When it fits. This is suitable when:

- volatility is an acceptable primary risk proxy,
- the investor tolerates symmetric risk framing,
- the objective is broadly "efficient frontier" selection.

Caution. Because $\hat{\mu}$ is noisy, unconstrained versions of the above constraint tend to over-concentrate. In practice, the constraints (position limits, sector caps, shrinkage) often matter more than the elegance of the objective.

Maximize Sharpe ratio (tangency portfolio)

Maximizing the Sharpe ratio can be written as

$$\max_{\mathbf{w}} \ \frac{\mathbf{w}^\top \hat{\mu} - R_f}{\sqrt{\mathbf{w}^\top \hat{\Sigma} \mathbf{w}}}$$

subject to constraints on $\mathbf{w}$.

When it fits. This is useful when the investor wants the best risk-adjusted return in volatility space and can lever/delever to a target risk level.

Caution. Sharpe can be misleading for skewed or tail-sensitive strategies. Many institutions therefore pair Sharpe optimization with tail constraints (e.g., ES limits) or replace the denominator with semi-deviation (Sortino).

Minimize variance for a target return (dual mean–variance form)

The dual form is

$$\min_{\mathbf{w}} \ \mathbf{w}^\top \hat{\Sigma} \mathbf{w}$$

subject to

$$\mathbf{w}^\top \hat{\mu} \geq \mu^{\min}.$$

This is often closer to the language of risk committees: "hit at least this return, with minimum risk."

Maximize geometric growth (growth-optimal / Kelly-style objective)

If the investor's true objective is long-horizon wealth compounding, it is natural to consider expected log wealth growth. In simplified settings this corresponds to maximizing

$$\max_{\mathbf{w}} \ \mathbb{E}\big[\ln(1 + \mathbf{w}^\top \mathbf{R})\big].$$

Connection to earlier sections. This objective internalizes volatility drag automatically because log utility penalizes variance.

Practical caution. Pure growth-optimal solutions can be aggressively levered and highly sensitive to estimation error. Institutions typically use "fractional Kelly" logic or impose strict drawdown/leverage constraints. In other words: geometric objectives are conceptually aligned with compounding, but require conservative constraints to be implementable.

Minimize shortfall or tail risk (downside-aware objectives)

When investor pain is asymmetric, an IPS may prioritize downside control. Examples include:

- **Minimize Expected Shortfall** at confidence level α:

$$\min_{\mathbf{w}} \ ES_\alpha(\mathbf{w}^\top \mathbf{R}).$$

- **Minimize probability of falling below a target** (shortfall probability):
$$\min_{\mathbf{w}} \ \mathbb{P}(\mathbf{w}^\top \mathbf{R} < \tau).$$

These objectives can be evaluated via historical simulation or scenario models. They are often more aligned with liability-driven or spending-driven mandates than volatility-based objectives.

Include trading costs directly in the objective

From the microstructure section, turnover is not free. A cost-aware objective often looks like

$$\max_{\mathbf{w}} \ \mathbf{w}^\top \hat{\mu} - \lambda \, \mathbf{w}^\top \hat{\Sigma} \mathbf{w} - \gamma \, C(\mathbf{w}, \mathbf{w}^{prev}),$$

where $C(\mathbf{w}, \mathbf{w}^{prev})$ is a trading cost model (often proportional to turnover or a nonlinear impact proxy), and γ controls how strongly the optimizer avoids trading.

Interpretation. This objective formalizes a real-world truth: the best portfolio on paper is not the best portfolio after implementation.

Step 3: encode constraints that reflect reality

Constraints transform a theoretical optimum into a portfolio that can be governed, implemented, and survived.

Hard vs soft constraints

A useful distinction:

Hard constraints. Must never be violated (policy, regulation, mandate):

- no leverage (or leverage cap),
- no shorting (or shorting limits),
- maximum allocation to illiquid assets,

- concentration limits.

Soft constraints. Preferences that can be traded off against performance:

- tracking error targets,
- turnover targets,
- mild factor exposure neutrality,
- tax-aware realizations.

Soft constraints are often implemented as penalties (as in the cost-aware objective) rather than strict bounds.

Common constraint families

Below are constraint types that appear repeatedly in multi-asset IPS design.

Long-only / leverage / gross exposure.

$$w_i \geq 0$$

(long-only)

$$\sum_{i=1}^{N} |w_i| \leq G^{\max}$$

(gross exposure cap)

$$\sum_{i=1}^{N} w_i = 1$$

(budget / fully invested)

Position and concentration limits.

$$w_i \leq w_i^{\max}$$

and

$$\sum_{i \in \mathcal{S}} w_i \leq W_{\mathcal{S}}^{\max}$$

where S might represent a sector, region, or asset-class sleeve.

Volatility (risk) limits.

$$\sqrt{\mathbf{w}^\top \hat{\Sigma} \mathbf{w}} \leq \sigma^{\max}.$$

Risk limits are often more stable than return targets because σ is easier to estimate than μ.

Tail-risk limits (ES/VaR constraints).

$$ES_\alpha(\mathbf{w}^\top \mathbf{R}) \leq ES^{\max}.$$

This is particularly relevant for portfolios containing nonlinear or negatively skewed exposures.

Drawdown constraints (path-aware). For each stress scenario considered:

$$MDD(\text{scenario path}) \geq -D^{\max}.$$

In practice, many institutions implement drawdown control via risk overlays, dynamic de-risking rules, or explicit stress scenario constraints.

Liquidity and capacity constraints. A practical IPS often limits exposure to assets that cannot be exited within a specified time:

$$\sum_{i=1}^{N} w_i \cdot \mathbb{I}\{\text{liquidation\_days}(i) > L\} \leq W_{illiquid}^{\max}.$$

For systematic strategies, capacity can be approximated by limiting trade size relative to ADV and limiting turnover.

Turnover constraints (implementation-aware).

$$\sum_{i=1}^{N} |w_i - w_i^{prev}| \leq TO^{\max},$$

or, more flexibly, a turnover penalty in the objective.

Tracking error constraints (benchmark-aware). If $\mathbf{w}^{bm}$ is benchmark weights and $\hat{\Sigma}$ is the covariance of asset returns, tracking error can be approximated as

$$TE(\mathbf{w}) = \sqrt{(\mathbf{w} - \mathbf{w}^{bm})^\top \hat{\Sigma} (\mathbf{w} - \mathbf{w}^{bm})} \leq TE^{\max}.$$

Constraints are not an afterthought: they are the portfolio

In real portfolio construction, constraints do more than "limit extremes." They often define the economic meaning of the portfolio:

- A leverage constraint determines whether a risk-parity concept is implementable.
- A liquidity constraint determines whether drawdown control is feasible under forced selling.
- A turnover constraint determines whether a signal-based overlay survives trading costs.
- A concentration constraint determines whether the portfolio is diversified in a way that committees can hold through stress.

This ties directly to earlier lessons on estimation error: constraints are a **regularizer**. They prevent the optimizer from translating tiny, noisy differences in estimated returns and correlations into extreme weights.

A structured IPS template: from words to math

A practical way to write an IPS for quantitative portfolio work is to use a structured template:

(1) Objective

Choose one primary objective (and optionally secondary penalties). Examples:

- maximize expected return net of costs at a risk target,
- maximize Sharpe subject to tail limits,
- minimize Expected Shortfall subject to minimum return,
- maximize expected log growth with conservative leverage caps.

(2) Primary risk definition

State the risk definition used in the constraint set:

- volatility,
- ES at α,
- drawdown under stress scenarios,
- a combination (e.g., volatility cap plus ES cap).

(3) Constraints

List hard constraints first, then soft preferences:

- long-only / leverage / gross exposure,
- asset-class caps and floors,
- liquidity limits,
- turnover limits,
- tracking error limits,
- regulatory and operational constraints.

(4) Inputs and estimation policy

Specify:

- data frequency (monthly vs daily),
- lookback windows,
- shrinkage and regularization choices,
- stress testing methodology,
- how costs are estimated and updated.

(5) Rebalancing and governance

Define:

- rebalance frequency or threshold bands,
- escalation rules when constraints are breached,
- documentation and change-control for model updates.

What to carry forward

The quantitative IPS is the bridge between investment intent and portfolio reality. The purpose of writing it as "objective + constraints" is not mathematical elegance; it is **accountability and robustness**. It forces the portfolio manager to answer:

- What outcome are we optimizing (and in what units)?
- Which risks are we controlling (volatility, tail loss, drawdown, liquidity)?
- What constraints reflect the true limits of implementation and governance?

Once these are explicit, the next step in portfolio engineering is straightforward in concept (though subtle in execution): solve the optimization problem, test sensitivity to estimation error, stress the portfolio under non-Normal scenarios, and evaluate implementation drag. Those are the building blocks of resilient multi-asset design—a theme that will recur throughout the subsequent portfolio construction chapters.

Chapter 2

The Asset Class Ecosystem

To the uninitiated, asset classes are merely ticker symbols moving in random unison. To the multi-asset strategist, they are distinct biological species that thrive or perish under specific economic conditions. This chapter strips away the marketing labels to reveal the mechanical engines beneath-explaining why equities are actually long-duration volatility instruments, why bonds provide convexity rather than just yield, and why the price of a commodity is rarely the return of the investor. By mastering these distinct risk profiles, we move beyond simple diversification into true structural harmony.

2.1 Equities: Decomposition of Growth and Risk

Equities occupy a special place in multi-asset portfolio design: they are typically the *primary engine of long-run real wealth creation*, but they are also the dominant contributor to drawdowns and portfolio-level volatility. In prior sections of this chapter, we established two foundational ideas that will now be applied directly to equities:

- **Portfolios are built from risk budgets, not return wishes.** A dollar allocated to a volatile asset class consumes more of the portfolio's risk capacity than a dollar allocated to a stable one.
- **Diversification is a correlation problem.** The usefulness of an asset is determined not only by its standalone expected return and volatility, but by how it behaves when the rest of the portfolio is under stress.

This section provides the allocator's practical bridge from *equity stories* ("stocks return 8%") to *equity mechanics* (what *must* happen for those returns to occur, and which parts are reliable versus speculative). The key tool is a disciplined decomposition of equity returns into:

- **Dividend yield** (cash paid to shareholders),
- **Earnings growth** (fundamental business compounding),
- **Valuation change** (how much investors are willing to pay per dollar of earnings).

The payoff is twofold:

- It improves **long-horizon forecasting** by separating slow-moving fundamentals from fast-moving sentiment.
- It clarifies **equity risk** as a layered set of exposures (market, region, sector) that must be sized and diversified intentionally.

Why decomposition matters: forecasting versus storytelling

A common forecasting mistake is to treat equity returns as a single "expected number." That approach ignores a crucial reality: the *most forecastable* components of equity return are not the ones that dominate short-run performance.

- Over **months to a few years**, equity returns are often dominated by **valuation changes** (multiple expansion or contraction), which are difficult to predict and can reverse abruptly.

- Over **many years**, equity returns are largely governed by **fundamentals** (earnings growth and dividends), which are slower-moving and more tightly connected to macroeconomic and corporate cash-flow realities.

Decomposition forces an investor to answer: *Am I forecasting a return because I expect businesses to compound, or because I expect others to pay higher prices for the same stream of earnings?* The former is an investment thesis; the latter is primarily a sentiment thesis.

A practical return decomposition (Grinold–Kroner style)

A convenient long-run approximation for the expected return on equities starts from a simple identity: the total return to shareholders comes from cash distributions plus growth in the underlying cash-generating capacity, plus any change in the valuation applied to that capacity.

One common form of the Grinold–Kroner decomposition expresses the expected equity return as

$$\mathbb{E}[R] \approx \frac{D}{P} + g + \Delta \ln\left(\frac{P}{E}\right) + \alpha$$

where:

- R is the total return on equities (price change plus dividends),
- D/P is the dividend yield,
- g is the long-run growth rate of earnings (or dividends, depending on implementation),
- P/E is the valuation multiple (price-to-earnings),
- $\Delta \ln(P/E)$ is the change in the log multiple (approximately the percentage change in the multiple),
- α collects smaller effects and modeling choices (e.g., net share repurchases/issuance if you choose to model per-share growth explicitly, or accounting adjustments).

Interpretation (what each term really means).

- **Dividend yield $\frac{D}{P}$:** the portion of return you receive even if the market price goes nowhere. It is "visible" and immediate, but it is not guaranteed (dividends can be cut).
- **Fundamental growth g:** the compounding engine. In aggregate, long-run earnings growth is tied to economic growth, inflation, and changes in corporate profit share of GDP.
- **Valuation change $\Delta \ln(P/E)$:** the sentiment accelerator (or brake). It can dominate short-term outcomes, but it is mean-reverting in many historical episodes and hard to forecast with precision.

From identity to intuition: two extreme worlds

It helps to visualize two extreme "worlds," both consistent with Equation (2.1).

World A: Fundamentals dominate. Assume the valuation multiple is stable over a decade:

$$\Delta \ln(P/E) \approx 0.$$

Then

$$\mathbb{E}[R] \approx \frac{D}{P} + g.$$

In this world, equity returns are largely the sum of *cash yield* and *business growth*. Forecasting becomes a macro-plus-micro exercise: What is sustainable growth? What payout policy is likely?

World B: Valuations dominate. Assume earnings growth disappoints but valuations expand sharply:

$$g \text{ low}, \qquad \Delta \ln(P/E) \text{ high}.$$

Returns can still be strong, but they are more dependent on *someone else paying more tomorrow for the same earnings today*. This tends to be a less stable foundation for strategic (long-horizon) return expectations.

Making the decomposition investable: a forecasting workflow

Decomposition is not just a conceptual lens; it is a forecasting workflow. A disciplined allocator can use the following sequence.

Step 1: Start with dividend yield as the observable anchor

Dividend yield is not a forecast of prosperity; it is a starting point that is *priced in today*. Two cautions matter in practice:

- **Dividends versus total payout:** Many markets return capital through repurchases rather than dividends. If you only use D/P, you may understate shareholder yield in repurchase-heavy markets.
- **Cyclicality of payouts:** In recessions, dividends can be cut; in expansions, they can be raised. The yield you observe today is not a promise, but it is still a useful baseline.

Step 2: Estimate sustainable long-run earnings growth

For long-horizon strategic allocation, the central question is: *What can the aggregate earnings base compound at without relying on ever-rising profit margins?*

A robust way to think about earnings growth is to break it into macro building blocks:

$$g \approx g_{real} + \pi + \Delta_{profitshare} + \Delta_{netdilutionrepurchases}$$

Here:

- g_{real} is real economic growth (productivity plus labor force growth),
- π is inflation (which tends to lift nominal revenues and earnings over time),

- profit share changes capture whether corporations are taking a larger or smaller slice of total income,
- net dilution/repurchases reflects whether earnings are spread across more shares (dilution) or fewer shares (repurchases), which matters for *per-share* earnings growth.

Practical principle. Long-run earnings growth that persistently exceeds nominal GDP growth usually requires either:

- a rising profit share,
- increasing leverage (which can be fragile), or
- sustained net share reduction.

Any of these may occur for extended periods, but none should be assumed indefinitely without explicit justification.

Step 3: Treat valuation change as a scenario variable, not a baseline

The term $\Delta \ln(P/E)$ is often the most tempting to "plug" with optimism, because it can quickly boost expected returns. A strategic allocator should instead treat it as mean-reversion-sensitive:

- If starting valuations are *high* relative to history, one should consider scenarios where $\Delta \ln(P/E)$ is negative over the horizon (multiple contraction).
- If starting valuations are *low*, positive valuation change is plausible, but still uncertain.

A clean way to operationalize this is:

$$\Delta \ln(P/E) \approx \frac{1}{T} \ln\left(\frac{(P/E)_{terminal}}{(P/E)_{today}}\right),$$

where T is the horizon in years. The key is that the investor must explicitly state a terminal valuation assumption rather than letting "hope" silently do the work.

Step 4: Combine components into a range, not a point estimate

Because valuation change and even growth are uncertain, the output should be a **range** of expected returns, not a single number. For example:

- a conservative case with lower growth and multiple contraction,
- a base case with stable multiples,
- an optimistic case with strong growth and mild multiple expansion.

This range becomes the input to risk budgeting: you are not only forecasting return, you are deciding whether the risk you must bear is *priced attractively*.

Equity risk: what you are actually holding

Return decomposition explains *where returns come from*. Risk decomposition explains *why equities can hurt you* and why equity allocations should almost never be treated as monolithic.

At a high level, equity risk can be layered as:

$$R_{equity} \approx \beta_{mkt} F_{mkt} + \sum_r \beta_r F_r + \sum_s \beta_s F_s + \varepsilon$$

where:

- F_{mkt} is the global equity market factor (the "risk-on / risk-off" engine),
- F_r are regional or country factors (policy regimes, currency and inflation dynamics, geopolitics),
- F_s are sector/industry factors (energy shocks, rate sensitivity of growth sectors, regulation),
- ε is idiosyncratic risk (security-specific outcomes).

The key allocator message. Most equity drawdowns that matter at the portfolio level are not idiosyncratic. They are driven by F_{mkt} plus clustered regional/sector exposures. In stress, correlations often rise, and the market factor dominates.

Geographic equity risk: more than international diversification

Geographic diversification is often presented as "own multiple countries." The deeper point is that regions embed *different macro sensitivities*:

- **Currency exposure:** A U.S.-based investor holding foreign equities holds both equity risk and currency risk unless hedged. Currency can diversify or amplify outcomes depending on the shock.
- **Inflation and policy regimes:** Some markets have a history of higher inflation volatility, different central bank reaction functions, and different fiscal dynamics.
- **Sector composition by market:** Many equity markets are effectively sector bets in disguise (e.g., heavy financials, heavy commodities, heavy tech).

Thus, geographic allocation is not just "more lines on a map"; it is a choice about macro factor exposure.

Sector equity risk: the hidden duration of equities

Sectors differ materially in their sensitivity to discount rates and economic cycles:

- **Long-duration equities:** High-growth sectors (often technology or biotech) can behave like long-duration assets because much of their value is tied to cash flows far in the future. Rising real rates can compress valuations sharply (a direct hit to $\Delta \ln(P/E)$).

- **Cyclical sectors:** Industrials, consumer discretionary, and some financials tend to be more sensitive to the business cycle; earnings growth g becomes highly pro-cyclical.

- **Defensive sectors:** Consumer staples and health care often display more stable earnings, but can still suffer valuation compression if starting multiples are high.

This sector "hidden duration" framing is essential: even within equities, you are choosing a term structure of cash flows, not merely a list of ticker symbols.

Linking decomposition to portfolio construction: what belongs in the risk budget?

A multi-asset portfolio is not improved by holding "more assets"; it is improved by holding *distinct sources of compensated risk* and by not unknowingly doubling up on the same risk factor.

Equities typically consume the largest share of risk budget because:

- equity volatility is structurally higher than high-quality bonds,

- equity drawdowns are deeper and more frequent,

- equity correlations across regions and sectors rise during crises.

Return decomposition gives a practical discipline for how much equity risk to own:

- If your expected return is mostly **dividend yield + plausible earnings growth**, you have a sturdier basis for a strategic allocation.

- If your expected return relies heavily on **multiple expansion**, you are implicitly increasing dependence on sentiment and reducing the margin of safety.

A compact allocator checklist

Before finalizing an equity allocation (and before arguing about "the" expected return), a professional allocator should be able to answer the following in plain language:

- **Dividend and payout:** What portion of expected return comes from cash returned to shareholders (dividends and/or net buybacks)?
- **Growth:** What macro and micro assumptions support earnings growth? Are they consistent with nominal GDP, margins, and competitive dynamics?
- **Valuation:** Are you assuming stable, rising, or falling multiples? What terminal valuation do you believe is plausible over your horizon, and why?
- **Risk layers:** Which regions and sectors dominate your equity sleeve? What macro factors are you implicitly overweighting?
- **Stress behavior:** In a severe risk-off event, do you expect this equity sleeve to behave differently from global equities, or will it converge toward the market factor?

Summary: the disciplined equity return narrative

Equities are not a single bet; they are a bundle of return components and a stack of risk exposures. The decomposition framework in Equation (2.1) gives the allocator a rigorous but practical narrative:

- **Dividend yield** is the near-term, observable anchor.
- **Earnings growth** is the compounding engine that justifies long-horizon equity ownership.
- **Valuation change** is the sentiment amplifier that dominates short horizons but should be treated as uncertain and scenario-driven.

In the next section, we extend this logic from "the equity market" to *systematic equity drivers*—factors such as Value, Momentum, and Quality—and show how factor tilts can reshape both the return decomposition and the risk decomposition of an equity allocation.

2.2 Equity Factors and Smart Beta Allocations

From cap-weighted beta to systematic premia

A traditional market-cap weighted index is often presented as "the market portfolio." In implementation terms, it is a portfolio whose weights are proportional to market capitalization:

$$w_i^{mkt} = \frac{MarketCap_i}{\sum_{j=1}^{N} MarketCap_j}.$$

This construction has useful properties—it is liquid, scalable, and self-rebalancing—but it is not neutral. A cap-weighted portfolio systematically allocates more capital to securities whose prices have already risen and whose market capitalizations are larger. That is neither "good" nor "bad," but it is a statement about what risks you are emphasizing.

Smart beta begins where cap-weighting ends: it keeps the transparency and rules-based implementation of indexing, while intentionally tilting the portfolio toward one or more systematic characteristics that have historically been associated with higher long-run returns, lower risk, or both.

A simple mental model. Think of cap-weighted beta as owning the *average* company in proportion to its size. Think of factor tilts as deciding that you want to own *more* of a certain type of company (e.g., cheap, improving, profitable, stable) and *less* of another type.

What exactly is a "factor"?

A factor is a systematic source of return (or risk) that is:

- **broad:** it applies to many securities,
- **persistent:** it has shown up across long samples (though not in every subperiod),
- **investable:** it can be captured with transparent, rules-based portfolios,
- **distinct:** it is not merely a relabeling of market beta.

A convenient way to express this in a portfolio context is to write the equity portfolio return as

$$R_p \approx \beta_{mkt}F_{mkt}+\beta_{val}F_{val}+\beta_{mom}F_{mom}+\beta_{qual}F_{qual}+\beta_{size}F_{size}+\beta_{lowvol}F_{lowvol}+\varepsilon,$$

where $F_{\cdot}$ are factor returns (market, value, momentum, quality, etc.), $\beta_{\cdot}$ are the portfolio's exposures, and ε is residual (idiosyncratic) return.

For allocators, the important point is not the exact regression specification. The important point is that **"equity risk" is a vector, not a scalar**. Two portfolios can both be "100% equities" and behave very differently because their factor exposures differ.

The big three: Value, Momentum, and Quality

Many factors have been proposed, but three are particularly central for allocators because they are intuitive, widely implemented, and interact in a useful way when blended: **Value**, **Momentum**, and **Quality**.

Value: paying less for a dollar of fundamentals

Definition (intuition first). Value strategies tilt toward securities that are "cheap" relative to fundamentals—for example, low price-to-book, low price-to-earnings, low price-to-cash-flow, or high dividend yield.

Why it might earn a premium. Two broad explanations are commonly offered:

1. **Risk-based:** value stocks may be fundamentally riskier (more cyclical, more financially levered, more exposed to distress). Investors demand compensation for bearing that risk.

2. **Behavioral:** investors may overpay for glamorous growth stories and underpay for dull, challenged, or unpopular firms; prices mean-revert as expectations adjust.

How it actually behaves (what allocators must respect). Value does not fail quietly. It tends to suffer in recognizable environments:

- **Growth-led markets** where long-duration "story stocks" command rising multiples,
- **recession scares** where distressed balance sheets are punished,
- **structural disruptions** where some "cheap" firms are cheap for a reason (value traps).

Implementation note. Naïve value screens can load heavily on sector bets (e.g., financials, energy) or on firms with deteriorating fundamentals. Many modern implementations therefore pair value with *quality screens* to avoid systematically buying the weakest businesses.

Momentum: owning what is already working

Definition. Momentum strategies tilt toward securities with strong recent performance (e.g., 6–12 month returns), and away from recent underperformers.

Why it might earn a premium. Two complementary stories are useful:

1. **Behavioral underreaction:** information diffuses slowly; investors update beliefs gradually; trends persist longer than a fully rational model would predict.
2. **Institutional frictions:** benchmarking, career risk, and slow-moving flows can reinforce trends.

The signature risk: momentum crashes. Momentum's worst drawdowns often occur during **sharp regime reversals**: the market snaps from "risk-off" to "risk-on" (or vice versa), and the previous winners become the new losers quickly. This is not a minor caveat; it is the defining risk of the factor.

Implementation note. Momentum needs explicit risk controls: turnover constraints, sector neutrality considerations, and often some form of volatility scaling. Without those, transaction costs and crash risk can dominate realized results.

Quality: paying up for resilience (but not overpaying)

Definition. Quality is a broad family of metrics that tilts toward firms with stronger profitability, cleaner balance sheets, and more stable earnings. Common inputs include:

- return on equity (ROE) or return on invested capital (ROIC),
- gross profitability or operating margins,
- leverage and interest coverage,
- earnings stability and accrual quality.

Why it might earn a premium. Quality can be interpreted as either:

1. **a behavioral anomaly:** investors underappreciate compounding from durable business models, or
2. **a structural preference:** constrained investors pay up for safety, leaving a premium for those willing to hold lower-quality firms; alternatively, quality can be seen as a way to avoid unrewarded tail risks (fraud, distress, dilution).

The key allocator nuance. Quality often behaves defensively in drawdowns, but it can become **expensive**. When the market prices quality as a "bond proxy" (high multiples for stable cash flows), the factor can suffer when discount rates rise and valuations compress. In other words, quality can drift toward *long-duration equity* characteristics if price is ignored.

Smart beta is portfolio engineering, not factor evangelism

A professional allocator should think of smart beta as **engineering the equity sleeve** to achieve a desired mix of:

- long-run expected return,
- drawdown behavior,
- sector and macro sensitivities,
- implementation robustness (liquidity, turnover, capacity, costs).

This framing avoids the most common mistake: treating a factor back-test as a perpetual "free lunch." Factors are better viewed as *cyclical premia with long-run positive expectation*, interrupted by periods of painful underperformance.

Factor cyclicality: why patience is not optional

If market beta is the tide, factors are the currents. They are persistent over long periods but highly variable over shorter ones. The practical implication is that a factor allocation is a **multi-year commitment**, not a quarterly trade.

A useful allocator rule of thumb. If a factor premium exists, it must be uncomfortable to hold at times; otherwise it would be arbitraged away. Therefore, a factor allocation plan should specify *in advance*:

- the intended role (return enhancement, risk reduction, diversification within equities),
- the maximum tolerated tracking error versus cap-weighted benchmarks,
- the rebalancing discipline (when you add after underperformance rather than abandon the exposure).

Without such pre-commitment, many investors mechanically buy factors after they perform well and sell after they disappoint—transforming a long-run premium into a behavioral penalty.

Factor crowding: when the trade becomes the risk

As smart beta has grown, an additional risk has become more relevant: **crowding.** Crowding occurs when too much capital targets similar signals, leading to:

- **valuation distortions** (the factor itself becomes expensive),
- **liquidity risk** (many investors try to exit the same trades at once),
- **correlation spikes** among strategies that look diversified on paper.

Crowding is especially important for allocators because it can cause factor behavior to become more "macro-like" during stress. A factor that is supposed to diversify within equities can instead become another source of synchronized de-risking.

Practical diagnostic questions. When evaluating a smart beta product or internal factor sleeve, ask:

1. Is the factor definition **standardized** (and therefore likely to be crowded), or does it incorporate robust variants?
2. Does the strategy rely on **less liquid names** (small cap, micro cap) that may not scale?
3. Is the reported historical performance **net of realistic trading costs** and turnover?
4. How does the strategy behave when **equity volatility spikes** and liquidity drops?

Blending factors: why Value and Momentum are natural complements

A central allocator insight is that factors can be combined to reduce the likelihood of catastrophic underperformance in any one regime. The most classic and practical blend is **Value + Momentum**:

- Value tends to like *mean reversion* (cheap gets less cheap).
- Momentum tends to like *trend continuation* (winners keep winning).

Because these are different return mechanisms, their payoffs often arrive in different market environments. When blended thoughtfully, one can partially offset the other's weakest periods. Importantly, the goal is not to eliminate drawdowns—it is to create a more stable path of relative performance so the allocator can **stick with the allocation**.

Adding **Quality** can further improve robustness by reducing exposure to fragile balance sheets that value screens might unintentionally emphasize and by improving the resilience of momentum winners.

A simple multi-factor construction (conceptual, implementable) A practical, transparent multi-factor equity sleeve often follows this blueprint:

1. **Define the universe:** liquid equities with minimum size and trading volume constraints.
2. **Compute standardized scores:** for each stock, compute z-scores for value, momentum, and quality metrics.
3. **Combine scores:** average or weighted sum to get a composite factor score.
4. **Portfolio formation:** tilt weights toward higher scores with constraints:
   - sector neutrality bands to avoid unintended macro bets,
   - single-name and country limits,
   - turnover and transaction cost controls,
   - volatility scaling if desired.
5. **Rebalance:** on a fixed schedule (e.g., quarterly) with explicit trading-cost awareness.

From an allocator's perspective, the primary decision is not the exact scoring formula; it is the **governance**: do you have a process designed to survive factor cycles, costs, and stress regimes?

How factors connect back to the equity return decomposition

Return decomposition (dividends, growth, valuation change) helps forecast broad equity returns. Factor investing changes the *mix* of those components:

- **Value tilts** often start with higher dividend yields and lower starting valuations, implicitly reducing reliance on future multiple expansion.
- **Momentum tilts** often embed a valuation component (winners may become more expensive), increasing sensitivity to reversals in $\Delta \ln(P/E)$.
- **Quality tilts** often emphasize earnings stability and profitability, potentially improving the *reliability* of the growth component g, but sometimes at the cost of higher starting valuations.

This is the unifying allocator insight: **factors are not separate from decomposition; they are ways of choosing which parts of equity return you want to lean on.**

Smart beta in the total portfolio: role clarity and risk budgeting

Within a multi-asset portfolio, factor tilts should be evaluated as changes to:

- **equity sleeve tracking error** versus cap-weighted benchmarks,
- **portfolio drawdown profile** (especially in equity stress),
- **cross-asset correlations** (e.g., rate sensitivity embedded via sector tilts or "bond-proxy" behavior).

A useful risk-budget framing is: *Treat factor tilts as an active risk allocation inside equities.* That means the allocator should size factor sleeves by **risk contribution** (tracking error, expected drawdown contribution), not by capital alone. A modest capital tilt can create a meaningful shift in risk if it concentrates exposures (for example, heavy momentum into a narrow set of large growth names).

Common implementation pitfalls (and how to avoid them)

Pitfall 1: Paying active fees for disguised beta Some products marketed as smart beta are primarily repackaged sector bets (e.g., implicit tech overweight) or leverage to market beta. The defense is to demand:

- factor exposure reports (betas to standard factor models),
- sector and country attribution,
- performance in multiple stress regimes (not only in a single bull market).

Pitfall 2: Ignoring trading costs and turnover Momentum and some quality signals can generate high turnover. If costs are ignored, paper premia disappear in live portfolios. Require:

- turnover statistics,
- realistic transaction cost assumptions,
- implementation details (rebalancing schedule, constraints, liquidity filters).

Pitfall 3: Allocating at the wrong time (performance chasing) Factor timing is notoriously difficult. The simplest defense is governance: commit to a diversified multi-factor allocation sized appropriately to the risk budget, then rebalance systematically rather than tactically chasing recent winners.

Summary: factors as the allocator's toolkit inside equities

Cap-weighted equities provide broad market exposure and scalability, but they embed implicit bets. Equity factors and smart beta are the allocator's toolkit for making those bets explicit and intentional.

- **Value** seeks cheapness; it can be powerful but cyclical and vulnerable to value traps.
- **Momentum** seeks trend persistence; it can be diversifying but carries crash risk in reversals.
- **Quality** seeks profitability and resilience; it can reduce fragility but may become expensive and rate-sensitive.

A well-designed smart beta allocation is not a claim that any single factor will "win" consistently. It is a structured choice to harvest multiple, distinct equity premia with controls that make the allocation *survivable* through inevitable cycles.

2.3 Fixed Income: Duration, Convexity, and Pricing

The prior sections built the equity sleeve from first principles: we decomposed equity returns into dividend yield, earnings growth, and valuation change, and then showed how factor tilts (Value, Momentum, Quality) reshape equity risk and return within a rules-based framework. The unifying message was that equity is the portfolio's growth engine—but it is also the portfolio's dominant source of drawdown risk, especially when correlations rise during stress.

Fixed income enters the multi-asset ecosystem as the *counterweight* to that equity-dominated risk budget. High-quality government bonds, in particular, have historically served two roles that are easy to state but often misunderstood in practice:

- **Volatility dampener:** bonds can reduce portfolio volatility because their price fluctuations are often smaller than equities and because their returns can be weakly correlated—or even negatively correlated—with equities during risk-off regimes.

- **Deflation / growth-shock hedge:** when inflation falls or growth expectations deteriorate, central banks often cut rates and investors demand safe assets. Yields decline, and bond prices rise.

To use bonds intelligently, the allocator must understand the mechanics: **bond pricing**, **duration** (first-order rate sensitivity), and **convexity** (second-order curvature that improves outcomes when rates move).

The bond as a priced stream of cash flows

A plain-vanilla bond is a contract that pays:

- periodic coupons C (often semiannual), and
- principal (face value) F at maturity T.

Ignoring default risk for the moment, the bond's price is the present value of these promised cash flows discounted at the market yield y:

$$P(y) = \sum_{t=1}^{T} \frac{C}{(1+y)^t} + \frac{F}{(1+y)^T}.$$

Two immediate implications follow:

- **Prices move inversely to yields.** If y rises, the discount rate increases, present values fall, and the bond price drops. If y falls, the bond price rises.
- **Longer cash flows are more sensitive.** The further in the future a cash flow arrives, the more sensitive its present value is to changes in y.

This is why maturity matters, but maturity alone is not the full story. The relevant concept is not "years to maturity" but the *timing-weighted average* of cash flows: **duration**.

Duration: the first-order risk of bonds

Duration answers a practical question: *If yields change a little, about how much does the bond price change?*

Modified duration as a price sensitivity

For small yield changes Δy, the bond's percentage price change is approximately linear:

$$\frac{\Delta P}{P} \approx -D_{mod}\,\Delta y,$$

where D_{mod} is the **modified duration** (measured in years), and Δy is in decimal form (so 100 basis points is 0.01).

Interpretation. If a bond has $D_{mod} = 7$, then:

- a $+1\%$ (100 bp) rise in yields implies roughly a -7% price change,
- a -1% fall in yields implies roughly a $+7\%$ price change.

The approximation above is the backbone of bond risk management because it translates a complex set of discounted cash flows into a single, tradable risk number. But it is only a *first-order* approximation; actual bond price-yield relationships are not straight lines.

Macaulay duration: the "center of mass" of cash flows

Modified duration is used for price sensitivity; Macaulay duration is the intuition-building version: it is the present-value-weighted average time to receiving cash flows. In discrete time:

$$D_{Mac} = \frac{1}{P}\sum_{t=1}^{T} t \cdot \frac{CF_t}{(1+y)^t}$$

and

$$D_{mod} = \frac{D_{Mac}}{1+y},$$

where CF_t are the bond's cash flows.

Two bonds with the same maturity can have different durations:

- A **high-coupon bond** returns more cash earlier $\Rightarrow$ lower duration.
- A **low-coupon bond** returns more cash later $\Rightarrow$ higher duration.

From a risk-budgeting perspective, duration is the bond market's analog to equity beta: it is the primary lever that scales exposure to the dominant systematic driver of high-quality bond returns—**interest rates**.

Convexity: the curvature that makes high-quality bonds special

Duration treats the price-yield relationship as a straight line. The true relationship is curved. This curvature is called **convexity**.

Mathematically, we can write a second-order approximation:

$$\frac{\Delta P}{P} \approx -D_{mod}\,\Delta y + \frac{1}{2}\,Conv\,(\Delta y)^2,$$

where $Conv$ is convexity (units of years squared, scaled appropriately).

Why allocators care. For a standard option-free bond, convexity is **positive**. Positive convexity means:

- When yields *fall*, the bond price rises *more* than the duration-only (linear) estimate.
- When yields *rise*, the bond price falls *less* than the duration-only estimate.

This is not merely a mathematical curiosity. It is one reason high-quality government bonds can be such effective portfolio insurance in acute risk-off episodes: the bigger the rally in bonds (from yields falling), the more the curve bends in your favor.

Why the curve bends: a cash-flow intuition

As yields fall, the present value of long-dated cash flows increases disproportionately because discounting becomes less severe. Those distant cash flows begin to "matter more" in today's price. The bond effectively behaves as if its duration is increasing when yields fall, and decreasing when yields rise. That state-dependent sensitivity produces the curved price-yield relationship.

Why bonds protect portfolios during flight-to-quality events

A portfolio manager does not own bonds for their elegance; they own them for what they do in stress.

A typical equity drawdown caused by a growth scare or deflationary impulse tends to coincide with:

- falling policy-rate expectations,
- declining term premia as investors seek safety,
- a bid for liquidity and high-quality collateral.

All three forces can push yields lower. Through the bond pricing formula above, lower yields mechanically raise bond prices. Duration tells you the *size* of that sensitivity; convexity tells you that the payoff can be *better than linear* when rates fall sharply.

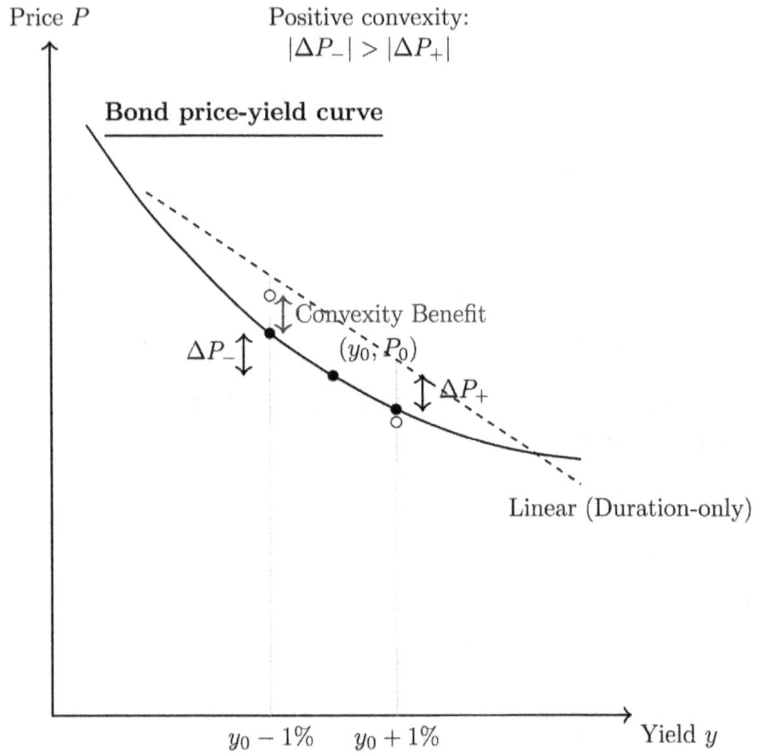

The "free lunch" has conditions: when convexity is not your friend

The positive convexity shown above describes **option-free** bonds. Many bonds in real portfolios are *not* option-free:

- **Callable bonds** (common in corporates and municipals) embed an issuer option: when rates fall, the issuer can refinance, limiting price appreciation. This creates **negative convexity** in the relevant range.
- **Mortgage-backed securities** embed borrower prepayment

options: when rates fall, prepayments accelerate and the investor gets principal back sooner, again limiting upside and changing duration dynamically ("contraction risk").

This is why the highest-quality government bond portfolio (Treasuries) often behaves as the cleanest "crisis hedge" instrument: it tends to be closer to option-free and dominated by rate exposure.

Total return of bonds: separating carry from price change

For allocators, the bond return over a horizon combines:

- **Carry / income:** the coupon and the pull-to-par effect if the bond is priced away from par,
- **Price change:** driven mainly by yield changes (duration and convexity effects),
- **Roll-down (for curves that slope upward):** as time passes, a bond "rolls" down the curve to a lower yield (higher price), all else equal.

This mirrors the equity decomposition conceptually: bonds also have components that are more "structural" (carry, roll) and components that are more "state-dependent" (rate moves). The key difference is that the bond components are governed by discounting mechanics rather than business growth.

Risk budgeting with duration: the bond sleeve's primary dial

In a multi-asset portfolio, the most important sizing decision inside high-quality fixed income is not "bonds yes/no," but **how much duration** you hold.

- **Short duration** provides stability and liquidity, but less protection in deep risk-off episodes because price sensitivity is small.

- **Long duration** provides more crisis convexity and stronger equity-hedging potential, but it also raises vulnerability to inflation shocks and rate spikes.

Thus, duration is the primary dial that translates the qualitative objective "defensive ballast" into a quantitative exposure that can be stress-tested and sized within the portfolio's risk budget.

Summary: why bonds belong in a resilient multi-asset portfolio

High-quality bonds are not held because they always "beat cash" or because they always diversify equities. They are held because their pricing mechanics produce a distinctive payoff pattern in key macro regimes.

- **Duration** explains the first-order protection: when yields fall, prices rise; longer duration increases sensitivity.

- **Convexity** explains why the protection can improve precisely when you need it most: price gains from large rate cuts can exceed losses from comparable rate hikes.

- **Option-free government bonds** tend to offer the cleanest version of this hedge because they preserve positive convexity and avoid embedded call/prepayment options.

With this foundation in place, we can now examine the hybrid middle ground between pure rate exposure and pure equity exposure: **credit markets**. Corporate credit introduces default risk and spread dynamics, and its diversification benefits can deteriorate sharply during market stress—a crucial consideration for allocators who rely on "fixed income" as a single, undifferentiated bucket.

2.4 Credit Markets: The Hybrid Risk Sleeve

The previous section established why high-quality government bonds occupy a privileged role in multi-asset portfolios: their cash flows are contractually fixed, their prices are primarily driven by interest rates, and their positive convexity can provide powerful protection in flight-to-quality episodes. In other words, *rates* are the dominant risk, and in deflationary or growth-shock regimes that risk often pays you.

Corporate credit changes the story. It still looks like a bond—a stream of promised coupons and principal—but now the promise depends on the issuer's ability and willingness to pay. The return becomes a blend of two distinct engines:

- **Interest-rate risk** (duration): the same discounting mechanics as Treasuries.
- **Credit risk** (spread/default): compensation for the possibility of downgrade, spread widening, and default.

That is why corporate credit belongs in the book's **ecosystem** as a **hybrid sleeve**: it often behaves like bonds in calm markets and *like equities in stress.* For allocators, that conditional behavior is the main point.

From Treasury yield to corporate yield: where spread enters

A simple way to express a corporate bond yield is:

$$y_{corp} \approx y_{gov} + s,$$

where:

- y_{gov} is the yield on a comparable-maturity government bond (the risk-free or near risk-free rate curve),
- s is the **credit spread**, quoted in basis points.

In practice, the spread you observe in the market is not only "expected default loss." It also embeds compensation for:

- **expected default losses** (probability of default times loss given default),
- **downgrade and migration risk** (a bond can lose value without defaulting),
- **liquidity risk** (corporate bonds can become hard to trade during stress),
- **risk aversion / risk premia** (spreads tend to widen when investors demand safety).

A useful conceptual approximation is:

$$s \approx EL + LR + RP.$$

The allocator's job is not to estimate each term perfectly; it is to understand which ones explode in crises and how that changes correlation behavior.

Credit as "short equity volatility" (a structural intuition)

Credit investors are paid to be confident that the firm will survive. Equity investors are paid to own the residual claim and benefit from upside. In calm periods, survival looks likely, and credit behaves bond-like: coupon carry dominates and spreads are stable.

But structurally, credit is exposed to the firm's downside tail. When the firm's asset value deteriorates, the probability of default rises nonlinearly, spreads widen, and bond prices fall. This produces a payoff profile that is often described as **negatively skewed**: many small gains (carry) punctuated by occasional large losses (spread blowouts, defaults).

This is the sense in which credit can resemble *selling insurance*:

- you collect a steady premium (spread/carry),

- you are vulnerable when risk aversion spikes and the left tail arrives.

This is not a moral judgment about credit; it is a risk-shape description that informs sizing and diversification assumptions.

A simplified Merton view: why spreads are linked to equity risk

A helpful intuition comes from the structural (Merton-style) view of the firm. In the simplest version:

- The firm has assets with value V.
- It has debt with face value F due at maturity.
- Equity is the residual claim: shareholders receive $\max(V - F, 0)$ at maturity.
- Debt holders receive $\min(V, F)$: they are paid in full unless assets fall below the debt level.

Two allocator-grade insights follow immediately:

- **Credit risk increases as the firm becomes more levered.** If V is only slightly above F, small negative shocks can push the firm into distress.
- **Credit spreads are linked to equity volatility.** Higher uncertainty about V (asset volatility) increases the likelihood that $V < F$ at maturity, raising expected loss and spread.

This is why high yield credit often co-moves with equities: the same underlying economic shocks that reduce earnings and raise equity volatility also worsen the firm's "distance to default," widening spreads.

Investment grade versus high yield: two different hybrids

Corporate credit is not one asset class. At minimum, it is two different sleeves with different dominant risks.

Investment grade (IG): more rate-like, until it isn't

Investment grade bonds generally have:

- lower default probabilities,
- tighter spreads,
- higher sensitivity to the risk-free curve because spread duration is smaller relative to interest-rate duration.

In calm regimes, IG often behaves closer to a duration instrument with extra carry. However, in systemic stress, even IG can experience abrupt spread widening due to liquidity evaporation and generalized de-risking. The default risk may not be the primary driver; the *spread risk* and *liquidity premium* can still dominate.

High yield (HY): equity-like in stress

High yield has:

- higher default probabilities and higher loss severity,
- larger spread component of yield (carry dominated),
- greater sensitivity to the business cycle and funding conditions.

HY therefore behaves more like an equity-adjacent risk asset. When growth slows, refinancing becomes harder, downgrade risk rises, and spreads can gap wider. In those environments, HY's correlation to equities tends to rise and its correlation to Treasuries often falls (or even becomes negative), because Treasuries rally as HY sells off.

Duration of spread: the often-missed risk measure

Bond investors are trained to measure interest-rate duration, but credit requires an additional lens: **spread duration**.

A simple approximation for a corporate bond's percentage price change is:

$$\frac{\Delta P}{P} \approx -D_{rate}\,\Delta y_{gov} - D_{spr}\,\Delta s,$$

where:

- D_{rate} is duration to the government curve,
- D_{spr} is duration to credit spreads (often similar in magnitude to interest-rate duration for plain bonds),
- Δs is the change in spread.

In risk-off episodes, it is common to see:

$$\Delta y_{gov} < 0 \quad \text{(Treasury yields fall)} \qquad \text{and} \qquad \Delta s > 0 \quad \text{(spreads widen)}.$$

Whether a corporate bond cushions the portfolio depends on which term dominates.

Key allocator implication. A corporate bond can lose money *even when rates fall* if spread widening is large. This is the mechanical reason credit is a hybrid sleeve rather than a pure diversifier.

The credit curve: why "more yield" can mean "less diversification"

Investors often treat credit as a linear trade: accept more credit risk, earn more yield. The portfolio reality is more subtle. As you move down in quality (from Treasuries to IG to HY), you often observe:

- higher average yield and higher carry,
- higher sensitivity to equity-like growth shocks,
- higher correlation with equities in stress,

- higher drawdown risk due to spread gaps and liquidity.

This produces what allocators should think of as a **credit curve in portfolio space**: *As credit quality declines, the asset behaves less like a hedge and more like a risk asset.*

The important point is not that HY is "bad." The point is that HY belongs in the portfolio's *risk-bearing* budget more than in the *crisis-hedging* budget.

The liquidity cliff: why credit behaves worst when you need it most

Corporate bonds are traded in dealer-intermediated markets and are less standardized than Treasuries. In stress, this matters. Liquidity can deteriorate quickly, leading to:

- **wider bid-ask spreads** and higher transaction costs,
- **price gaps** (discontinuous repricing),
- **forced selling dynamics** from leveraged holders, mutual fund outflows, or risk-parity deleveraging,
- **basis risk** between cash bonds and derivatives (e.g., CDS indices) as hedging demand surges.

In calm markets, credit's extra yield can look like a steady return source. In stress, liquidity premia and risk premia rise simultaneously, amplifying drawdowns. This is the mechanism behind the empirical observation that credit correlations can "break"—not randomly, but systematically—during crises.

Default is not the only loss channel

A frequent misunderstanding is: "Credit is safe unless there are defaults." In reality, investment performance can be damaged well before default occurs:

- **Spread widening:** mark-to-market losses as required yields rise.
- **Downgrades:** forced selling by constrained investors (e.g., fallen angels) and higher required yields.
- **Refinancing risk:** especially for HY, the ability to roll debt maturities is sensitive to the level of rates and the openness of capital markets.
- **Recovery uncertainty:** loss given default can be regime-dependent (recoveries can be low when many firms default at once).

Therefore, for portfolio design, credit risk should be treated as a **continuum of states**, not a binary "default/no default" event.

Where credit fits in a multi-asset portfolio

Credit earns its place because it can provide:

- higher income than Treasuries,
- potentially attractive risk-adjusted returns in stable growth regimes,
- diversification within fixed income relative to pure duration (because spreads and rates are not perfectly correlated).

But the hybrid nature demands role clarity:

A practical role-based map

Sleeve	Primary job	Primary failure mode
Treasuries / gov't	Crisis hedge, deflation protection, liquidity	Inflation shock / rate spike
IG credit	Income enhancement with moderate spread risk	Liquidity-driven spread widening in stress
HY credit	Risk-bearing carry (equity-adjacent)	Equity-like drawdowns; default cycle

The table highlights a core allocator discipline: do not fund an equity risk budget with instruments that behave like equity in the left tail, and do not expect an equity hedge from instruments whose spread risk dominates in crises.

Sizing and governance: treating credit as a risk allocation

Because credit risk is cyclical and negatively skewed, prudent governance emphasizes:

- **risk contribution sizing** (spread DV01, scenario drawdowns), not just market value weights,
- **stress testing** that explicitly combines falling rates with widening spreads,
- **liquidity planning** (ability to meet cash needs without selling credit at the worst time),
- **diversification within credit** (industries, issuers, maturity buckets, and avoiding excessive concentration in the most levered capital structures).

A simple stress-test template. A portfolio manager can sanity-check a credit allocation by applying a two-factor shock using the price-change relation above:

$$\Delta y_{gov} = -100 \text{ bp}, \qquad \Delta s = +300 \text{ bp}$$

(HY-like shock) and observing whether the spread term overwhelms the rate hedge. The point is not to predict the exact magnitude; it is to ensure the portfolio's risk budget is aligned with the intended role of the sleeve.

Summary: credit is the bridge between bonds and stocks

Corporate credit is best understood as the bridge between the clean interest-rate world of government bonds and the residual-claim world of equities:

- Credit inherits **duration** from fixed income and **downside sensitivity** from corporate balance sheets.
- **Spreads** are the price of bearing default, downgrade, liquidity, and risk-premium variability.
- As quality declines, credit becomes more **equity-correlated in stress**, reducing its usefulness as a diversifier precisely when diversification is most valuable.

With this hybrid sleeve mapped, the ecosystem can now expand into **commodities**, where the key complexities are not default and duration, but *futures mechanics*, *term structure*, and the crucial distinction between spot price changes and total return.

2.5 Commodities: Supply Shocks and Term Structure

The chapter has now covered three foundational building blocks of the liquid portfolio:

- **Equities**, whose long-run returns are anchored in dividends and earnings growth but whose short-run outcomes are often dominated by valuation changes and factor cycles.
- **Government bonds**, whose defensive value comes from duration and positive convexity—a mechanical tendency to gain when yields fall during growth scares or deflationary shocks.
- **Corporate credit**, a hybrid sleeve that can behave bond-like in calm regimes but equity-like in stress because spreads widen, liquidity evaporates, and default risk becomes salient.

Commodities enter the ecosystem for a different reason. They are not primarily a claim on corporate cash flows (like equities) and they are not primarily a discounted stream of fixed payments (like bonds).

Instead, commodities are linked to **physical scarcity** and **supply–demand imbalances**. This makes them particularly relevant for one portfolio problem that stocks and bonds can struggle with:

> *unexpected inflation and supply shocks.*

When inflation rises because of supply disruptions (energy shocks, weather events, geopolitical constraints, inventory shortages), both equities and bonds may suffer at the same time: equities face margin pressure and policy tightening; bonds face rising yields. Commodities can help precisely because they are often *the source* of the price pressure.

However, commodities are also one of the most misunderstood asset classes in institutional portfolios. The main misunderstanding is deceptively simple:

> *You cannot usually buy "spot oil" or "spot wheat" in a portfolio. Commodity exposure is typically obtained through futures.*

Once you accept that commodity exposure is usually **futures-based**, you must accept a second implication: commodity returns are not just about where the spot price goes. They are also about **term structure** and **roll yield**. Those mechanics determine whether commodities are a powerful hedge or a slow leak of performance.

Spot versus futures: what you own when you "own commodities"

Spot commodity

The **spot price** is the price for immediate delivery of the physical commodity. It reflects:

- current supply and demand,
- inventories and storage constraints,

- immediate disruptions (refinery outages, harvest shortfalls, shipping bottlenecks).

Most investors cannot efficiently hold spot commodities due to storage, insurance, spoilage, and operational constraints. Even if you could, many commodities are costly to carry.

Futures-based exposure

A **futures contract** is an agreement to buy or sell the commodity at a future date for a price agreed today. Futures are standardized, exchange-traded (for many commodities), and require margin rather than full cash payment upfront.

For an investor, a commodity futures position is typically implemented as:

- holding a near-dated futures contract, and
- periodically **rolling** it into a later-dated contract as it approaches expiration.

This rolling process is where many long-run commodity outcomes are made or lost.

Commodity futures total return: the three-part decomposition

A useful allocator-grade decomposition of commodity futures total return is:

$$\text{Futures Total Return} \approx \underbrace{\Delta\text{Spot}}_{\text{spot price change}} + \underbrace{\text{Roll Yield}}_{\text{term structure effect}} + \underbrace{\text{Collateral Yield}}_{\text{cash on margin}}$$

where:

- ΔSpot is the change in the spot price over the holding period,
- **Roll yield** is the gain or loss from selling an expiring contract and buying the next one,

- **Collateral yield** is the return on the cash collateral (often short-term rates) posted against the futures position.

The decomposition is the commodity counterpart to the earlier equity and bond decompositions. Equities split into yield, growth, and valuation; bonds split into carry and price change via duration/convexity; commodities split into spot, roll, and collateral.

Practical implication. Even if spot prices are flat over a period, a commodity futures strategy can have positive or negative returns depending on roll yield and collateral yield. Conversely, even if spot prices rise, a persistently negative roll yield can materially reduce realized total return.

Term structure: contango versus backwardation

The **futures curve** (term structure) plots futures prices across maturities: 1-month, 3-month, 6-month, etc.

Two shapes dominate commodity discussions:

- **Contango:** longer-dated futures prices are *higher* than near-dated prices (an upward-sloping curve).
- **Backwardation:** longer-dated futures prices are *lower* than near-dated prices (a downward-sloping curve).

Term structure is not cosmetic; it determines the sign of roll yield.

Roll yield: the mechanical gain or loss from rolling

Consider a long-only strategy that holds the front-month contract and rolls it forward each month.

- In **contango**, the next-month contract tends to be *more expensive* than the expiring contract. Rolling means selling low and buying high, creating a **negative roll yield**.
- In **backwardation**, the next-month contract tends to be *cheaper* than the expiring contract. Rolling means selling high and buying low, creating a **positive roll yield**.

This is a key reason commodities can be "powerful but costly" to hold long term: many commodities spend meaningful time in contango, especially when inventories are ample and storage/carry costs are high.

Term structure diagram and the roll mechanism

The following diagram makes the roll mechanics visually explicit. The investor is assumed to be long the front contract and rolling into the next contract.

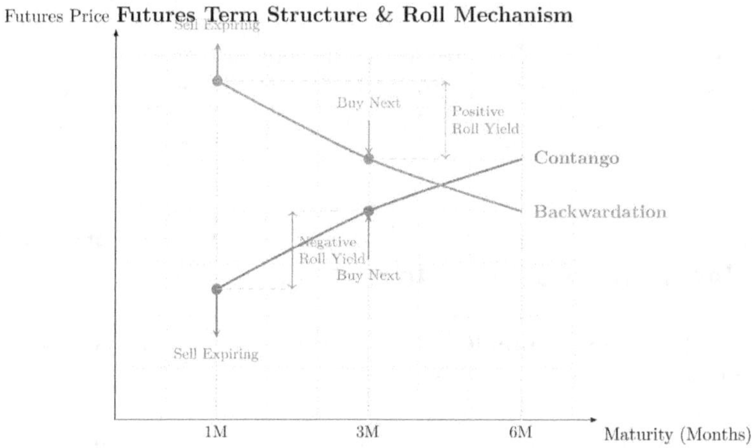

Why contango and backwardation occur (the economics behind the curve)

The curve shape reflects real-world frictions and incentives. A useful starting point is the **cost of carry** idea: holding physical inventory can involve storage, insurance, financing, and spoilage. These carrying costs tend to push futures prices above spot (contango), especially when inventories are plentiful.

At the same time, holding physical inventory can provide a benefit: the ability to meet unexpected demand, avoid stockouts, or keep production running. This benefit is often called a **convenience yield**. When convenience yield is high—typically when inventories are scarce and the commodity is "tight"—near-term prices can rise relative to deferred prices, producing backwardation.

A simplified intuition is:

- **Plentiful inventories** $\Rightarrow$ low convenience yield, storage dominates $\Rightarrow$ more contango $\Rightarrow$ negative roll for long-only.
- **Scarce inventories** $\Rightarrow$ high convenience yield, immediate delivery valuable $\Rightarrow$ more backwardation $\Rightarrow$ positive roll for long-only.

This inventory link is one reason commodities can hedge inflation shocks: when supply is constrained and inventories are tight, spot prices often surge and backwardation may appear, improving both the *spot* and *roll* components.

Commodities as an inflation hedge: what they hedge, and what they do not

It is tempting to say "commodities hedge inflation." The more accurate statement is:

> *Commodities tend to hedge unexpected inflation, especially inflation caused by commodity-driven supply shocks.*

Why the hedge can work

Unexpected inflation that comes from energy and food price shocks can quickly feed into headline CPI and into inflation expectations. In these environments:

- spot commodity prices often rise directly,
- some commodity curves move toward backwardation as inventories tighten,

- equities can struggle (input costs rise, margins compress),
- bonds can struggle (yields rise as inflation compensation increases).

Commodities may therefore provide diversification precisely when the traditional stock–bond mix is challenged.

Why the hedge is imperfect

Commodities are not a clean hedge for all inflation regimes:

- **Demand-driven inflation** (overheating growth) can raise many prices, but commodity spot moves may be less direct or may arrive late.
- **Disinflation with strong growth** can be benign for equities but negative for commodities if supply is ample.
- **Persistent contango** can impose a long-run headwind even if inflation is elevated.

Thus, the commodity sleeve is best justified as a hedge against a specific class of macro risk: **supply-driven inflation surprises** and **inventory shocks**.

The roll decision is an allocation decision

In fixed income, duration is the key dial. In commodities, **the roll** is a key dial. Seemingly small implementation choices can materially change the realized experience:

- **Front-month roll:** highest sensitivity to spot shocks, but often worst contango bleed.
- **Longer-dated exposure:** sometimes lower roll costs, but also less responsiveness to immediate supply shocks (and potentially different risk drivers).

- **Dynamic roll / curve-aware strategies:** attempt to reduce negative roll yield by selecting contracts along the curve, but introduce model risk and potentially higher turnover.

From a portfolio-manager's perspective, these are not details; they determine whether the commodity sleeve behaves like an insurance policy with a manageable premium or like a chronic drag that investors abandon at the wrong time.

Risk profile and governance: why commodities are "powerful but costly"

Commodities have distinctive risks that should be acknowledged explicitly in an investment policy:

- **High volatility and episodic spikes:** supply disruptions can create sharp moves.
- **Weak long-run drift in spot prices:** unlike equities, commodities do not naturally compound via reinvested cash flows.
- **Term structure regime risk:** contango/backwardation regimes can persist for long periods, dominating total return.
- **Correlation instability:** commodities may diversify equities and bonds in some regimes, but correlations can vary widely by commodity and macro environment.

These characteristics push allocators toward two governance principles:

- **Size commodities as a risk allocation, not a return engine.** The sleeve is often justified by drawdown protection in specific inflation shock scenarios.
- **Evaluate commodities by scenario performance, not by benchmark envy.** The objective is not to "beat equities"; it is to improve the portfolio's resilience when inflation shocks impair both stocks and bonds.

Summary: commodities in the ecosystem

Commodities earn their place in the multi-asset ecosystem not because they are always high returning, but because they provide exposure to a different macro risk: **physical scarcity and supply shocks**. The key professional insight is that commodity investing is usually *futures investing*, and futures returns decompose into:

- **spot price change** (what most people focus on),
- **roll yield** (what most people miss),
- **collateral yield** (which can be meaningful when short-term rates are high).

Contango and backwardation determine whether rolling futures is a performance headwind or tailwind. This is why commodities can be a powerful inflation hedge—and why they can also be costly to hold if the term structure persistently works against you.

With these mechanics in place, we can now move to **real assets** such as real estate and infrastructure, where inflation protection is often mediated through contractual cash flows, cap rates, and the crucial distinction between public market volatility and the appraisal-smoothing that masks risk in private valuations.

2.6 Real Assets: Real Estate and Infrastructure

The prior sections covered the liquid backbone of most institutional portfolios: equities as the long-run growth engine; government bonds as the duration/convexity-based shock absorber; credit as the hybrid sleeve whose diversification can vanish in stress; and commodities as a supply-shock hedge whose real-world performance depends critically on futures term structure and roll yield.

Real assets sit at the intersection of these themes. Like equities, they are ultimately claims on cash flows that can grow. Like bonds, many real-asset cash flows are contract-like, anchored by leases, regulated tariffs, or inflation-linked agreements. And like commodities, real assets are tied to the real economy and can benefit when nominal prices rise.

In portfolio construction, real assets are typically owned for two strategic reasons:

1. **Yield enhancement:** stable, distributable cash flows that can support spending policies or liability-like needs.
2. **Inflation protection:** the potential for rents, tariffs, or replacement costs to rise with the price level, supporting real (inflation-adjusted) purchasing power.

This section focuses on two major real-asset categories:

- **Real estate** (often implemented via REITs in public markets and via private funds in private markets),
- **Infrastructure** (often implemented via listed infrastructure, private funds, or direct ownership).

The allocator's task is to understand what is truly being purchased: not "buildings" or "roads," but a particular **mix of cash-flow duration, inflation linkage, leverage, and liquidity**.

Real assets as cash-flow machines: a unified view

A real asset can be described by a simple economic identity:

$$\text{Value} \approx \frac{\text{NOI}}{\text{CapRate}}$$

where **NOI** is income after operating expenses (but before financing), and the **capitalization rate** (cap rate) is the market's required yield for owning that stream of income.

Equation (2.6) is not a pricing law; it is a practical lens. It immediately highlights the two central drivers of real-asset performance:

1. **Cash-flow growth (NOI growth):** rent increases, occupancy changes, operating efficiency, tariff escalators, demand growth.

2. **Valuation change (cap rate movement):** changes in discount rates, risk premia, financing conditions, and investor appetite for stable income.

This parallels earlier decompositions:

- equities: dividends + earnings growth + valuation,
- bonds: carry + duration/convexity-driven price change,
- commodities: spot + roll + collateral.

Real assets similarly combine **income** (NOI distributions) and **valuation sensitivity** (cap rates), with an additional twist: valuations can be *observed daily* in public markets but are often *appraised infrequently* in private markets.

Real estate: bond-like leases and equity-like cyclicality

Real estate is easiest to understand when split into two components:

1. **Contracted income from leases** (bond-like),
2. **Residual exposure to occupancy, re-leasing, and property values** (equity-like).

The bond-like component: contractual rent. A leased building often resembles a bond in a very specific sense: tenants have a legal obligation to pay rent. This produces cash-flow visibility, especially when:

- tenants are high-quality and diversified,
- lease terms are long,
- escalation clauses are explicit (fixed annual bumps or CPI-linked increases),
- operating expenses are passed through (e.g., triple-net structures).

For allocators, the key question is: *How much of the income stream is truly contractual, and how long does that contract last?* The longer and more enforceable the lease, the more the asset behaves like a long-duration income instrument.

The equity-like component: re-leasing risk and economic sensitivity. Even the best lease expires. At that moment, the asset's income becomes a function of market conditions:

- tenant demand (linked to the business cycle),
- new supply (construction pipelines),
- local economic health and migration,
- the property's competitive position (location, amenities, obsolescence risk).

This is where real estate becomes equity-like. Occupancy declines and rent concessions during downturns can reduce NOI at the same time that cap rates rise (a double hit: lower numerator, higher denominator in Equation (2.6)).

Cap rates and interest rates: the hidden duration of real assets

If bonds are explicitly priced by yields, real assets are implicitly priced by cap rates. A useful (approximate) relationship is:

$$\text{CapRate} \approx r_f + \text{RiskPremium} - g_{NOI},$$

where r_f is the risk-free rate and g_{NOI} is expected NOI growth. The signs matter:

- Higher risk-free rates tend to **push cap rates higher** (all else equal), reducing values.
- Higher expected NOI growth tends to **push cap rates lower** (all else equal), raising values.

This creates a critical portfolio insight: many real assets have **equity-like exposure to growth** but also **bond-like exposure to rates** through cap rates. In inflationary tightening cycles, that can produce uncomfortable outcomes: financing costs rise, cap rates reprice upward, and valuations fall even if nominal rents are increasing.

Debt amplifies cap-rate sensitivity. Real estate and infrastructure are commonly levered. Leverage magnifies valuation changes and introduces refinancing risk. When cap rates rise and credit tightens simultaneously, the equity slice of a levered real asset can behave much more like a high-beta equity than investors expect.

Inflation protection: what is real, what is aspirational

Real assets are often described as inflation hedges, but the strength of the hedge depends on the *contract structure* and the *speed of repricing*.

Fast repricing versus slow repricing.

- **Fast repricing segments** (often more inflation-responsive): hotels (daily pricing), self-storage (monthly), multifamily residential (annual or shorter in many markets).
- **Slow repricing segments** (more bond-like, potentially inflation-lagged): long-lease office or single-tenant net lease, some regulated infrastructure with periodic (not continuous) resets.

The allocator should interpret "inflation protection" as *the ability to raise cash flows in nominal terms without losing occupancy or political/regulatory support.*

Replacement cost and the long-run anchor. A deeper inflation linkage comes through **replacement cost**. In the long run, construction costs (labor, materials, financing) influence the economics of new supply. Higher replacement costs can support rents and asset values by limiting new supply and raising the cost of substitutes. This channel is slow and regime-dependent, but it helps explain why high-quality real assets can preserve purchasing power over long horizons.

Infrastructure: contracted cash flows with regulatory and political overlays

Infrastructure is often described as "essential assets": toll roads, airports, ports, pipelines, utilities, cell towers, and similar systems. From a portfolio standpoint, infrastructure tends to be defined more by its **cash-flow architecture** than by its physical form.

Two broad subtypes matter:

Regulated or quasi-regulated infrastructure (more bond-like). Examples include many utilities and regulated networks. Cash flows may be supported by:

- regulated allowed returns on a rate base,
- long-term contracts,
- in some cases, explicit inflation pass-through mechanisms.

These assets can be stable, but they carry **regulatory risk**: the rules can change, allowed returns can be reset, and political pressures can cap price increases in periods of high inflation.

User-pay / volume-sensitive infrastructure (more equity-like). Examples include airports, toll roads, and some ports. Revenue depends on usage volumes and sometimes on discretionary travel and trade flows. These assets can have inflation-linked pricing power, but they are exposed to:

- economic cycles,
- demand shocks (pandemics, recessions),
- technological disruption (e.g., changing transportation patterns).

Inflation linkage is not free. If inflation is high because growth is weak (stagflation), volume-sensitive infrastructure can face lower volumes even as pricing rises. In that case, the net effect on NOI may be ambiguous.

Public versus private implementation: liquidity changes what you observe

Real assets can be accessed through:

- **public vehicles** (REITs, listed infrastructure),
- **private funds or direct holdings** (private real estate, private infrastructure).

These two implementation routes often own similar underlying assets, yet their reported risk can look dramatically different.

Public real assets: priced continuously. Public REITs and listed infrastructure trade daily. Their prices embed:

- changes in rates and risk premia in real time,
- equity-market sentiment and liquidity conditions,
- expectations about future cash flows.

As a result, public real assets can exhibit equity-like volatility and drawdowns, particularly when risk premia reprice quickly.

Private real assets: appraised and smoothed. Private funds often report valuations based on appraisals and transactions that occur infrequently. This creates **appraisal smoothing**:

- reported volatility appears artificially low,
- drawdowns appear delayed and gradual,
- correlations to equities and rates appear lower than the underlying economic reality.

This is not deception; it is measurement. But for risk budgeting, it is dangerous if taken at face value.

Allocator rule. Private real assets may *report* lower volatility, but they do not necessarily *have* lower economic volatility. Liquidity transforms how quickly prices adjust, not whether fundamentals changed.

Real assets in the portfolio: defining the role precisely

Real assets can play multiple roles, but the role must be stated explicitly to avoid mismatched expectations.

Role 1: Income-oriented diversifier. A portfolio may use real assets to harvest relatively stable cash distributions. In this role, the key underwriting variables are:

- lease duration and tenant quality (real estate),
- contract terms and regulatory regime (infrastructure),
- leverage and refinancing schedule,
- cap-rate sensitivity and exit assumptions.

The main risk is that the investor unknowingly buys a long-duration asset at a tight cap rate just before rates rise.

Role 2: Inflation linkage. In this role, the key underwriting variables are:

- explicit CPI escalators versus fixed rent bumps,
- repricing frequency (fast versus slow),
- the political economy of passing through higher costs (especially in regulated infrastructure),
- exposure to input costs (maintenance capex can rise with inflation).

The main risk is assuming inflation protection in name, while the actual contract structure delays repricing and caps pass-through.

Role 3: Illiquidity premia (mostly private). Some investors allocate to private real assets seeking an illiquidity premium. If that is the goal, then governance must address:

- capital lockups and pacing,

- the inability to rebalance during drawdowns,
- valuation lag and the risk of "stale" NAVs,
- the need to fund capital calls (especially when liquid assets are down).

This role naturally foreshadows the private markets section, where commitment pacing becomes a core design constraint.

A practical due diligence checklist (real estate and infrastructure)

Before sizing a real-asset sleeve, a portfolio manager should be able to answer:

1. **Cash-flow contract:** What proportion of NOI is contractual, and what is the weighted average time to reprice?
2. **Inflation linkage:** Are escalators fixed or CPI-linked? How quickly do they reset?
3. **Cap-rate sensitivity:** What happens to valuation if cap rates rise 100–200 bp? Is that consistent with the portfolio's rate risk budget?
4. **Leverage and refinancing:** How much debt is used? When does it mature? What happens if refinancing spreads widen?
5. **Public vs private:** Are reported volatilities and correlations economic realities or appraisal artifacts?
6. **Tail risks:** What are the regime-specific risks (regulatory, political, obsolescence, climate, demand shocks)?

Summary: real assets are "income + cap-rate duration + repricing optionality"

Real estate and infrastructure are best understood as income-generating engines whose performance is governed by:

- **NOI growth** (linked to leases, usage, and pricing power),
- **cap-rate movements** (a rate- and risk-premium-driven valuation channel),
- **repricing speed and inflation pass-through** (the true source of inflation protection),
- **liquidity and leverage** (which shape both measured and realized risk).

Real assets can enhance yield and provide meaningful inflation linkage, but they are not "set-and-forget" hedges. Their diversification value depends on how quickly cash flows reprice relative to inflation, and their drawdown behavior depends on cap-rate sensitivity and financing conditions.

With the real-asset sleeve mapped, we are ready to enter the most structurally complex part of the ecosystem: **private markets**, where the central challenge is not only valuation and risk, but also *cash-flow timing*—capital calls, distributions, and the J-curve that can force portfolio-level decisions at exactly the wrong moment if commitments are not paced correctly.

2.7 Private Markets: Liquidity and Commitment Pacing

The asset-class ecosystem now reaches its most operationally demanding corner. In public markets, reallocating is largely a question of risk budgets, correlations, and trading costs. In private markets, those same questions remain—but they are constrained by two additional realities:

- **Illiquidity:** you cannot reliably rebalance on demand.
- **Cash-flow uncertainty:** you do not control the timing of capital calls and distributions.

This changes portfolio construction. A private allocation is not merely an expected-return choice; it is a **multi-year cash-flow commitment** that can force portfolio-level decisions at exactly the wrong time if it is not paced correctly.

This section focuses on the mechanics that matter most to multi-asset allocators:

- why private equity (PE) and private credit (PC) are structurally illiquid,
- the **J-curve** and what it really represents,
- the difference between **commitment** and **funded exposure**,
- a practical **commitment pacing** framework designed to avoid forced selling of liquid assets during drawdowns.

What investors mean by the "illiquidity premium"

Private markets are often justified by an **illiquidity premium**: the idea that investors earn excess return because they accept:

- lockups and limited redemption,
- valuation uncertainty and lag,
- complexity and higher fees,
- the inability to rebalance dynamically.

Whether an illiquidity premium is reliably available is a debated empirical question and depends heavily on manager selection, fees, vintage, and implementation. For our purposes, the allocator takeaway is more practical:

Even if private markets offer higher expected returns, the portfolio only benefits if the investor can hold through the illiquid cycle without becoming a forced seller of liquid assets.

Thus, the critical design problem is not just *how much* private exposure to target, but *how to fund it through time.*

The basic mechanics: commitment, capital calls, and distributions

A private fund commitment is not the same as buying a public security.

Commitment versus funded exposure. When you commit $100 million to a private equity fund, you do *not* hand over $100 million on day one. Instead:

- the fund calls capital over time (the **investment period**),
- the fund returns capital over time (the **harvest period**).

Therefore, at any point in time, your actual invested amount ("paid-in capital") can be far below your commitment. The remainder is **uncalled capital** ("dry powder"), which is not optional–it is a legally binding obligation.

Allocator implication. Uncalled commitments are a hidden liability on the portfolio. They may not appear as a mark-to-market loss, but they can create a liquidity crunch if calls arrive when liquid assets are down.

A minimal cash-flow vocabulary. Private market cash flows are commonly summarized by:

- **Capital calls:** cash outflows from the investor to the fund.
- **Distributions:** cash inflows from the fund to the investor (from exits, refinancings, income).
- **Net cash flow:** distributions minus calls (negative early, positive later for many PE funds).

These mechanics apply to both private equity and private credit, but their timing patterns differ meaningfully.

Private equity: why the J-curve exists

Private equity funds typically buy and build businesses, improve operations, and exit over several years. The cash-flow path reflects this lifecycle and creates the **J-curve**: cumulative net cash flow is often negative early and positive later.

What drives the early dip. The early years are dominated by:

- capital deployment into portfolio companies,
- management fees and fund expenses,
- conservatively valued early-stage positions (especially before clear operating improvements or exit comps are observed).

Even if the underlying companies are performing, the *net cash flow* to the limited partner is typically negative at first.

What drives the later rise. The later years are dominated by:

- realizations (sales, IPOs, recapitalizations),
- distributions of proceeds,
- the compounding of improvements and potential multiple expansion at exit (uncertain, cycle-dependent).

The J-curve diagram (cash-flow management is the point). The diagram below should be read as a liquidity planning tool, not as a promise of returns. The crucial feature is the **timing mismatch**: outflows come earlier and more predictably than inflows.

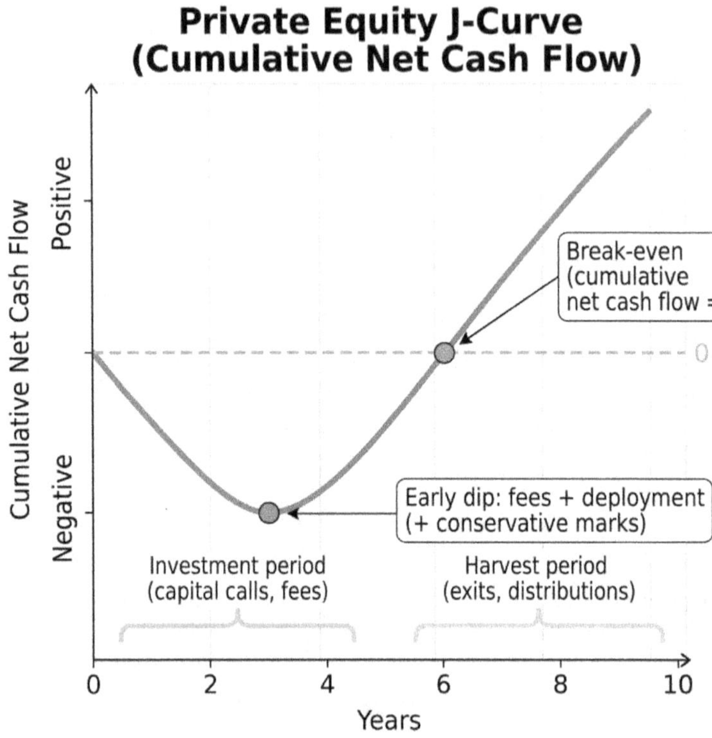

Private credit: a different cash-flow animal

Private credit is often grouped with private equity under "alternatives," but its mechanics are typically closer to **credit** than to **equity**:

- cash flows are driven by contractual interest payments,
- return dispersion is influenced by underwriting discipline and recoveries,
- the left tail is dominated by defaults and restructurings rather than by equity multiple compression.

Why private credit can reduce J-curve severity. Many private credit strategies generate current income earlier than private equity because:

- interest accrues and is often paid periodically (or PIKed, depending on structure),
- principal amortization or refinancing events can occur throughout the fund's life.

As a result, private credit may exhibit a flatter cumulative cash-flow path than private equity. But it introduces its own liquidity and valuation complexities:

- marks can be stale (especially for bespoke loans),
- covenants, restructurings, and workouts can delay recoveries,
- liquidity can disappear precisely when defaults rise.

Allocator implication. Private credit can be an income-oriented complement to private equity, but it is not a substitute for liquid high-quality bonds as a crisis hedge. In stress, credit risk can dominate and correlations can rise—a theme already established in the public credit section.

The central portfolio problem: uncalled capital as a liquidity stressor

Private allocations create a distinctive liquidity profile:

- **known obligation, unknown schedule:** you must fund calls, but you do not control the timing,
- **pro-cyclical stress:** calls may arrive when liquid assets are down and financing conditions are tight,
- **rebalancing friction:** you cannot easily sell private positions to raise cash.

This leads to the classic failure mode:

The investor commits too aggressively, then funds capital calls by selling liquid risk assets at depressed prices during a drawdown.

The portfolio consequence is worse than the private market underperformance itself: you crystallize losses in liquid assets and reduce the portfolio's capacity to recover.

Commitment pacing: turning a target allocation into a feasible plan

A private market program must distinguish between:

- **target NAV allocation** (e.g., "10% in private equity"),
- **commitment schedule** (how much to commit each year),
- **liquidity resources** (how calls will be funded without forced selling).

Step 1: Define the role and the risk budget. Before mechanics, role clarity:

- Is the private allocation intended to increase long-run return?
- Is it intended to diversify (often limited in crisis)?
- Is it intended to deliver income (more applicable to private credit)?

Then size the sleeve by risk-bearing capacity, recognizing that private assets often embed:

- equity beta-like exposure (private equity),
- credit spread/default exposure (private credit),
- leverage and refinancing risk (both).

Step 2: Translate NAV target into an approximate commitment multiple. Because NAV builds slowly, many institutions commit more than their target NAV in early years to reach the desired steady-state exposure. A simplified relationship is:

Steady-state NAV $\approx$ Commitments $\times$ Funding ratio,

where the **funding ratio** depends on:

- call pace (how quickly capital is drawn),
- distribution pace (how quickly capital is returned),
- reinvestment and recycling provisions.

In practice, the result is often a **commitment multiple** greater than 1 (i.e., commitments exceed target NAV) to offset uncalled capital and distributed capital. The precise number is program-specific; the allocator's job is to ensure it is consistent with liquidity capacity.

Step 3: Stagger vintages to diversify timing risk. Private returns and exit opportunities are strongly influenced by entry valuations, credit conditions, and macro cycles. "Vintage year" diversification is therefore a first-order risk control.

A pacing program typically aims to:

- commit a relatively stable amount each year,
- maintain diversification across managers, strategies, and geographies,
- avoid concentrating commitments into euphoric periods when valuations are high and leverage is cheap.

Staggering vintages does not eliminate risk, but it reduces the chance that the entire private sleeve is exposed to the same entry environment.

Step 4: Build an explicit liquidity funding plan. The funding plan should specify:

- a **liquidity bucket** (cash, T-bills, short duration high-quality bonds),

- rules for when and how liquid assets are sold to meet calls,
- constraints on selling risk assets during drawdowns (to avoid procyclical de-risking),
- whether lines of credit are permitted (and their governance).

A conservative operating assumption. Assume capital calls accelerate during stressed periods for at least some strategies (e.g., opportunistic funds, distressed credit), while liquid asset values may be down. Liquidity planning should be robust to that joint stress.

Rebalancing reality: private allocations drift

In public markets, rebalancing is a choice. In private markets, allocation drift is often unavoidable:

- strong public-market rallies can mechanically reduce private NAV as a % of total portfolio,
- public drawdowns can mechanically increase private NAV as a % of total (even if private marks lag),
- distributions can arrive when they are least convenient for maintaining exposure (forcing reinvestment decisions).

A well-run program accepts that perfect rebalancing is impossible and instead focuses on:

- steady pacing,
- liquidity resilience,
- discipline around commitment decisions in different market regimes.

Appraisal smoothing and the illusion of low volatility

As discussed in real assets, private valuations are often appraisal-based and lagging. In private equity and private credit, this can create:

- artificially low reported volatility,
- delayed drawdown recognition,
- understated correlations with public equities and credit.

For risk budgeting, the correct stance is:

Treat private market risk as real even when marks are slow. Liquidity is not a volatility reducer; it is a price-discovery delay.

This matters most in stress: capital calls do not wait for marks to catch up.

Sizing private allocations: a portfolio manager's checklist

Before finalizing a private market target and pacing schedule, the allocator should be able to answer:

- **Commitment capacity:** What is the maximum uncalled capital the portfolio can fund under stress without selling risk assets at a drawdown?
- **Liquidity bucket:** What assets will fund calls, and what is their expected behavior in crises?
- **Vintage diversification:** How many years of commitments are you diversified across, and how concentrated are you in any single cycle?
- **Fee and leverage awareness:** How much of expected excess return is consumed by fees and financing costs, especially when exit multiples are not expanding?
- **Downside governance:** What happens if distributions dry up for several years? Is the plan still feasible?

Summary: private markets are a cash-flow program, not a ticker symbol

Private equity and private credit can provide attractive exposure to long-horizon premia and specialized underwriting opportunities, but they impose a binding operational constraint: **illiquidity plus uncertain cash-flow timing**.

- The **J-curve** is a reminder that early-period net cash flows are typically negative, even for ultimately successful funds.
- The key portfolio risk is not only mark-to-market volatility; it is **liquidity risk**—the possibility of needing cash when you cannot sell private positions.
- A sustainable private allocation therefore requires **commitment pacing**, **vintage diversification**, and an explicit **liquidity funding plan**.

In the broader ecosystem, private markets complete the allocator's toolkit by adding illiquid return sources. But they also impose the discipline that defines professional multi-asset management: *the portfolio must be able to survive its own commitments through the full cycle.*

Chapter 3

Portfolio Theory, Dynamics, and Regimes

Modern Portfolio Theory (MPT) promised investors a 'free lunch' through diversification, but in the trenches of global markets, the bill often arrives when least expected. This chapter moves beyond static textbook definitions to explore the dynamic physics of finance-why correlations breakdown during crises, how central banks manipulate the gravity of discount rates, and why the most robust portfolios are built not on asset class labels, but on fundamental economic regimes.

3.1 Covariance, Correlation, and Diversification Math

Portfolio construction begins with a deceptively simple question: *what makes a collection of individually risky assets become less risky when held together?* The answer is not "more names" or "more asset classes" by itself. The mathematical engine of diversification is the interaction between assets—captured by **covariance** and its standardized cousin, **correlation**.

This section builds on the prior foundational idea that *portfolio risk is not the weighted average of individual risks.* Instead, portfolio risk is driven by:

- how large each position is (weights),
- how volatile each asset is (standalone variance), and
- how assets co-move (covariance/correlation).

The first two terms are usually observable and relatively stable over short horizons. The third term—co-movement—is the critical one for diversification, and it is the least stable precisely when you need it most.

Returns as random variables: why "co-movement" is a risk input

Let r_i be the (excess) return on asset i over some horizon (e.g., daily or monthly). Treat each r_i as a random variable. A portfolio with weights w_i has return

$$r_p = \sum_{i=1}^{N} w_i r_i = \mathbf{w}^\top \mathbf{r},$$

where $\mathbf{w}$ is the $N \times 1$ weight vector and $\mathbf{r}$ is the $N \times 1$ return vector.

Risk, in the mean–variance tradition, is summarized by the variance of portfolio returns:

$$\sigma_p^2 = \mathrm{Var}(r_p).$$

The key step is to expand $\mathrm{Var}(\sum_i w_i r_i)$ using variance algebra.

Deriving the portfolio variance formula (the diversification identity)

Start with the two-asset case. Let

$$r_p = w_1 r_1 + w_2 r_2, \quad w_1 + w_2 = 1.$$

Then

$$\begin{aligned}\sigma_p^2 &= \mathrm{Var}(w_1 r_1 + w_2 r_2)\\ &= w_1^2\mathrm{Var}(r_1) + w_2^2\mathrm{Var}(r_2) + 2w_1 w_2 \mathrm{Cov}(r_1, r_2).\end{aligned}$$

This single equation contains the entire diversification story:

- The first two terms, $w_1^2\sigma_1^2$ and $w_2^2\sigma_2^2$, are the *standalone* risk contributions.
- The third term, $2w_1w_2\mathrm{Cov}(r_1, r_2)$, is the *interaction term.* It can either increase risk (positive covariance) or reduce it (negative covariance).

For N assets, the expression generalizes cleanly. Define the covariance matrix $\boldsymbol{\Sigma}$ where $\Sigma_{ij} = \mathrm{Cov}(r_i, r_j)$. Then

$$\sigma_p^2 = \mathbf{w}^\top \boldsymbol{\Sigma}\, \mathbf{w}.$$

Written out explicitly:

$$\sigma_p^2 = \sum_{i=1}^{N}\sum_{j=1}^{N} w_i w_j\, \Sigma_{ij} = \sum_{i=1}^{N} w_i^2 \sigma_i^2 + 2\sum_{i<j} w_i w_j\, \mathrm{Cov}(r_i, r_j).$$

Equation (3.1) is the "diversification identity": portfolio variance is *own-risk plus cross-risk.* In real portfolios, the cross-terms are numerous: for N assets there are $\frac{N(N-1)}{2}$ distinct pairwise covariances. That count grows quickly, and it is why estimating the covariance structure is both central and treacherous.

Covariance vs. correlation: standardizing co-movement

Covariance is measured in squared return units, making it hard to compare across pairs of assets with different volatilities. Correlation rescales covariance into a unitless number between -1 and $+1$:

$$\rho_{ij} = \frac{\mathrm{Cov}(r_i, r_j)}{\sigma_i \sigma_j}, \qquad \mathrm{Cov}(r_i, r_j) = \rho_{ij}\sigma_i\sigma_j.$$

Substituting (3.1) into (3.1) yields an equivalent and highly intuitive form:

$$\sigma_p^2 = \sum_{i=1}^{N} w_i^2 \sigma_i^2 + 2 \sum_{i<j} w_i w_j \rho_{ij} \sigma_i \sigma_j.$$

Interpretation.

- If $\rho_{ij} = +1$, the two assets move perfectly together; the cross-term is maximally risk-increasing. You should not expect meaningful diversification.
- If $\rho_{ij} = 0$, the two assets have no linear co-movement; the cross-term vanishes (in expectation), and diversification is substantial.
- If $\rho_{ij} < 0$, the cross-term becomes negative and actively *hedges* risk; this is the strongest form of diversification.

Note the asymmetry in practice: negative correlations are precious, but they are also the least reliable across regimes. Many strategies that appear diversifying in calm markets become merely "less positively correlated" under stress.

A clean benchmark: equal weights, equal vol, equal pairwise correlation

To see the mathematical limit of diversification, use a stylized but clarifying case:

- N assets,
- equal weights $w_i = \frac{1}{N}$,
- identical volatility $\sigma_i = \sigma$,
- constant pairwise correlation $\rho_{ij} = \rho$ for $i \neq j$.

Then (3.1) becomes

$$\begin{aligned}\sigma_p^2 &= \sum_{i=1}^{N}\left(\frac{1}{N}\right)^2\sigma^2 + 2\sum_{i<j}\left(\frac{1}{N}\right)\left(\frac{1}{N}\right)\rho\sigma\sigma \\ &= N\cdot\frac{1}{N^2}\sigma^2 + 2\cdot\frac{N(N-1)}{2}\cdot\frac{1}{N^2}\rho\sigma^2 \\ &= \frac{\sigma^2}{N} + \rho\sigma^2\left(1-\frac{1}{N}\right).\end{aligned}$$

Rearranging:

$$\sigma_p^2 = \rho\sigma^2 + (1-\rho)\frac{\sigma^2}{N}.$$

The diversification limit falls out immediately. As $N \to \infty$,

$$\lim_{N\to\infty}\sigma_p^2 = \rho\sigma^2, \qquad \lim_{N\to\infty}\sigma_p = \sigma\sqrt{\rho}.$$

You can diversify away the idiosyncratic component (the $\frac{1}{N}$ term), but you *cannot* diversify away the common component implied by ρ.

Connecting the math to intuition: idiosyncratic vs. systematic risk

Equation (3.1) decomposes risk into two parts:

- **Diversifiable risk:** $(1-\rho)\frac{\sigma^2}{N}$ shrinks as you add assets.
- **Non-diversifiable risk (systematic floor):** $\rho\sigma^2$ remains even with infinitely many holdings.

This is the mathematical version of a practical truth: most multi-asset portfolios are not under-diversified because they lack names; they are under-diversified because their positions share *common drivers*. Common drivers show up as positive average correlations and covariances, which create a hard floor under risk.

Why correlation stability is the Achilles' heel

Mean–variance optimization and most risk models assume the covariance matrix $\boldsymbol{\Sigma}$ is a reasonably stable object that can be estimated from history. In reality, correlations are:

- **Time-varying:** The same pair of assets can switch from low to high correlation across macro regimes.
- **State-dependent:** Correlations tend to rise during sell-offs and liquidity stress (a phenomenon often called *correlation clustering*).
- **Estimation-sensitive:** Small sampling noise in ρ_{ij} can materially change optimized weights because the cross-terms are numerous and interact nonlinearly through $\mathbf{w}^\top \boldsymbol{\Sigma} \mathbf{w}$.

The practical consequence is not merely that your risk forecast is imperfect. The deeper issue is that traditional optimizers can *over-trust* a fragile covariance estimate and allocate aggressively into what appears diversifying—until the regime changes and the diversification disappears.

Crisis correlation (and the "when you need it" problem). In many historical stress episodes, assets that were only modestly correlated in normal times become strongly positively correlated as investors de-risk simultaneously, funding costs rise, and liquidations become forced rather than discretionary. In the language of (3.1), many ρ_{ij} drift upward toward $+1$ *at the same time* that volatilities σ_i rise. Both effects raise the cross-terms:

$$2w_i w_j \rho_{ij} \sigma_i \sigma_j,$$

exactly when the portfolio is most vulnerable.

The mathematical "diminishing returns" of diversification

A useful way to internalize (3.1) is to focus on *how quickly* risk falls as you add more truly uncorrelated bets. When $\rho = 0$ (uncorrelated assets), (**??**) becomes:

$$\sigma_p^2 = \frac{\sigma^2}{N}, \quad \sigma_p = \frac{\sigma}{\sqrt{N}}.$$

The first few additions matter a lot; later additions matter less. For example, moving from $N = 1$ to $N = 4$ cuts volatility in half, but moving from $N = 25$ to $N = 36$ only cuts volatility from $\sigma/5$ to $\sigma/6$.

When $\rho > 0$, the effect is even more sharply limited because the portfolio approaches a non-zero floor $\sigma\sqrt{\rho}$. Diversification is not a bottomless well; it is a curve that quickly flattens.

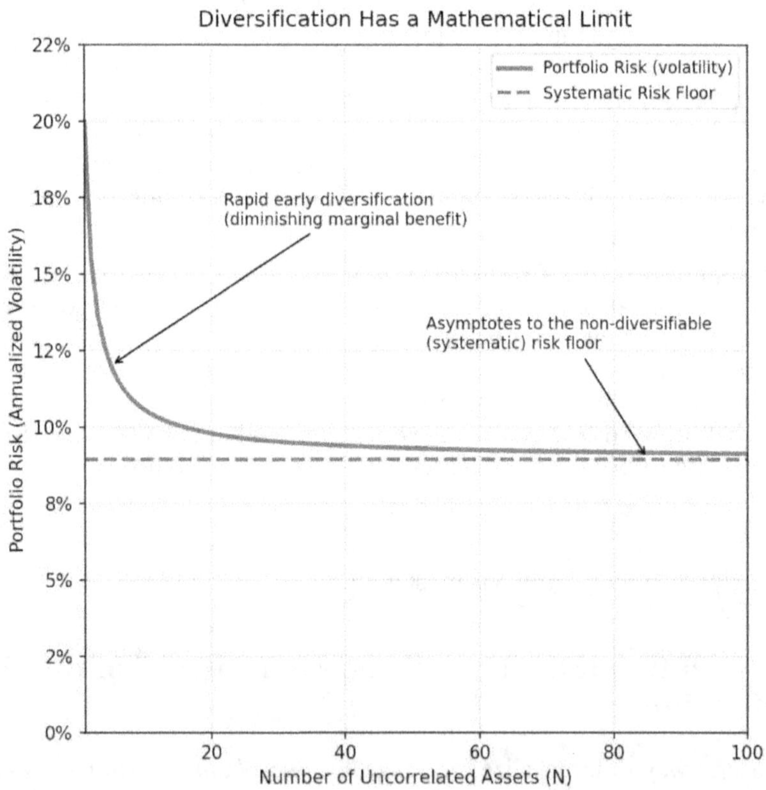

What this implies for real multi-asset portfolios

The formulas above are simple, but their implications are operationally demanding.

1) Volatility is observable; correlation is a forecast. Volatility σ_i can be measured directly from recent price history and is often persistent (it clusters). Correlation ρ_{ij} must be treated as a model output: it is an estimate of a relationship that can shift with policy, liquidity, leverage, and macro shocks.

2) Diversification is about *independent drivers*, not labels. Two instruments with different names can share the same core risk. For example, a long position in high yield credit and a long position in equities can both embed a significant exposure to growth and risk appetite. In the covariance matrix, that shared exposure shows up as positive covariance that does not diversify.

3) "More assets" can be cosmetic if the covariance structure is concentrated. If a portfolio is built from many positions that are all tied to the same dominant driver (e.g., a global risk-on factor), then ρ is effectively high and the systematic floor in (3.1) is large. The portfolio may look diversified by count, but not by risk.

4) Correlation shocks are multiplicative with volatility spikes. In stress, both ρ_{ij} and σ_i often rise together. Because the cross-term in (3.1) contains the product $\rho_{ij}\sigma_i\sigma_j$, the portfolio can experience a nonlinear jump in realized risk relative to a calm-regime forecast.

A practitioner's checklist: making the math usable

To translate diversification math into robust portfolio design, sophisticated investors typically:

- **Model correlations conditionally** (e.g., by macro regime or volatility state), rather than assuming a single constant matrix.
- **Shrink or regularize covariance estimates** to reduce the optimizer's tendency to overfit noisy correlations.

- **Stress test correlation regimes** explicitly (e.g., "risk-off" matrices with elevated correlations).
- **Distinguish diversifiers from return-seekers** by asking: *what happens to this asset's correlation when equity volatility spikes?*

Key takeaway

The portfolio variance identity $\sigma_p^2 = \mathbf{w}^\top \boldsymbol{\Sigma} \mathbf{w}$ is not just a formula; it is a warning label. Diversification lives in the covariance terms, and those terms are numerous, estimated, and regime-dependent. You can diversify idiosyncratic risk quickly, but you will inevitably hit a systematic risk floor determined by common drivers—and correlations often rise toward one precisely when the market forces those drivers to dominate.

3.2 The Mean-Variance Framework and Efficient Frontiers

The previous section reduced diversification to its engine: portfolio variance,

$$\sigma_p^2 = \mathbf{w}^\top \boldsymbol{\Sigma} \mathbf{w},$$

and emphasized the practical vulnerability: correlation (and therefore covariance) is the least stable input. Markowitz's mean–variance framework takes that variance identity and turns it into a full capital allocation program: choose weights $\mathbf{w}$ to trade off expected return against risk.

This section develops three ideas in sequence:

- 1) how the Efficient Frontier is constructed (and what it means),
- 2) how the Tangency Portfolio links the frontier to a risk-free asset and the Sharpe ratio, and

- 3) why the optimizer is fragile in practice—leading to corner solutions and portfolios that maximize estimation error rather than long-run utility.

The Markowitz objective: return and risk in one problem

Let $\boldsymbol{\mu}$ be the vector of expected (excess) returns for N risky assets and $\boldsymbol{\Sigma}$ their covariance matrix. For a weight vector $\mathbf{w}$, the portfolio's expected excess return is

$$\mathbb{E}[r_p] = \mathbf{w}^\top \boldsymbol{\mu},$$

and the portfolio variance is

$$\sigma_p^2 = \mathbf{w}^\top \boldsymbol{\Sigma} \mathbf{w}.$$

There are two standard equivalent ways to pose the Markowitz problem.

Formulation A: minimize variance for a target return.

$$\min_{\mathbf{w}} \quad \mathbf{w}^\top \boldsymbol{\Sigma} \mathbf{w}$$

subject to

$$\mathbf{w}^\top \boldsymbol{\mu} = \mu^\star, \qquad \mathbf{1}^\top \mathbf{w} = 1,$$

optionally with constraints such as $w_i \geq 0$ (long-only) or leverage limits.

Formulation B: maximize expected return for a risk budget.

$$\max_{\mathbf{w}} \quad \mathbf{w}^\top \boldsymbol{\mu}$$

subject to

$$\mathbf{w}^\top \boldsymbol{\Sigma} \mathbf{w} \leq (\sigma^\star)^2, \qquad \mathbf{1}^\top \mathbf{w} = 1.$$

Both formulations produce the same object: the **Efficient Frontier**, the set of portfolios that are *not dominated*. A portfolio is dominated if there exists another portfolio with higher expected return for the same risk, or lower risk for the same expected return.

The Efficient Frontier: the boundary of what is achievable

If you plot portfolio volatility σ_p on the x-axis and expected return $\mathbb{E}[r_p]$ on the y-axis, every feasible set of weights produces a point in the plane. The Efficient Frontier is the upper-left boundary of that cloud: it represents the best expected return you can achieve for each level of risk (or, equivalently, the least risk for each level of expected return).

Two special points on the frontier matter in almost every allocation discussion.

Global Minimum Variance (GMV) portfolio. This is the risky-asset portfolio with the lowest possible variance:

$$\mathbf{w}_{GMV} = \arg\min_{\mathbf{w}} \; \mathbf{w}^\top \boldsymbol{\Sigma} \mathbf{w} \quad \text{s.t.} \quad \mathbf{1}^\top \mathbf{w} = 1.$$

It is the leftmost point of the frontier. Note what it does *not* require: expected returns. GMV depends only on $\boldsymbol{\Sigma}$. That does not make it immune to estimation risk, but it avoids the most unstable input in the entire framework: $\boldsymbol{\mu}$.

What the frontier is really saying. The frontier is a statement about trade-offs under a model:

- Moving up the frontier increases expected return but requires accepting more risk.
- Moving off the frontier means you are leaving return on the table for the same risk (or taking extra risk for the same return).

For a portfolio manager, the frontier is best viewed as a *diagnostic* and *budgeting* tool: it clarifies which risks are being paid and which are simply being taken.

Introducing a risk-free asset: the Tangency Portfolio and the Sharpe ratio

Now introduce a risk-free rate r_f (or a cash proxy). If you can combine a risk-free asset with a risky portfolio, you can create a straight line in mean–variance space:

$$\mathbb{E}[r_c] = r_f + y\left(\mathbb{E}[r_p] - r_f\right), \qquad \sigma_c = |y|\sigma_p,$$

where y is the capital allocated to the risky portfolio (with $1-y$ in cash). When $y > 1$, the portfolio is leveraged (borrowing at or near r_f in the model).

Among all risky portfolios, the one that produces the steepest line from $(0, r_f)$ to the risky frontier is the **Tangency Portfolio**. The slope of that line is the maximum achievable Sharpe ratio:

$$\text{Sharpe}(\mathbf{w}) = \frac{\mathbf{w}^\top \boldsymbol{\mu} - r_f}{\sqrt{\mathbf{w}^\top \boldsymbol{\Sigma} \mathbf{w}}}.$$

The tangency portfolio weights (in the unconstrained case) are proportional to

$$\mathbf{w}_{tan} \propto \boldsymbol{\Sigma}^{-1}\left(\boldsymbol{\mu} - r_f\mathbf{1}\right),$$

then scaled to satisfy $\mathbf{1}^\top\mathbf{w} = 1$.

Capital market line (CML) intuition. Once $\mathbf{w}_{tan}$ is identified, an investor's risk level is set by a single dial: the mix between cash and the tangency portfolio. In theory, this is elegant:

- **Portfolio selection:** everyone holds the same tangency portfolio of risky assets.
- **Risk preference:** everyone differs only in how much they lever or de-lever it with cash.

In practice, the tangency portfolio is exactly where the model's most dangerous sensitivity sits, because it depends on both $\boldsymbol{\mu}$ and $\boldsymbol{\Sigma}^{-1}$.

Why the optimizer is fragile: three sources of instability

Mean–variance optimization is mathematically correct given correct inputs. The challenge is that portfolio weights can be a wildly unstable function of slightly incorrect inputs. There are three compounding reasons.

1) Expected returns are hard to estimate, and the optimizer treats them as precise Expected returns are small signals observed through noisy realizations. A simple mental model is:

$$\text{signal (expected return)} \ll \text{noise (realized return volatility)}.$$

Even if you estimate μ_i with reasonable econometrics, errors of 1–3% per year are common, while the cross-sectional differences in true expected returns might also be only a few percent.

In the Markowitz machinery, those small differences are the engine that determines which assets you own more of. So the optimizer tends to interpret estimation noise as alpha and expresses it through large relative tilts.

2) Covariance matrices are high-dimensional, and inversion amplifies noise Equation (3.2) contains $\mathbf{\Sigma}^{-1}$. Inverting a noisy estimate of a large covariance matrix is numerically and statistically unstable:

- Small errors in correlations can imply large changes in optimal weights.
- If assets are highly correlated, $\mathbf{\Sigma}$ can be close to singular (ill-conditioned), making the inverse extremely sensitive.

This is not a technical footnote; it is the core of why optimized portfolios often look unreasonable without constraints.

3) The optimizer likes extremes because extremes are the easiest way to satisfy equations If one asset has a slightly higher estimated Sharpe ratio than another, the optimizer can increase expected return for a given modeled risk by concentrating weight in the 'best' asset and hedging its covariance footprint with other assets. With shorting allowed, this can produce large long/short positions that look brilliant in-sample and unstable out-of-sample.

This is the origin of **corner solutions**: allocations that pin against constraints (e.g., 0% or 100% weights, max leverage, max position size). The optimizer is not "wrong"—it is faithfully exploiting the inputs you gave it. The problem is that the inputs are not stable enough to deserve that level of trust.

The Efficient Frontier as a picture of estimation error

In a textbook diagram, the frontier is smooth and stable. In real life, it is an estimated object. If you slightly perturb μ or Σ and recompute the frontier, you often get a noticeably different curve and materially different "optimal" portfolios.

A practical way to interpret this: *The Efficient Frontier is not a single line; it is a band whose width reflects estimation uncertainty.* The optimizer, however, typically behaves as though the line is exact.

Where multi-asset investors get fooled

In multi-asset allocation (stocks, bonds, alternatives), the mean–variance framework often produces intuitively appealing stories:

- Bonds diversify equities because correlation is low or negative.
- Alternatives diversify both because their vol is moderate and correlation appears low.

Those statements can be true in some regimes. The trap is that the optimizer embeds them as persistent facts. As emphasized in the prior section, correlations are regime-dependent; in stress, they can rise sharply ('crisis correlation').

So the specific Achilles' heel of Markowitz optimization is not merely that the future differs from the past. It is that the diversification terms in Σ—the cross-covariances that justify allocations—are the ones most likely to change when liquidity and policy regimes shift.

Constraints and robustness: how professionals make Markowitz usable

This book's goal is not to discard mean–variance logic; it is to use it without being used by it. In practice, professionals add structure to prevent the optimizer from overfitting noise:

- **Long-only or limited shorting:** prevent fragile levered hedges.
- **Position limits and group constraints:** avoid 0/100 outcomes and enforce diversification across sleeves (e.g., equities, rates, credit, alternatives).
- **Volatility and tracking-error budgets:** keep risk consistent with the investor's mandate.
- **Return shrinkage / Bayesian priors:** pull μ toward reasonable baselines (e.g., equilibrium premia).
- **Covariance shrinkage and factor structure:** stabilize Σ by reducing estimation error and conditioning problems.
- **Resampling / bootstrapping:** evaluate how stable allocations are across plausible input draws.

The guiding principle is simple: if small input changes cause large allocation changes, then the optimization problem is telling you that you are *not optimizing investment opportunity*; you are optimizing the noise in your estimates.

Efficient Frontier visualization: assets, frontier, GMV, and tangency

The figure below shows the core geometry:

- Individual assets appear as dots (stocks, bonds, alternatives), typically inside the feasible region.
- The Efficient Frontier forms the upper-left boundary.
- The Global Minimum Variance portfolio is the leftmost point on the frontier.
- The Tangency Portfolio is the point where the line from the risk-free rate is tangent to the frontier (maximum Sharpe).

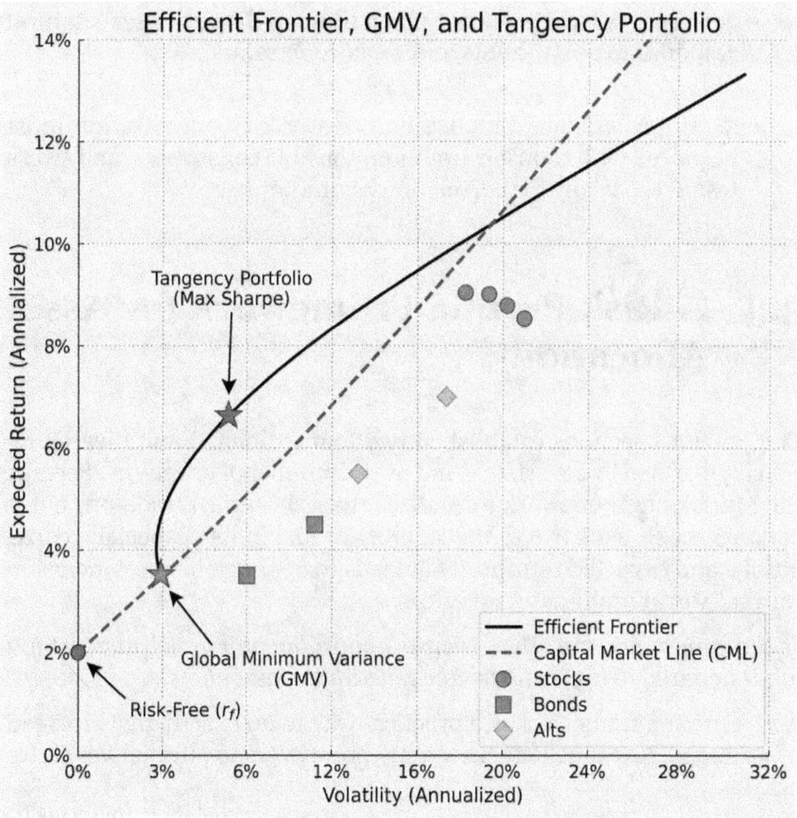

Key takeaways for the multi-asset strategist

- 1. The Efficient Frontier formalizes the best achievable risk–return trade-offs given inputs (μ, Σ).

- 2. The GMV portfolio is a covariance-driven anchor; it avoids expected returns but still depends on correlation stability.

- 3. The Tangency Portfolio maximizes Sharpe ratio, but it is the most input-sensitive object in the framework because it depends on both expected returns and the inverse covariance matrix.

- 4. Corner solutions are not a bug; they are the optimizer's natural response to noisy inputs and weak constraints.

- 5. In professional practice, mean–variance optimization must be paired with robust estimation, sensible constraints, and stress tests—especially for correlation regime shifts.

3.3 A Risk Premia Framework for Asset Allocation

The previous sections established two foundations. First, diversification is governed by covariance, not by the number of line items. Second, the Markowitz framework formalizes the risk–return trade-off, but it is dangerously sensitive to the stability of its inputs—especially correlations and expected returns. That leads to an unavoidable conclusion for real-world multi-asset investors:

If the inputs are unstable, then a good allocator must understand what actually drives returns underneath the asset labels.

A risk premia framework is a practical way to do exactly that. Instead of asking, "How much stocks versus bonds versus alternatives?" we ask:

- What economic risks am I being paid to bear?

- Which premia are independent, and which are redundant?

- In which regimes do these premia *compress* (i.e., pay less or become unreliable)?

This section introduces a simple, usable set of underlying drivers—**carry**, **growth**, and **convexity**—and shows how to map common assets and strategies into these drivers. The goal is not to create a perfect taxonomy. The goal is to allocate capital in a way that is robust to shifting correlations because it is grounded in economic mechanism.

From asset classes to "return engines"

Asset class labels are helpful for governance and benchmarks, but they can be misleading for risk control. Two different labels can hide the same engine:

- High yield credit and equities are different instruments, but both often rely on benign growth and stable risk appetite.
- Trend-following and long volatility may look like "alternatives," but their payoff is often linked to crisis dynamics rather than growth.
- Private equity may be labeled "alternative," yet much of its economic exposure resembles levered public equity plus liquidity and valuation smoothing.

The risk premia approach starts with a decomposition:

Asset Return = Compensation for bearing risks + Idiosyncratic outcomes + Implementation frictions.

The terms we can plan around are the systematic risk premia. The terms we must manage are the frictions (fees, slippage, financing, taxes, liquidity). And the terms we should not overfit are the idiosyncratic outcomes.

Three building blocks: carry, growth, and convexity

Many professional frameworks exist (factors, styles, macro sensitivities). For multi-asset allocation, a compact and highly actionable view is that most returns come from some mix of:

- **Carry:** earning a yield, spread, or roll-down for holding/financing risk.
- **Growth:** exposure to improving real activity, earnings, and risk appetite.

- **Convexity:** non-linear payoff that tends to monetize large moves or crises (often at a cost in calm markets).

These are not mutually exclusive; they are *components*. The same instrument can embed all three.

Carry (being paid to hold risk today)

Carry is the return you expect if markets do "nothing dramatic" and prices do not move against you. It is often visible, sometimes contractual, and frequently seductive.

Examples.

- **Bonds:** coupon income plus potential roll-down (depending on the curve).
- **Credit:** spread income for bearing default and downgrade risk.
- **FX carry:** interest rate differentials across currencies.
- **Option selling:** premium collected for warehousing volatility (short convexity).

Carry as a trade.

Carry is rarely free. It is typically payment for providing insurance or liquidity:

- Credit carry compensates you for loss severity in downturns.
- Short-vol carry compensates you for tail risk.
- Emerging market carry can compensate you for funding stress and capital flight.

A critical discipline for allocators is to ask: *what must remain true for carry to be realized?* Usually, it requires stable funding conditions and the absence of large adverse moves.

Growth (being long the economic cycle)

Growth exposure is the portfolio's sensitivity to the real economy and risk appetite. It is not the same thing as "equities," but equities are the most obvious carrier of it.

Where growth lives.

- **Equities:** earnings and multiple expansion are typically strongest when growth is improving and financial conditions are supportive.
- **Credit (especially HY):** behaves like a hybrid of bond duration and equity beta; it often benefits when growth is steady and defaults are low.
- **Cyclical commodities and industrials:** can be pro-growth, though commodities can also be inflation-driven.

Growth is a portfolio "center of gravity."

Most institutional portfolios are structurally long growth because:

- liabilities and spending needs implicitly assume nominal growth over time,
- career risk and benchmarks are usually equity-centric, and
- long-only mandates constrain explicit hedging.

A risk premia lens forces a portfolio manager to measure and budget growth exposure explicitly rather than letting it emerge accidentally through multiple sleeves.

Convexity (owning non-linearity)

Convexity refers to payoff curvature: the return changes *non-linearly* with the underlying risk factor. In practical terms, convexity is what tends to help when markets gap, correlations jump, and diversification fails.

Two kinds of convexity matter.

- **Positive convexity (long convexity):** tends to gain in large moves (often crisis-friendly). Classic examples include protective equity puts, long volatility strategies, and certain trend-following profiles that profit from persistent large moves.
- **Negative convexity (short convexity):** tends to earn small steady gains but can suffer outsized losses in tail events. Classic examples include option selling, certain carry trades, and levered spread products.

The convexity "budget" problem.

Convexity is often expensive in calm markets (premium decay, negative carry). This creates a behavioral trap: when volatility is low and carry looks attractive, investors sell convexity to boost returns. That choice can increase hidden correlation risk because many short-convexity positions lose simultaneously during stress.

A core multi-asset design principle emerges:

Carry and growth pay the bills most of the time; convexity keeps you solvent when the regime changes.

Decomposing familiar asset classes into risk premia

A risk premia framework becomes actionable when you can translate common holdings into drivers. The goal is not a perfect equation; the goal is a *map* that reveals concentration.

A practical decomposition template

For many instruments, you can write a simple decomposition:

$$\begin{aligned}\text{Expected Return} \approx{} & \text{Cash Rate} + \text{Term Premium} + \text{Credit Premium}\\ & + \text{Liquidity Premium} + \text{Equity (Growth) Premium}\\ & \pm \text{Convexity Premium.}\end{aligned}$$

The signs matter:

- If you *own* convexity, you often *pay* a convexity premium (expected drag).
- If you *sell* convexity, you often *earn* a convexity premium (expected carry), while warehousing tail risk.

Examples (conceptual, but operationally useful)

Investment-grade corporate bonds.

Often decomposed as:

$$\text{IG Credit} \approx \text{Rates Duration (term premium)} + \text{Credit Spread Carry} + \text{Liquidity}$$

In benign conditions, credit spread carry can look bond-like. In stress, spreads widen and IG can behave more like an equity risk-off asset (through credit beta).

High yield credit.

A useful mental model is:

$$\begin{aligned}\text{High Yield} \approx\ & \text{Short/Intermediate Duration} + \text{Credit Carry}\\ & + \text{Equity-like Growth Beta} - \text{Crisis Convexity}\end{aligned}$$

The last term is the warning: HY often embeds negative convexity to the cycle. Defaults and forced selling are nonlinear.

Equities.

A stylized decomposition:

$$\begin{aligned}\text{Equities} \approx\ & \text{Growth Premium} + \text{Inflation Pass-Through (imperfect)}\\ & - \text{Discount-Rate Sensitivity}\end{aligned}$$

Equities can be thought of as long growth and (usually) short real-rate shocks through valuation.

Commodities.

Commodities can contain:

$$\text{Commodities} \approx \text{Inflation Shock Exposure} + \text{Carry/Backwardation/Contang}$$

This is why commodities can be diversifying in inflationary regimes but unreliable in disinflationary slowdowns.

Trend-following / managed futures (stylized).

Many implementations exhibit:

$$\text{Trend} \approx \text{Crisis Convexity (often)} + \text{Rate/FX/Commodity Diversification} - \text{Ch}$$

The key point is not the label "alternative" but the role: it can be a source of convexity when traditional correlations break.

Redundant risk: the illusion of diversification

Once you decompose holdings into drivers, you can identify redundancy that is otherwise invisible.

A common institutional redundancy.

Consider a portfolio with:

- a large equity allocation (explicit growth),
- a high yield allocation (growth plus carry),
- an "alternative credit" sleeve (carry plus growth beta), and
- a volatility-selling overlay to "enhance yield" (carry via short convexity).

The labels look diversified, but the underlying drivers are concentrated:

- a heavy **growth** bet,

- a large **carry** bet that depends on stable funding, and
- a structurally **short convexity** profile that is vulnerable in drawdowns.

In a regime shift, these sleeves can become highly correlated because they are all exposed to the same underlying state variable: tightening financial conditions.

This is the practical bridge between this section and the earlier covariance discussion:

Correlations are not magic numbers; they are symptoms of shared underlying drivers.

When risk premia compress (and why it matters more than point forecasts)

A risk premium "compresses" when the compensation for bearing a risk declines relative to the risk itself. Compression can show up as lower expected return, worse forward Sharpe, or an unfavorable skew (small gains, rare large losses). Understanding compression is central because it explains why allocations that looked strong in one period disappoint in the next.

Carry compression

Carry tends to compress when:

- **spreads tighten:** credit spreads, term spreads, or volatility risk premia fall, leaving less income to buffer losses,
- **funding becomes fragile:** leverage and crowded positioning increase the chance of forced unwind,
- **tail risk is underpriced:** low realized volatility encourages short-convexity behavior, shrinking the premium available.

A useful operational heuristic is: *the better carry looks, the more you should ask what risk is being ignored.*

Growth premium compression

Growth exposure disappoints when:

- growth expectations are already high (little room for positive surprise),
- margins mean-revert or earnings revisions turn negative,
- discount rates rise (valuation compression can dominate earnings growth), or
- policy shocks tighten liquidity (raising cross-asset correlations).

This is one reason equity returns can be weak even when the economy is "fine": the growth premium depends on *surprises* and the *discount rate* environment, not just the level of growth.

Convexity premium compression (or: why hedges feel expensive)

Convexity is often purchased through instruments with negative carry (options, explicit hedges) or through strategies that underperform in choppy, mean-reverting markets. Convexity can feel "compressed" in two ways:

- **too expensive:** implied volatility is high, so hedges cost a lot and bleed.
- **doesn't pay when expected:** the portfolio hedges the wrong scenario (e.g., equity puts help in crashes but not in slow grind-downs with rising rates).

The implication is not that convexity is useless, but that it must be sized and diversified. Convexity is a role in the portfolio, not a single instrument.

A portfolio-manager's workflow: allocating by premia

A risk premia framework becomes practical when it drives a repeatable workflow:

- **Inventory exposures:** For each sleeve, state its dominant premia (carry/growth/convexity) and its likely behavior in stress.
- **Risk-budget premia, not assets:** Decide how much portfolio risk you want in growth, how much in carry, and how much convexity you are willing to pay for (or sell).
- **Diversify within premia:** If you want carry, do not source it from a single crowded trade. If you want growth, diversify across geographies and cyclicality. If you want convexity, avoid relying on a single hedge.
- **Stress regimes explicitly:** Ask what happens if correlations rise, funding tightens, or inflation surprises—because these are the states where premia tend to compress simultaneously.
- **Translate back to implementable assets:** Only after the risk-premia plan is clear do you decide the instruments (cash bonds, futures, options, ETFs, swaps, managers).

Key takeaways

- Asset labels often hide the true drivers of risk and return; a risk premia lens makes those drivers explicit.
- **Carry** is typically payment for providing insurance or liquidity; it is most vulnerable when funding conditions tighten.
- **Growth** exposure is the portfolio's pro-cyclical engine; it can be undermined by valuation (discount-rate) shocks even when growth is positive.
- **Convexity** is the regime-change stabilizer; it often has negative carry, but it can reduce the portfolio's dependence on stable correlations.

- Premia *compress* in predictable circumstances (tight spreads, crowded carry, policy tightening, volatility repricing). Recognizing compression is often more valuable than producing precise point estimates of returns.

3.4 Macro Regimes: Growth and Inflation Quadrants

The prior sections made two points that set up this one. First, diversification depends on covariances, and correlations can shift abruptly. Second, a risk premia framework helps you see through asset labels by identifying underlying drivers such as carry, growth exposure, and convexity. A macro regime framework goes one step further: it organizes those drivers around two forces that repeatedly dominate cross-asset returns over medium horizons:

- **Growth shocks:** are we getting better or worse real activity than the market expected?

- **Inflation surprises:** is inflation running hotter or cooler than expected?

The emphasis is on *direction relative to expectations*, not just the level. Markets price levels quickly; they re-price when reality deviates from the path that was discounted.

The regime map (mental model)

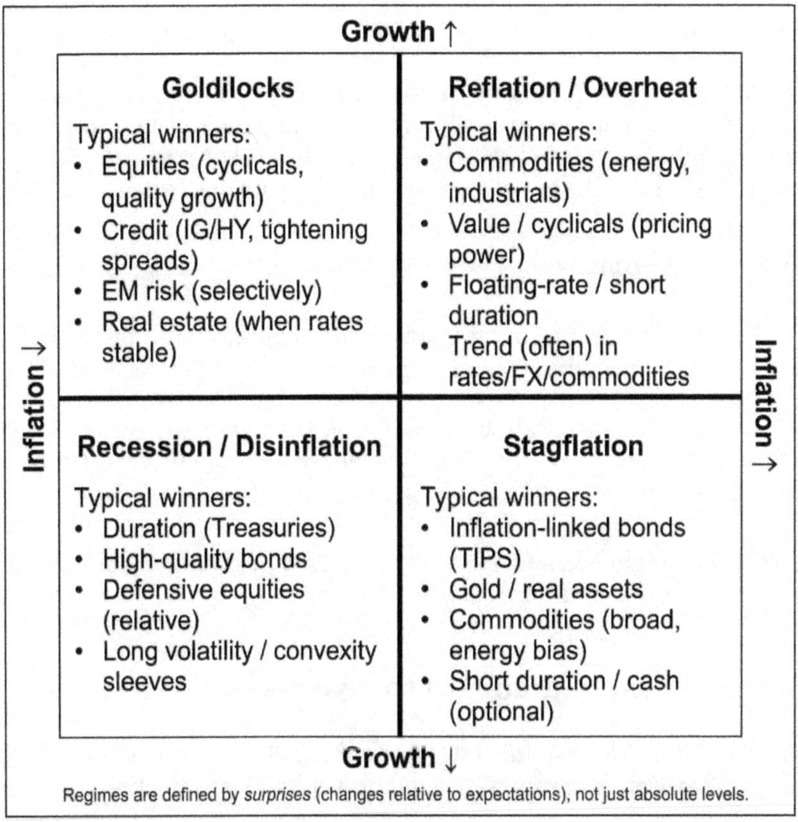

This 2×2 is not meant to predict the future with precision. It is meant to discipline portfolio thinking:

- Which direction are growth and inflation surprises moving *right now*?
- Which premia am I relying on (carry, growth, convexity), and how do they behave in this quadrant?
- If the regime shifts, which correlations are likely to break or con-

verge?

Why "surprises" drive returns (the pricing logic)

Markets are forward-looking discounting machines. Asset prices embed a baseline path for growth, inflation, and policy. The return you earn over the next period is driven less by the level of growth/inflation and more by the delta between realized macro path and expected macro path.

Two concrete examples:

- If growth is strong but *less strong than expected*, equities can fall. That is a negative growth surprise even in a healthy economy.
- If inflation is high but *cooling faster than expected*, long-duration bonds can rally strongly even with inflation still above target.

This is why regime labels must be tied to *changes* (rising/falling) and *surprises*, not to static thresholds.

Mapping each quadrant to cross-asset behavior

The quadrants are best understood as combinations of two shocks that propagate through earnings, discount rates, and risk appetite.

Quadrant I: Goldilocks (Growth ↑, Inflation ↓)

Narrative. The economy improves while inflation pressures ease. This is the regime where the market can plausibly have both: improving cash flows and a stable or falling discount rate.

Typical asset behavior.

- **Equities:** tend to do well because earnings expectations rise and valuation multiples can hold up.

- **Credit:** tends to perform as spreads tighten (default risk perceived to be lower) and carry is realized.

- **Duration:** can perform if inflation is falling and the central bank has room to be less restrictive, but the direction depends on how much growth pushes real rates higher.

Risk premia translation. Goldilocks is usually friendly to **growth** and **carry**. The danger is complacency: investors often sell convexity here because volatility is low, making the portfolio fragile if the regime flips.

Quadrant II: Reflation / Overheat (Growth $\uparrow$, Inflation $\uparrow$)

Narrative. Demand is strong and inflation pressures build. The market begins to price tighter monetary policy and/or higher real rates. The conflict is that cash flows improve but the discount rate rises.

Typical asset behavior.

- **Commodities:** often perform well because they are closer to the inflation impulse (especially energy and industrial metals).

- **Equities:** can be mixed. Cyclicals and value may outperform defensives; overall equity performance depends on whether the inflation impulse triggers aggressive tightening.

- **Bonds (duration):** often struggle because yields rise.

- **Floating-rate / short duration:** tends to be more resilient as higher front-end rates raise carry.

Risk premia translation. Carry can remain attractive, but it becomes more rate-sensitive. Growth premia can still be positive, but dispersion across equity styles increases. Convexity can become valuable if policy tightening creates instability.

Quadrant III: Recession / Disinflation (Growth ↓, Inflation ↓)

Narrative. Demand slows and inflation pressure fades. Earnings expectations drop, default risk rises, and central banks often have room to ease. This is the classic "risk-off" environment.

Typical asset behavior.

- **Nominal government bonds (duration):** often perform well as yields fall (though this can fail if inflation is not truly falling or if fiscal risk dominates).
- **Equities:** generally struggle due to weaker earnings and risk appetite.
- **Credit:** can be doubly hit (widening spreads plus impaired liquidity).
- **Convexity sleeves:** tend to be most valuable; correlation spikes and diversification within risky assets weakens.

Risk premia translation. The **growth** premium is negative. **Carry** often compresses sharply because spreads widen and funding becomes dear. **Convexity** is the stabilizer: it is designed for the state where correlations converge and cross-asset hedges matter most.

Quadrant IV: Stagflation (Growth ↓, Inflation ↑)

Narrative. This is the most difficult quadrant for traditional 60/40 thinking: growth deteriorates but inflation remains problematic. Central banks face a trade-off, and real income is squeezed.

Typical asset behavior.

- **Nominal duration:** can struggle because inflation pushes yields up even as growth slows.
- **Equities:** can struggle because earnings weaken and margins compress.

- **Inflation hedges (TIPS, commodities, gold):** often perform relatively well.
- **Quality of convexity matters:** some hedges help (e.g., inflation-linked exposure), while others may not if the sell-off is driven by rates rather than pure equity crash dynamics.

Risk premia translation. Carry is dangerous if it is sourced from nominal bonds or tight credit spreads. Growth is weak. The portfolio needs **inflation protection** and often benefits from **real-asset** exposure or explicit inflation-linked instruments.

Regimes as a correlation framework (why this helps diversification)

Recall the earlier warning: correlations are unstable. The regime framework explains *why*.

- In Goldilocks, risky assets may diversify each other modestly because liquidity is abundant and shocks are small. Correlations can appear stable.
- In Recession, many risky assets share the same dominant driver (risk aversion and tightening financial conditions). Correlations rise, often sharply.
- In Stagflation, the dominant driver can become inflation and the discount rate, flipping the sign of stock–bond correlation relative to disinflationary regimes.

In other words, the covariance matrix is not one matrix. It is closer to a *set of matrices,* one per regime. A portfolio that is robust across regimes must be built with that in mind.

Implementation: using the quadrant model without turning it into a forecasting contest

A frequent misuse of regime frameworks is to treat them as a macro trading call: "We are in quadrant X, therefore buy asset Y." That is too brittle. A more robust use is to treat the quadrant model as a **risk budgeting and tilt framework**:

Step 1: Define the strategic core
Start with a diversified strategic allocation (the "core") designed to survive all quadrants:

- a long-term growth engine (global equities, diversified),
- a defensive ballast (high-quality duration, sized realistically),
- inflation protection (TIPS/real assets), and
- convexity/ crisis response (explicit or implicit).

The weights should reflect the investor's risk capacity, not a tactical view.

Step 2: Nowcast, don't prophecy
Use a small set of observable indicators to assess the *direction* of growth and inflation surprises:

- growth: PMIs, unemployment claims, earnings revisions, credit conditions,
- inflation: CPI/PCE trend, wage growth, inflation expectations, commodity impulse.

The goal is to identify whether the marginal news flow is pushing the economy toward a different quadrant.

Step 3: Tilt exposures rather than flip allocations
Rather than wholesale reallocation, tilt:

- In growth-up regimes, modestly increase growth beta and diversify carry sources.
- In inflation-up regimes, increase inflation protection and reduce nominal duration vulnerability.
- In recession risk, reduce fragile carry and add convexity or high-quality duration.

This keeps the portfolio stable and reduces turnover and behavioral error.

Step 4: Stress test the quadrant transition
The highest risk is often the *transition* between quadrants:

- Goldilocks → Overheat: rates rise; long-duration and long-multiple equities can reprice quickly.
- Overheat → Stagflation: growth rolls over but inflation stays sticky; both stocks and nominal bonds can struggle.
- Goldilocks → Recession: carry trades unwind; correlations jump.

A disciplined manager asks: *What breaks if my quadrant read is wrong by one step?*

Common pitfalls (and how to avoid them)

Pitfall 1: confusing "inflation up" with "rates up."
Inflation surprises can raise nominal yields, but yields also move with real rates, term premia, and policy expectations. The quadrant model gives the macro impulse; you still need to consider the rate channel and the policy response.

Pitfall 2: treating alternatives as regime-proof.
Many "alts" are still long growth or short convexity in disguise. In recessionary transitions, their correlations can rise with other risk assets. The regime framework helps you test whether the alternative truly changes your quadrant behavior.

Pitfall 3: ignoring implementation frictions.
Real portfolios face constraints: tracking error limits, liquidity, governance, and taxes. The quadrant model should guide *risk budgeting* and incremental tilts, not constant regime-chasing.

Key takeaways

1. The most useful macro regime lens for multi-asset allocation is the interaction of **growth shocks** and **inflation surprises**.

2. Quadrants are defined by *direction relative to expectations*; levels alone are not enough.

3. Each quadrant has a characteristic pattern of winners and losers because cash flows, discount rates, and risk appetite move differently.

4. Regimes provide an economic explanation for **time-varying correlations**, including the tendency for correlations to rise in stress.

5. Use the quadrant model as a **risk budgeting and tilting framework** with explicit stress tests around transitions, not as a brittle forecasting game.

3.5 Monetary Policy and the Discount Rate Channel

The previous section organized multi-asset behavior into growth and inflation regimes. That framework is powerful, but it still leaves a practical question unanswered: *what is the mechanism that often makes correlations rise, valuation multiples compress, and "safe" duration suddenly become either a hedge or a hazard?*

One of the most important mechanisms is the **discount rate channel**. Central banks influence the economy and markets primarily by shifting the level and expected path of interest rates, and by shaping financial conditions through liquidity operations and balance sheet policy. Those policy choices transmit into asset prices through a common denominator: the rate at which future cash flows are discounted.

In multi-asset portfolios, that common denominator is exactly where "diversification math" can break: when the discount rate moves as a dominant common factor, multiple asset classes can reprice together.

The discount rate as the common denominator across assets

A simple present value identity captures the intuition. If an asset delivers expected cash flows CF_t and is discounted at rate r, its price is

$$P = \sum_{t=1}^{\infty} \frac{\mathbb{E}[CF_t]}{(1+r)^t}.$$

All else equal, a higher discount rate r lowers P. This is sometimes called the **denominator effect**: the denominator grows, compressing present value.

The key multi-asset point is that many assets can be viewed as discounted cash flow claims:

- **Bonds:** fixed coupons discounted at yields.
- **Equities:** uncertain dividends/free cash flows discounted at an equity discount rate (risk-free rate plus an equity risk premium).
- **Real estate and infrastructure:** long-duration contractual or quasi-contractual cash flows discounted at rates linked to risk-free yields plus spreads.
- **Credit:** bond-like cash flows discounted at risk-free yields plus credit spreads.

When the discount rate shifts materially, it can move several asset classes in the same direction, raising correlations.

Nominal rates, inflation, and real rates: the decomposition you must track

Policy rates are nominal, but the economy and valuations are often driven by **real** rates. The foundational relationship is:

$$y_{nominal} \approx y_{real} + \pi^e,$$

where $y_{nominal}$ is a nominal yield, y_{real} is a real yield, and π^e is expected inflation (plus, in practice, various premia).

For portfolio managers, this decomposition matters because different assets respond differently to which component is moving:

- Rising **expected inflation** can help real assets and inflation-linked bonds while hurting nominal duration.
- Rising **real rates** tend to pressure valuation multiples broadly, especially for long-duration cash flow assets (growth equities, long-duration credit, real estate).

This connects directly back to the regime map: stagflation risk is uniquely challenging because inflation pressures can keep nominal and/or real discount rates elevated while growth weakens.

How monetary policy transmits to markets (a practical chain)

Monetary policy affects markets through several linked channels. A useful practitioner's chain is:

Policy & Liquidity $\rightarrow$ Real Rates & Credit Conditions $\rightarrow$ Discount Rates –

We can make each step concrete.

Step 1: Policy rates shape the front end and expectations

Central banks set an administered short rate (or a corridor) and provide forward guidance. The market then prices an expected path of future short rates. This is why the entire yield curve can move on policy communication, not just the overnight rate.

Portfolio implication. Assets that are sensitive to the expected path of rates (long-duration bonds, long-multiple equities) can reprice sharply on guidance changes even without any change in current economic data.

Step 2: Real rates and financial conditions transmit to risk appetite

Policy influences borrowing costs, discounting, and liquidity. When conditions tighten:

- financing becomes more expensive (margin and funding stress can rise),
- risk-free yields compete more effectively with risky assets,
- credit spreads can widen as default risk and liquidity premia increase.

This is the bridge between "macro" and "correlation." In tightening cycles, correlations often rise because the *shared* driver becomes financial conditions rather than idiosyncratic fundamentals.

Step 3: Discount rates compress valuation multiples (the denominator effect)

Equity valuation can be summarized as a multiple on earnings or cash flow. A simplified intuition: P/E multiple $\sim$

$$\frac{1}{r-g},$$

where r is the equity discount rate and g is expected growth. This is not a literal formula you should plug numbers into; it is a directional map:

- If r rises and g is unchanged, multiples tend to fall.
- If g falls and r is unchanged, multiples tend to fall.
- If both move against you, multiple compression can be severe.

Bonds are even more directly exposed: higher yields reduce bond prices mechanically. Credit adds a spread component that can widen at the same time, producing a double hit.

Why stock–bond correlation flips sign (and why that matters)

A central practical question for multi-asset design is whether nominal duration hedges equity risk. Historically, stock–bond correlation has not been stable. A useful way to understand the sign is to ask the dominant shock: growth (bad for stocks, good for bonds) or inflation/policy (bad for both)?

Growth shock dominance (often negative correlation). If equities sell off due to growth deterioration, yields often fall as markets price easier policy and lower inflation. Bonds rally, and the stock–bond correlation turns negative. This is the classic "60/40 works" regime.

Inflation/policy shock dominance (often positive correlation). If equities sell off because the discount rate rises (higher real rates, tighter policy, inflation concerns), bonds can also sell off. The stock–bond correlation can turn positive. This is the regime where traditional balanced portfolios experience simultaneous drawdowns across stocks and bonds.

This is not a small technicality. In portfolio variance terms,

$$\sigma_p^2 = \sum_i w_i^2 \sigma_i^2 + 2 \sum_{i<j} w_i w_j \rho_{ij} \sigma_i \sigma_j,$$

a sign flip in $\rho_{stocks,bonds}$ changes whether duration is a hedge or a source of correlated risk.

Balance sheet policy: QE/QT as a term-premium and liquidity channel

Beyond policy rates, central banks can expand or shrink their balance sheets:

- **Quantitative easing (QE):** purchases of longer-dated assets intended to compress term premia and ease financial conditions.
- **Quantitative tightening (QT):** allowing securities to roll off (or selling), which can increase term premia and tighten conditions.

Even without specifying a single model of QE/QT, the practical implication is clear: balance sheet policy can move **long-end discount rates** and **liquidity premia**. Those are cross-asset inputs:

- higher term premia can pressure long-duration bonds and long-duration equity styles,
- tighter liquidity can widen credit spreads and increase cross-asset correlation,
- risk premia can reprice quickly when market depth deteriorates.

For the multi-asset strategist, QE/QT is best treated not as an abstract debate but as a regime variable that influences the stability of correlations.

The "Fed put" as a regime-dependent volatility anchor

Market participants often speak of a "Fed put": the idea that severe market stress may elicit policy easing or liquidity support. Whether or not one accepts the phrasing, the mechanism matters:

- If investors believe policy will respond to disorderly tightening of financial conditions, then risk premia may compress in calm periods (lower implied volatility, tighter credit spreads).
- If inflation constraints limit easing, that perceived backstop weakens, and risk premia can expand abruptly.

This belief interacts with portfolio construction in a subtle way: it can encourage crowded carry and short-convexity behavior (because "the central bank will step in"), increasing fragility exactly when policy flexibility is least.

A practical multi-asset playbook: what to watch and how to position

This section is about mechanism, not market timing. Still, a portfolio manager needs observable anchors to translate mechanism into risk controls.

Watchlist: indicators that the discount rate channel is dominating

Signs the discount rate channel is becoming the primary driver include:

- rising real yields (or rising inflation-adjusted discount rates),
- simultaneous weakness in stocks and nominal bonds (positive stock–bond correlation),
- multiple compression leadership (growth/long-duration equities underperforming),
- widening credit spreads alongside rising risk-free yields (a "double tightening").

Portfolio implications (expressed as risk budgeting, not point forecasts)

When discount rates are the dominant shock, portfolio construction typically benefits from:

- **reducing unintended long-duration exposure** (in both bonds and equity style tilts),
- **diversifying inflation protection** (TIPS, commodities, real assets where appropriate),
- **being cautious with carry** that is implicitly short volatility or reliant on tight spreads,
- **maintaining some convexity budget** so the portfolio is not relying solely on stock–bond diversification.

When growth deterioration is the dominant shock, the playbook often flips:

- high-quality nominal duration can again serve as a hedge,

- quality and defensiveness tends to matter more than pure cyclical exposure,
- credit beta should be treated carefully because spreads can dominate carry.

The key is that these are *regime-conditional* statements, consistent with the quadrant framework. Monetary policy and real rates are a primary reason regimes change, and a primary reason correlations fail when investors assume they are stable.

Connecting back to optimization: why Markowitz breaks hardest during policy shocks

Mean–variance optimization implicitly assumes that:

- expected returns are stable enough to estimate, and
- the covariance matrix is a reliable guide to future co-movement.

Policy shocks attack both assumptions at once:

- expected returns shift because discount rates and risk premia move,
- correlations shift because multiple assets are repriced by the same denominator.

This is why optimized portfolios can experience "model surprise" precisely when the market experiences macro surprise.

In other words, monetary policy is not merely one more macro variable. It is a correlation engine.

Key takeaways

- The discount rate is a **common denominator** across bonds, equities, credit, and many alternatives; when it moves, cross-asset correlations can rise.

- Decomposing nominal yields into **real rates** and **inflation expectations** is essential because different assets respond to different components.
- Tightening policy and rising real rates tend to compress valuation multiples and can produce **positive stock–bond correlation**, undermining traditional diversification.
- Balance sheet policy (QE/QT) influences term premia and liquidity, affecting risk premia and the stability of correlations.
- For robust multi-asset portfolios, treat monetary policy shocks as **regime shifts** and budget risk accordingly (duration, carry, growth beta, and convexity).

3.6 Yield Curve Mechanics and Rate Cycles

What the yield curve is (and what it is not)

The yield curve is the set of yields (or discount rates) across maturities for a given issuer, typically the government curve (e.g., U.S. Treasuries). Let $y(\tau)$ be the yield at maturity τ.

Three reminders to keep the discussion grounded.

1. **Yields are summaries, not primitives.** Prices and discount factors are more fundamental; yields are convenient compressions.
2. **The curve mixes multiple components.** A long yield is not just future short rates. It also includes term premia and risk compensation.
3. **Different parts of the curve respond to different shocks.** The front end is policy-sensitive; the long end is more sensitive to inflation expectations, real rate regimes, and term premia.

Decomposing the curve: expectations and term premium

A standard conceptual decomposition of an n-year yield is

$$y_n \approx \frac{1}{n}\sum_{t=1}^{n}\mathbb{E}[r_t] + \mathrm{TP}_n,$$

where:

- $\mathbb{E}[r_t]$ is the expected short rate in year t (policy expectations),
- TP_n is the term premium (compensation for bearing duration risk, plus other effects such as supply/demand and liquidity).

This decomposition is conceptually essential even if you never estimate TP_n explicitly. It tells you why the same curve shape can occur for different reasons:

- An inverted curve can reflect expected policy cuts (growth risk), or a depressed term premium (strong demand for duration), or both.
- A steep curve can reflect expected hikes (inflation/overheat risk) or a rising term premium (fiscal supply risk), or both.

Curve geometry: level, slope, and curvature

To manage curve risk, you need a minimal vocabulary that maps directly to trade construction.

Level. The **level** is the general height of yields across maturities. A parallel shift is a change in level.

Portfolio translation. Level risk is primarily **duration risk**. If you are long duration, rising yields cause price losses. If you are short duration (or hedged), rising yields help (or hurt less).

Slope. The **slope** measures the difference between long and short yields. A common proxy is

$$\text{slope} = y_{10} - y_2.$$

Steepness reflects how restrictive policy is relative to the market's expected long-run rate environment.

Portfolio translation. Slope risk can be expressed through curve trades (e.g., 2s10s steepeners/flatteners) or through portfolio construction choices that overweight one maturity bucket relative to another.

Curvature. Curvature captures how humped the curve is: whether intermediate maturities are high or low relative to a line connecting the front and long end. A common proxy is

$$\text{curvature} \approx y_5 - \frac{1}{2}(y_2 + y_{10}).$$

Curvature matters because many portfolios concentrate in the belly (e.g., 5-year exposure) for carry/roll reasons, while hedging is often done with the long bond. That maturity mismatch is curvature risk.

Price sensitivity: duration and convexity as the bond analog of equity multiples

For a bond (or a bond portfolio), the first-order price response to a yield change is

$$\frac{\Delta P}{P} \approx -D\,\Delta y,$$

where D is (modified) duration. The second-order correction is convexity:

$$\frac{\Delta P}{P} \approx -D\,\Delta y + \frac{1}{2}C(\Delta y)^2,$$

where C is convexity.

Why this belongs in a multi-asset chapter. Duration is the bond-market equivalent of "multiple exposure" in equities: it measures sensitivity to the discount rate. When discount rates are the dominant shock, duration and equity multiples can compress together, creating positive stock–bond correlation.

Carry and roll-down: why the curve shape matters for expected bond returns

Bond returns over a horizon are not only about forecasting yield changes. They also reflect **carry** and **roll-down**:

- **Carry:** the yield (or income) you earn by holding the bond.
- **Roll-down:** if the curve is upward sloping, a bond rolls down the curve over time (its maturity shortens), potentially gaining price if shorter maturities have lower yields.

A simplified decomposition for expected return over a short horizon Δt is

$$\mathbb{E}[\text{Bond Return}] \approx y(\tau)\Delta t + \text{roll}(\tau, \Delta t) - D\,\mathbb{E}[\Delta y].$$

Practical implication. Two portfolios with the same duration can have very different expected carry/roll profiles depending on where they sit on the curve. This is one reason curve positioning is not just a rates view; it is a return engineering choice.

Rate cycles and curve moves: steepeners and flatteners

Market narratives often say rates up or rates down. For portfolio construction, that is too blunt. You need to know which part of the curve is moving and why. A useful taxonomy combines direction (bull/bear) with shape (steepener/flattener):

- **Bull steepener:** yields fall and the curve steepens (front end falls more). Often associated with the market pricing policy cuts (recession risk).
- **Bull flattener:** yields fall and the curve flattens (long end falls more). Often occurs when inflation fears recede and duration rallies.
- **Bear steepener:** yields rise and the curve steepens (long end rises more). Often associated with rising term premium, inflation risk, or fiscal supply concerns.

- **Bear flattener:** yields rise and the curve flattens (front end rises more). Often associated with active tightening: policy rates rise faster than long-run expectations.

This taxonomy connects directly to the earlier macro quadrant framework:

- Overheat/reflation regimes frequently coincide with bear moves (yields rising), though whether steepening or flattening depends on policy credibility and term premium.
- Recession/disinflation regimes frequently coincide with bull moves (yields falling), often with front-end-led steepening when cuts are priced.
- Stagflation can produce bear steepening (inflation/term premium pressure) even as growth weakens, which is exactly why it is difficult for balanced portfolios.

Curve positioning: translating a macro view into implementable exposures

Curve positioning means choosing where along the curve you want interest rate exposure (and where you want to neutralize it). There are three common objectives:

1. maximize carry/roll for a given duration,
2. hedge a specific macro risk (growth shock vs inflation shock),
3. reduce correlation with equities by avoiding the wrong duration in the wrong regime.

Front-end vs long-end exposure

Front end (e.g., 0–3 years). Dominated by policy expectations and current policy stance. Advantages:

- typically lower price volatility (lower duration),

- higher sensitivity to near-term policy path (useful for expressing monetary policy views),
- carry can be attractive when cash rates are high.

Risks.

- can be vulnerable in bear flatteners (front-end rates rising sharply),
- provides less crisis convexity than long duration.

Long end (e.g., 10–30 years). Dominated by real rate regimes, inflation expectations, and term premium. Advantages:

- strong hedge potential in growth shocks (bull moves),
- higher convexity (can help in large rate rallies).

Risks.

- vulnerable to term premium shocks and inflation shocks (bear steepeners),
- can become positively correlated with equities when discount rate shocks dominate.

The belly (e.g., 3–7 years): the carry/roll battleground

Intermediate maturities often offer attractive roll-down in normal upward-sloping curves. Many managers concentrate exposure here to optimize carry per unit duration. The hidden risk is that belly-heavy portfolios can be exposed to curvature changes and can under-hedge tail scenarios if the long end is the primary shock absorber.

Barbell vs bullet: shaping duration to express views and manage risk

Two classic portfolio shapes help translate curve views and hedging needs into construction.

Bullet portfolio

A **bullet** concentrates maturity exposure around a single point (e.g., mostly 5-year bonds). It is clean and often efficient for targeting a benchmark duration.

When bullets make sense.

- You want to maximize carry/roll in the belly.
- You want simple, concentrated exposure to a specific part of the curve.
- You have a strong view about that maturity segment (e.g., policy path affects 2–5 years).

Bullet risks.

- greater vulnerability to local curve repricing (curvature shifts),
- potential underperformance if the regime changes and a different segment becomes the key hedge.

Barbell portfolio

A **barbell** splits exposure between short and long maturities, with less in the belly.

When barbells make sense.

- You want **policy sensitivity** at the front end and **convexity/hedge potential** at the long end.
- You want to reduce exposure to belly-specific curvature risk.
- You are uncertain about the shape of curve moves and want a more robust distribution of exposures.

Barbell trade-off. Barbells can sacrifice some carry/roll that the belly may offer in normal times, but they can improve robustness across regimes—especially when the curve's movement is driven by different shocks at different maturities.

Hedging macro risks with curve tools (practical principles)

Yield curve tools are among the cleanest macro hedges because they target the discount rate channel directly. The objective is not to predict every basis point move; it is to align hedges with the portfolio's macro vulnerabilities.

Hedging growth shocks

If the portfolio is structurally long growth (most are), a classic hedge is exposure to high-quality duration that tends to rally when growth deteriorates and policy cuts are priced. The hedge is most reliable when inflation is not the binding constraint.

Hedging inflation/policy shocks

If inflation is the dominant risk, nominal duration can fail as a hedge. Managers may reduce long-end exposure, use inflation-linked bonds, shorten duration, or diversify with real assets and other inflation-sensitive exposures. The curve framework clarifies that the hedge target is the real discount rate and inflation expectation complex, not simply own bonds.

Hedging correlation instability

When policy shocks dominate, stock–bond correlation can turn positive. A robust framework therefore avoids relying on a single hedge relationship. Practically, this means:

- diversify defensive assets (some nominal duration, some inflation protection, some convexity),
- monitor the regime in which duration is expected to hedge (growth-driven) versus amplify risk (policy-driven).

A concise taxonomy for portfolio meetings

To make yield curve conversations actionable, it helps to standardize the questions asked in investment committees:

1. **What is our duration?** (Level exposure)
2. **Where is our duration?** (Front/belly/long concentration)
3. **What curve move hurts us most?** (Bear steepener vs bear flattener vs bull steepener vs bull flattener)
4. **What macro shock are we hedging?** (Growth vs inflation/policy)
5. **What is the carry/roll trade-off we are accepting?**

This aligns curve mechanics with the earlier risk premia framework:

- carry/roll is a form of carry premium,
- long duration can provide convexity in growth shocks,
- the discount rate channel is the link between curve moves and equity valuation.

Chapter 4

Modern Portfolio Construction and Risk Budgeting

Most investors believe they are diversified because they hold many distinct assets; in reality, they are often concentrating risk in a single economic factor. This chapter dismantles the illusion of capital-weighted diversification, introducing the rigorous machinery of risk budgeting. We move beyond simple mean-variance optimization-which often acts as an 'error maximization' engine-to explore how leverage, robust optimization, and Bayesian frameworks like Black-Litterman allow us to build portfolios that respect uncertainty rather than ignoring it.

4.1 Risk Budgeting: Allocating Risk, Not Capital

Most portfolios are described in the language of *capital weights*: "60% equities, 40% bonds," "10% alternatives," and so on. Capital weights are easy to communicate, easy to implement, and they match how custodians and statements report holdings. But they are not the right language for answering the question that matters most to a multi-asset strategist:

How much risk is each sleeve actually contributing to the whole?

Risk budgeting is the discipline of allocating *risk* rather than dollars. It is the bridge between (i) an investor's desired exposure profile—growth, deflation-hedge, inflation-hedge, liquidity, convexity—and (ii) a portfolio that behaves as intended under stress.

The practical motivation is simple: in most environments, equities are far more volatile than high-quality bonds. As a result, a portfolio that is "balanced" by capital can be severely *unbalanced* by risk. This mismatch is the core of what practitioners sometimes call the *60/40 fallacy*: the belief that a 60/40 split implies anything close to a 60/40 balance of risk.

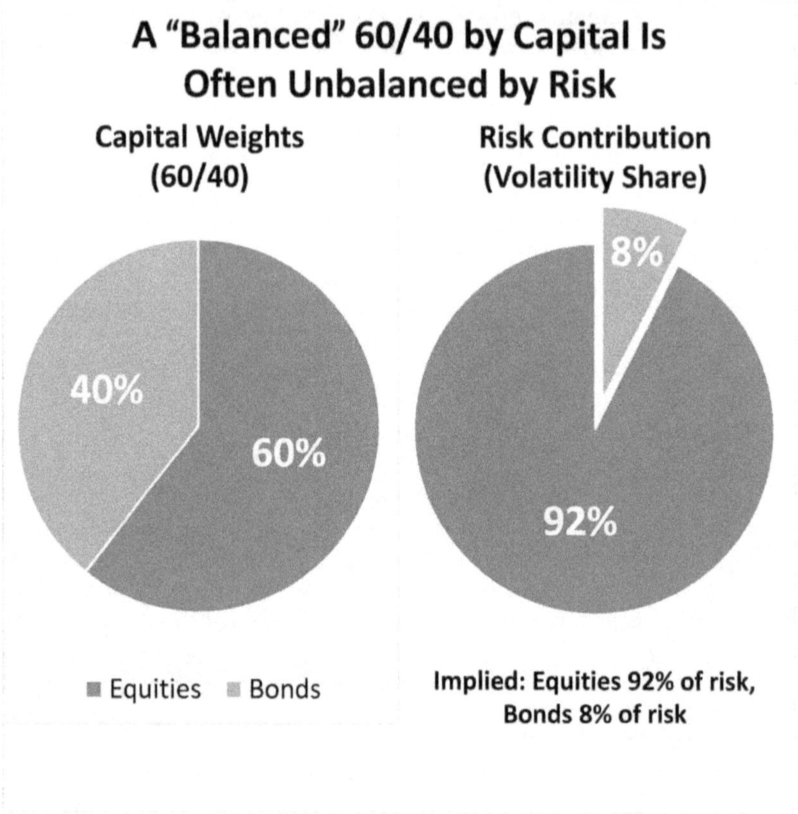

From capital weights to risk weights

A capital allocation answers: *What fraction of dollars are invested in each asset?* A risk allocation answers: *What fraction of portfolio uncertainty is coming from each asset?*

In this section we focus on volatility as the risk measure because (i) it is the building block for many other risk systems (tracking error, VaR under elliptical assumptions, stress test scaling), and (ii) it supports a clean decomposition: we can attribute total portfolio volatility back to the underlying holdings in a way that is mathematically coherent and practically actionable.

Let the portfolio have weights vector $w \in \mathbb{R}^n$ and covariance matrix $\Sigma \in \mathbb{R}^{n \times n}$. Portfolio variance is

$$\sigma_p^2 = w^\top \Sigma w.$$

Portfolio volatility is

$$\sigma_p = \sqrt{w^\top \Sigma w}.$$

Two immediate observations are worth making:

- **Volatility depends on covariances, not just volatilities.** A low-volatility asset can still add meaningful risk if it is highly correlated with the dominant risk factor.
- **Risk is nonlinear in the weights.** Doubling a weight does not double portfolio volatility. This is why "risk budgeting" is not a simple re-labeling of capital weights.

Marginal Contribution to Total Risk (MCTR): the portfolio's risk "sensitivities"

When a portfolio manager asks, "Where is my risk coming from?" there are two closely related questions:

- 1. *If I increase weight w_i a little, how much does total portfolio volatility increase?*
- 2. *Given my current w_i, how much of today's portfolio volatility can I attribute to asset i?*

The first question is answered by the **Marginal Contribution to Total Risk (MCTR)**. Define MCTR with respect to volatility (not variance) as the partial derivative:

$$\text{MCTR}_i \equiv \frac{\partial \sigma_p}{\partial w_i}.$$

Using $\sigma_p = \sqrt{w^\top \Sigma w}$, differentiate:

$$\begin{aligned}\frac{\partial \sigma_p}{\partial w} &= \frac{1}{2}(w^\top \Sigma w)^{-1/2} \cdot 2\Sigma w \\ &= \frac{\Sigma w}{\sigma_p}.\end{aligned}$$

So the i-th component is

$$\text{MCTR}_i = \frac{(\Sigma w)_i}{\sigma_p}.$$

Interpretation (why MCTR is intuitive).

- $(\Sigma w)_i$ is the covariance of asset i with the portfolio (in variance units).
- Dividing by σ_p converts it into the units of volatility per unit of weight.
- If $(\Sigma w)_i$ is large, then asset i is "moving with" the portfolio in a way that matters; adding more of it increases total volatility quickly.
- If $(\Sigma w)_i$ is small or negative, adding more of it increases volatility slowly or may even reduce it (a true diversifier).

From MCTR to risk contributions: diagnosing concentration

MCTR is a *marginal* object: it tells you what happens at the margin. Risk budgeting, however, needs an *attribution*: we want the portion of the current portfolio risk that is "due to" each holding.

The standard, internally consistent attribution uses Euler's theorem for homogeneous functions. Portfolio volatility $\sigma_p(w)$ is *homogeneous of degree 1* in the weights: scaling all weights by $k > 0$ scales volatility by k:

$$\sigma_p(kw) = k\sigma_p(w).$$

Euler's theorem implies

$$\sigma_p = \sum_{i=1}^{n} w_i \frac{\partial \sigma_p}{\partial w_i} = \sum_{i=1}^{n} w_i \,\mathrm{MCTR}_i.$$

This gives a natural definition of each asset's **(absolute) risk contribution** to portfolio volatility:

$$\mathrm{RC}_i \equiv w_i \,\mathrm{MCTR}_i = w_i \frac{(\Sigma w)_i}{\sigma_p}.$$

And the **percentage risk contribution** is

$$\mathrm{PRC}_i \equiv \frac{\mathrm{RC}_i}{\sum_{j=1}^{n} \mathrm{RC}_j} = \frac{\mathrm{RC}_i}{\sigma_p}.$$

Why this decomposition matters operationally. A capital-weight report might say you are "diversified" because no position exceeds 10%. A risk report can reveal the opposite: one sleeve can quietly dominate the portfolio's behavior. Risk contributions are the diagnostic tool that converts diversification from a *story about holdings* into a *measurement about outcomes.*

The 60/40 fallacy: a two-asset illustration

Consider a portfolio with two assets: equities (E) and bonds (B). Capital weights are

$$w_E = 0.60, \qquad w_B = 0.40.$$

Suppose (stylized) annualized volatilities are $\sigma_E = 16\%$ and $\sigma_B = 5\%$, and their correlation is $\rho_{EB} = 0.20$. The covariance matrix is

$$\Sigma = \begin{bmatrix} \sigma_E^2 & \rho_{EB}\sigma_E\sigma_B \\ \rho_{EB}\sigma_E\sigma_B & \sigma_B^2 \end{bmatrix}.$$

Even without doing the full arithmetic, the intuition is clear:

- Equities have roughly three times the volatility of bonds.

- Equities typically have a much higher covariance with the portfolio because the portfolio itself is materially equity-driven.
- Therefore, the equity MCTR is much larger than the bond MCTR.

The result is that the equity sleeve often accounts for the overwhelming majority of portfolio volatility. This is not an "error" in 60/40 construction; it is simply what happens when you mix a high-volatility return engine (equities) with a low-volatility stabilizer (bonds) without explicitly budgeting risk.

A practical workflow: compute MCTR and risk contributions before you rebalance

Risk budgeting is most powerful when it becomes part of the rebalance routine. A simple workflow for any multi-asset portfolio is:

- 1. **Estimate Σ.** Use a covariance estimate appropriate to your horizon (daily/weekly/monthly) and your regime assumptions. (Later sections will address how to stabilize this step.)
- 2. **Compute portfolio volatility.** $\sigma_p = \sqrt{w^\top \Sigma w}$.
- 3. **Compute MCTR.** $\text{MCTR} = \Sigma w / \sigma_p$.
- 4. **Compute risk contributions.** $\text{RC}_i = w_i \text{MCTR}_i$ and $\text{PRC}_i = \text{RC}_i / \sigma_p$.
- 5. **Diagnose concentration.** Compare PRC to your desired risk budget. Concentration is present when one sleeve's PRC is meaningfully above its policy risk share.

Two practical points make this more than a spreadsheet exercise:

(1) MCTR is the "shadow price" of risk. If your equity sleeve has a very high MCTR, then every incremental dollar allocated to equities buys a large increment of portfolio volatility. MCTR converts vague statements like "equities are risky" into an actionable number: how risky for this portfolio, right now.

(2) Risk concentration can exist even with many holdings. A portfolio with 20 ETFs can still have 80–90% of its volatility explained by a single underlying factor (often global equity beta). Risk contributions can be computed at multiple levels:

- by asset (ETF-by-ETF),
- by sleeve (equities vs. rates vs. credit vs. commodities),
- by factor (equity beta, duration, inflation sensitivity, carry, etc.).

The math is the same; only the mapping from holdings to risk buckets changes.

Common misconceptions (and how risk budgeting resolves them)

Misconception: "Bonds are 40% of my portfolio, so they must meaningfully offset equity drawdowns." Capital weights do not guarantee diversification. Bonds help when they are negatively correlated (or at least weakly correlated) with equities during equity stress and when their own volatility is sufficient (or their weight is sufficient) to matter. Risk contribution makes this visible: if bonds contribute only a small share of volatility, their ability to change the portfolio's path is mechanically limited except in large bond moves.

Misconception: "If I just add more asset classes, I am diversified." If the new assets are all highly correlated with the dominant risk driver, the portfolio can remain concentrated. Risk contributions reveal whether the new positions are true diversifiers (low/negative MCTR relative to the portfolio) or simply additional expressions of the same bet.

Misconception: "Low volatility means low risk." Low standalone volatility does not imply low *portfolio* risk contribution. A low-volatility asset can have a high MCTR if it covaries strongly with the existing portfolio and is held in large size. Conversely, a high-volatility asset can have a modest MCTR if it is diversifying.

What risk budgeting sets up next

This section's goal is diagnostic: to replace capital-based intuition with a risk-based measurement system. Once you can compute MCTR and risk contributions, two natural questions follow:

- 1. If a capital-balanced portfolio is risk-concentrated, *how do we build portfolios that are balanced by risk on purpose*? (This leads directly to Equal Risk Contribution and risk parity construction.)
- 2. If balancing risk pushes us toward larger allocations to low-volatility assets, *what are the operational constraints* (leverage, margin, funding) that determine whether the theory survives contact with markets?

In other words, MCTR is not merely a statistic. It is the first tool in a practical sequence: *diagnose* concentration, then *re-allocate* risk deliberately, then *manage* the implementation realities that risk-balanced portfolios require.

4.2 Risk Parity and Balanced Portfolios

The previous section established a diagnostic fact that surprises many investors the first time they measure it: a portfolio can look diversified by *capital* and still be highly concentrated by *risk*. The natural next step is prescriptive:

> If we want a portfolio that is truly "balanced," what does it mean to balance *risk*—and how do we implement it in practice?

Risk parity is best understood as a *risk-budgeting framework* rather than a single product. Its core idea is the construction of portfolios where each sleeve contributes a specified share of total portfolio risk, often (but not always) equally. The most common formulation is **Equal Risk Contribution (ERC)**: every asset (or sleeve) is sized so its percentage risk contribution matches a target, typically $1/n$.

From a diagnostic to a design target: Equal Risk Contribution (ERC)

Recall the volatility-based risk decomposition from the prior section. With weights $w \in \mathbb{R}^n$ and covariance matrix Σ, portfolio volatility is

$$\sigma_p = \sqrt{w^\top \Sigma w},$$

and the marginal contribution to total risk (MCTR) is

$$\text{MCTR} = \frac{\Sigma w}{\sigma_p}.$$

The absolute risk contribution of asset i is

$$\text{RC}_i = w_i \, \text{MCTR}_i = w_i \frac{(\Sigma w)_i}{\sigma_p},$$

and the percentage risk contribution is

$$\text{PRC}_i = \frac{\text{RC}_i}{\sigma_p}.$$

An ERC portfolio targets

$$\text{PRC}_i = b_i \qquad (i = 1, \ldots, n),$$

where $b_i \geq 0$ and $\sum_{i=1}^n b_i = 1$. The special case $b_i = 1/n$ is *equal* risk contribution. More generally, b is your *risk budget*: you can equalize risk across broad sleeves (e.g., equities, rates, credit, commodities), or you can intentionally overweight certain risks (e.g., allocate more risk to inflation hedges) while still controlling concentration.

Why ERC is a sensible baseline. ERC is not claiming that all assets have equal expected returns. It is claiming something narrower and more operational: if you do not have high conviction about relative Sharpe ratios, a reasonable starting point is to avoid letting any single sleeve dominate portfolio outcomes. ERC replaces the vague mandate "be diversified" with a concrete, measurable requirement: *no single asset gets to own the portfolio's volatility by accident.*

The first implementation step: inverse-volatility scaling (what it solves, and what it ignores)

A common entry point to risk parity is the **inverse-volatility** heuristic:

$$\tilde{w}_i \propto \frac{1}{\sigma_i}, \qquad w_i = \frac{\tilde{w}_i}{\sum_{j=1}^{n} \tilde{w}_j},$$

where σ_i is the standalone volatility of asset i.

Intuition. If one asset is twice as volatile as another, inverse-volatility scaling roughly halves its weight. This tends to push capital away from the highest-volatility assets (often equities or commodities) and toward the lowest-volatility assets (often high-quality bonds), which is the mechanical antidote to the 60/40 fallacy.

When inverse-vol works well. Inverse-volatility weights are most effective when:

- correlations are low or roughly uniform across pairs, and
- the portfolio has a small number of broad, liquid sleeves.

In that setting, equalizing standalone volatility is often close to equalizing *risk contribution*.

The limitation (the part investors miss). Inverse-volatility scaling does *not* explicitly control for correlation. But risk contributions depend on Σw, not just $\mathrm{diag}(\Sigma)$. Two assets can have identical volatilities and still contribute very different amounts of risk if one is highly correlated with the rest of the portfolio and the other is not.

Said differently: inverse-vol answers "how risky is the asset by itself?" ERC answers "how much does this asset drive the whole portfolio's movement given everything else we hold?" Those are not the same question.

Correlation is not a footnote: it is the entire diversification engine

To see why correlation matters, separate portfolio variance into volatility and correlation terms. For two assets:

$$\sigma_p^2 = w_1^2\sigma_1^2 + w_2^2\sigma_2^2 + 2w_1w_2\rho_{12}\sigma_1\sigma_2.$$

The cross term is where diversification lives. If ρ_{12} rises during stress, the diversification term weakens (or disappears), and the portfolio behaves more like a single concentrated position.

For n assets, the same logic holds: the covariance matrix Σ governs whether adding a sleeve reduces risk (through low/negative correlation) or simply adds another expression of the same underlying bet.

The practical implication for risk parity. A portfolio is not "risk parity" because its weights happen to look balanced. It is risk parity when *its risk contributions* are balanced *under the covariance structure you are assuming*. Therefore:

- ERC is fundamentally a **covariance-aware** construction.
- The quality and stability of your correlation estimates directly determine whether the portfolio is balanced in the real world.

Defining ERC precisely: the optimization problem

There are multiple mathematically equivalent ways to formulate ERC. A common and practical form is to choose weights that make risk contributions close to the target budget b.

Let RC(w) be the vector of risk contributions:

$$\mathrm{RC}_i(w) = w_i\frac{(\Sigma w)_i}{\sigma_p(w)}.$$

ERC seeks w such that

$$\mathrm{RC}_i(w) = b_i\sigma_p(w) \qquad (i = 1, \ldots, n).$$

Because $\sigma_p(w)$ itself depends on w, this is nonlinear. A widely used implementation is to solve

$$\min_w \sum_{i=1}^{n} \left(\text{PRC}_i(w) - b_i\right)^2,$$

subject to $\sum_{i=1}^{n} w_i = 1$ and $w_i \geq 0$ for all i. The long-only constraint is optional (many institutional implementations allow limited shorting, especially within rates), but long-only is a clean baseline for multi-asset policy portfolios.

A useful engineering note. In practice, you rarely optimize directly over PRC without additional safeguards because:

- multiple solutions can exist when assets are very correlated,
- small estimation errors in Σ can change the optimizer's preferred mix, and
- constraints (caps, floors, liquidity, regulatory limits) often matter as much as the objective.

Later sections on robust optimization revisit these issues. For now, the key point is conceptual: *ERC is implemented by explicitly targeting the decomposition of volatility using MCTR and Euler risk attribution.*

A step-by-step implementation recipe (what a PM actually does)

A workable ERC process is more of a pipeline than a single optimization. The following steps translate the concept into an operational routine.

Step 1: Choose the risk buckets and the measurement horizon Decide whether you are balancing risk across:

- individual instruments (e.g., ETFs), or
- sleeves (e.g., global equities, nominal duration, credit, commodities, trend, etc.).

Most serious multi-asset portfolios risk-budget at the sleeve level first, then build sub-portfolios within sleeves.

Choose the volatility horizon (e.g., daily returns with a 60-day window, weekly with a 3-year window). The right choice depends on rebalance frequency and the stability of your exposures. Fast rebalancers can use shorter windows; strategic allocators should prefer longer windows with robustness adjustments.

Step 2: Estimate Σ with explicit attention to correlation At minimum, compute a covariance matrix from returns and ensure it is positive semi-definite. Then ask: are the correlations you are feeding into the optimizer plausible under stress?

Many teams implement a **correlation floor** or **stress correlation overlay** for assets that are known to "go to one" in crises (e.g., equity regions, equity factors, credit with equities). This is not pessimism; it is acknowledging that correlations are state-dependent.

Step 3: Initialize with inverse-volatility weights Inverse-volatility weights are an excellent initial guess for ERC optimization. They deliver a portfolio that is usually closer to balanced risk than naive capital weights, and they speed convergence for nonlinear solvers.

Step 4: Solve for weights that match the risk budget Compute $\sigma_p(w)$, MCTR, and risk contributions. Update weights until $\text{PRC}(w)$ is sufficiently close to b.

Step 5: Apply real-world constraints Typical constraints include:

- max weight per sleeve (to avoid overconcentration in low-vol assets),
- min weight (to keep exposure meaningful and avoid churn),
- turnover controls (transaction costs matter),
- instrument-level liquidity constraints,
- maximum leverage (if leverage is allowed),
- tracking-error constraints vs. a policy benchmark (for institutional mandates).

Step 6: Rebalance with a "risk drift" trigger, not a calendar alone A calendar rebalance (monthly/quarterly) is simple but blunt. ERC portfolios are naturally suited to **risk drift** monitoring: rebalance when PRC_i deviates from b_i by more than a threshold. This focuses trades on moments when the portfolio has actually become unbalanced, often due to volatility changes and correlation shifts rather than just price drift.

What "balanced" really means: balancing risk is not balancing outcomes

A crucial clarification for sophisticated readers: ERC balances *contributions to volatility*, not expected returns, not drawdown, and not tail risk. A few implications follow:

Balanced volatility does not guarantee balanced drawdowns. Equities and commodities can have the same contribution to volatility as bonds and still dominate left-tail outcomes because their return distributions are more negatively skewed and more sensitive to liquidity shocks.

Balanced risk contributions are conditional on the covariance regime. If correlations shift, risk contributions shift. ERC is a *model-based balance*. That is not a flaw; it is simply the nature of multi-asset diversification.

Balanced is a policy choice. Equal risk contribution is one choice. Many investors should not target equal risk across everything:

- A pension plan might deliberately allocate more risk to growth assets to meet actuarial return needs.
- An inflation-sensitive liability stream might allocate more risk to inflation hedges.
- A liquidity-constrained allocator might avoid large allocations to assets whose correlations become unstable when liquidity disappears.

Risk parity is best viewed as a *framework for expressing these choices cleanly* through a vector b of risk budgets.

A minimal numerical intuition: why correlation-adjusted ERC differs from inverse-vol

Consider three sleeves: equities (E), nominal duration (D), and commodities (C). Suppose E and C have similar volatilities, but C is less correlated with E than E is with D. Inverse-vol might give E and C similar weights. Correlation-aware ERC will often allocate more to C than inverse-vol does because C delivers more diversification per unit of volatility: its MCTR is smaller relative to its standalone σ_C.

This is the key idea to internalize:

$$\sigma_i \neq \text{MCTR}_i.$$

Risk parity is the practice of sizing exposures off the right-hand side.

Implementation pitfalls (the most common ways ERC goes wrong)

Pitfall 1: Treating the covariance matrix as a static truth. ERC portfolios are only as good as the covariance estimate. If you feed in a covariance regime that is too optimistic (low correlations, low bond volatility, stable negative stock/bond correlation), the portfolio may look balanced on paper and behave concentrated in stress.

Pitfall 2: Confusing "risk parity" with "bond-heavy." Many risk parity allocations do allocate substantial capital to bonds in order to equalize volatility contributions. That is not the thesis; it is the arithmetic. The thesis is *balanced risk.* In some regimes (e.g., higher bond volatility, positive stock/bond correlation), the risk-parity solution can look very different.

Pitfall 3: Ignoring the funding/implementation layer. If you want a higher expected return than a low-volatility risk-balanced portfolio can provide unlevered, you will be tempted to lever the portfolio. At that point, the strategy's dominant risk often becomes *funding liquidity* and *forced deleveraging* rather than market volatility alone. This is the natural bridge to the next section.

Where this leads next

At this point we have moved from measurement (MCTR and risk contributions) to construction (ERC/risk parity). But a practical multi-asset strategist must now confront the real-world constraint that makes risk parity both powerful and dangerous: to target equity-like returns with a risk-balanced mix of low-volatility assets, you often need leverage, derivatives, or both.

The next section addresses the operational "plumbing"—margin, financing rates, haircuts, and the risk of deleveraging spirals—that determines whether a risk-parity design remains resilient when markets become discontinuous.

4.3 Leverage, Margin, and Funding Constraints

The previous section showed how Equal Risk Contribution (ERC) portfolios can be engineered by controlling marginal and total risk contributions under an assumed covariance structure. That construction step is intellectually clean: compute Σ, solve for w such that risk contributions match a budget, and rebalance as correlations and volatilities drift.

Implementation is not clean.

The moment you attempt to make a risk-balanced portfolio *competitive on expected return*, you run into the defining operational reality of multi-asset risk parity: many of the diversifying sleeves (high-quality duration, cash-like carry, defensive relative-value) are low-volatility. Balanced risk often implies large *capital* allocations to these sleeves, and to reach an equity-like return target, the portfolio often uses leverage (explicitly via borrowing or implicitly via derivatives).

This section is a practical manual for that leverage layer. If risk budgeting is the *architecture*, leverage is the *plumbing*. Plumbing failures are what turn theoretically balanced portfolios into forced sellers.

Why leverage shows up in risk-balanced portfolios

In a two-asset caricature (equities and high-quality bonds), an ERC-like solution often gives bonds a large weight because their standalone volatility is low. Unlevered, that portfolio can have substantially lower expected return than a traditional equity-heavy mix. The temptation is to scale the whole portfolio up by a leverage factor λ:

$$w^{(\lambda)} = \lambda w, \qquad \lambda > 1.$$

Under the volatility model,

$$\sigma_p\left(w^{(\lambda)}\right) = \lambda\sigma_p(w),$$

so leverage is a straightforward way to map a low-volatility diversified mix to a target risk level.

But leverage changes the portfolio's risk profile in a crucial way:

Without leverage, the dominant risk is usually market risk. With leverage, a large fraction of the dominant risk becomes funding and liquidity risk.

A manager who only optimizes weights w and ignores funding mechanics is solving the wrong problem.

Three distinct concepts: leverage, gross exposure, and effective leverage

Practitioners often use the word "leverage" loosely. For implementation, it helps to distinguish:

- **Gross exposure**: $\sum_i |w_i|$. A long-only unlevered portfolio has gross exposure $= 1$. A 1.5× levered long-only portfolio has gross exposure $= 1.5$.
- **Net exposure**: $\sum_i w_i$. Long-only portfolios have net exposure $= 1$ even when levered via borrowing (because the asset weights sum to more than 1 and the difference is funded by cash borrowing).

- **Effective leverage**: a practical measure tied to financing and margin, often defined as

$$\text{effective leverage} \approx \frac{\text{market value of positions}}{\text{equity (collateral) supporting the positions}}.$$

  This is the ratio that determines how quickly you are forced to de-risk when prices move against you or margin requirements rise.

ERC portfolios can look conservative in volatility space while having high effective leverage because the low-vol sleeves are held in large size with financing.

The financing identity: expected return must pay for funding

At the portfolio level, leveraged implementation creates a simple but unforgiving arithmetic. Consider an unlevered portfolio of risky assets with weights w that sum to 1. If you scale to gross exposure λ by borrowing, a stylized one-period return model is

$$R_p \approx \lambda\, w^\top R - (\lambda - 1)\, r_f - \text{costs},$$

where R is the vector of asset returns, r_f is the financing rate on borrowed cash (or the relevant funding benchmark), and "costs" include transaction costs, financing spreads, roll costs, margin frictions, and slippage.

Taking expectations:

$$\mathbb{E}[R_p] \approx \lambda\, w^\top \mathbb{E}[R] - (\lambda - 1)\, r_f - \mathbb{E}[\text{costs}].$$

Key implication: leverage amplifies both returns and the funding bill. The common conceptual error is to treat leverage as a free scaling knob. It is not. The incremental unit of leverage $\Delta\lambda$ is only valuable if the portfolio's expected excess return over funding is sufficiently positive *after* all implementation costs:

$$w^\top \mathbb{E}[R] - r_f \qquad \text{must compensate for costs and risk.}$$

When funding rates rise, or when the carry in the low-vol sleeves turns negative (e.g., rising yields hurting duration carry/roll), the same levered structure can become unattractive quickly.

Margin mechanics: how leverage becomes fragile

Leverage is implemented through mechanisms that require collateral and impose maintenance rules. The details vary by instrument (cash bonds, futures, swaps, repo), but the economic structure is similar.

Initial margin, variation margin, and maintenance

A simplified margin account evolves as follows:

- **Initial margin (IM)**: collateral posted to open the position.
- **Variation margin (VM)**: daily (or intraday) cash settlement of mark-to-market P&L.
- **Maintenance margin**: a minimum equity level. If your equity falls below it, you face a margin call.

If a position loses money, VM requires cash *now*. This is not an accounting issue; it is a liquidity demand. Even a temporary drawdown can force de-risking if you cannot post cash.

Why risk parity portfolios are exposed. Risk parity portfolios often hold large notionals in low-vol instruments (especially rates futures or swaps). These instruments are *capital efficient* but *liquidity intensive* under adverse moves, because VM is settled in cash. The portfolio can be solvent in a long-horizon sense and still fail operationally due to cash-flow timing.

Haircuts, repo, and financing of cash securities

When leverage is implemented by borrowing against cash securities (e.g., financing bonds in repo), lenders apply a **haircut** h, meaning only $(1-h)$ of the security's market value can be borrowed. A position of market value V supports borrowing

$$B \le (1-h)V.$$

Haircuts tend to rise precisely when you least want them to: in volatility spikes and liquidity stress. Rising haircuts are economically equivalent to a sudden reduction in allowed leverage.

Cost of carry: the hidden "expense ratio" of leveraged diversification

In multi-asset portfolios, the financing cost is only the beginning. The **cost of carry** differs by sleeve and instrument:

- **Duration exposure via futures/swaps**: the implied financing is embedded in pricing; P&L reflects both yield changes and the term structure effects. In addition, margin cash typically earns a short rate, but the opportunity cost is the spread between that rate and the portfolio's required return.
- **Commodity futures**: returns include spot change, collateral yield, and roll yield. "Diversification" can be expensive when curves are in persistent contango (negative roll).
- **FX forwards**: carry equals the interest rate differential; hedging can be a return drag or a tail-risk reducer depending on rate differentials and risk objectives.

In a levered portfolio, small persistent carries compound into large performance differences.

This is why sophisticated implementations treat carry and funding as first-class citizens in the portfolio design, not as implementation afterthoughts.

The dangerous feedback loop: forced deleveraging and the volatility spiral

The most important operational risk in levered risk-balanced portfolios is not that volatility rises. Volatility rising is expected. The danger is that rising volatility triggers *mechanical* actions that worsen the environment:

1. **Volatility rises** $\Rightarrow$ risk models (VaR, stress tests, margin models) demand lower exposure.
2. **Margin requirements and haircuts rise** $\Rightarrow$ more collateral is required for the same positions.

3. **The portfolio sells to raise cash** $\Rightarrow$ prices fall, liquidity thins, bid-ask spreads widen.
4. **Price declines increase measured volatility** $\Rightarrow$ the risk model demands even more deleveraging.

This is the **deleveraging spiral**. It is not a theory; it is a mechanism that appears whenever leverage meets procyclical risk constraints.

The portfolio-manager translation. Even if your strategic thesis is correct, you can lose because of *path dependency*. In levered portfolios, the order of returns matters more. A sequence of adverse moves early in the holding period can force you to cut risk before mean reversion or diversification benefits materialize.

Funding constraints as risk constraints: a more realistic risk budget

Traditional risk budgeting allocates contributions to volatility:

$$\mathrm{PRC}_i \quad \text{targets.}$$

Levered portfolios need an additional risk budget: **a funding and liquidity budget**. In practice, many teams implement explicit constraints such as:

- **Cash buffer constraint**: maintain a minimum cash or T-bill buffer as a fraction of NAV to meet VM without selling core positions.
- **Margin utilization limit**: cap the fraction of available liquidity that is pledged as margin (e.g., do not exceed 50–70% utilization).
- **Stress haircut constraint**: re-calc leverage assuming stressed haircuts and require survivability.
- **Liquidity ladder**: ensure that a specified fraction of the portfolio can be liquidated within T days under stressed bid-ask assumptions.

The conceptual shift is important: the relevant "risk" is not only the standard deviation of returns, but the probability of forced selling given your cash-flow mechanics.

Practical margin management: rules that prevent avoidable blowups

A disciplined levered portfolio typically follows rules that look conservative in calm markets but prove essential in turbulence.

Rule 1: Treat margin as a liquidity reserve, not as buying power

Using all available margin is a common failure mode. The correct mental model is that unused margin is a *liquidity reserve* that keeps you from selling at the worst time.

Rule 2: Size positions to "margin in stress," not margin today

Because margin requirements are procyclical, sizing to current margin is equivalent to assuming markets will remain calm. A more robust approach uses a stressed margin schedule:

$$\text{position size} \leq \frac{\text{available collateral}}{\text{stressed margin per unit notional}}.$$

Rule 3: Separate "diversifiers" from "funding liabilities"

Some positions diversify *market* risk but consume liquidity under stress (large VM). Others might lose money in a crisis but do not create immediate cash demands. Good implementation classifies sleeves by their liquidity profile and prevents the portfolio from being "diversified on paper but liquidity-concentrated in reality."

Rule 4: Rebalance with volatility caps and speed limits

Risk parity implementations often rebalance as volatilities shift. Without guardrails, this can produce procyclical trading: selling into falling markets and buying into rising markets purely due to volatility changes. Many practitioners add:

- **volatility caps** (do not lever beyond a maximum target vol),
- **rebalance bands** (only trade if risk contributions drift beyond thresholds),
- **turnover limits** (avoid reacting to noise).

A compact checklist: before you lever a risk-balanced portfolio

For portfolio managers, the most useful question is not "Can I lever?" but "Can I survive leverage when markets are discontinuous?" A minimal pre-flight checklist:

1. **Funding rate exposure:** What happens to expected return if funding rises by 200 bps?
2. **Correlation regime shift:** What happens if your diversifiers become positively correlated with equities for a quarter?
3. **Margin stress:** What is the required cash outflow under a 3–5σ move in the largest notional exposures?
4. **Haircut shock (if using repo):** What if haircuts double?
5. **Liquidity:** If you must reduce gross exposure by 30% in five trading days, what instruments do you sell first, and what is the estimated slippage?

If these questions do not have explicit answers, the portfolio is not fully specified. It is an idea, not an implementation.

Where this fits in the chapter's progression

We have now built a coherent chain:

- **Risk budgeting** gave us the measurement system: MCTR and risk contributions.
- **Risk parity/ERC** turned that measurement into a construction method: balance contributions intentionally, not accidentally.
- **Leverage, margin, and funding constraints** showed the operational layer that determines whether a theoretically balanced portfolio can be held through stress without forced selling.

The next challenge is that even if we manage leverage perfectly, ERC portfolios still depend on estimates of volatilities and correlations. Those estimates are noisy and unstable. The next section therefore focuses on robust optimization techniques—how to keep portfolio design from being whipsawed by estimation error in Σ and by the optimizer's tendency to produce brittle, overfit solutions.

4.4 Robust Optimization Techniques

The previous sections built a coherent portfolio-construction stack: measure risk contributions (MCTR), design balanced portfolios (ERC/risk parity), and then confront the operational realities of leverage and funding. There is, however, a quieter failure mode that can destroy even an unlevered portfolio: *estimation error.*

Portfolio optimizers are not fragile because the mathematics is wrong. They are fragile because the inputs are noisy. The problem is structural: expected returns and covariances must be estimated from finite samples, while the optimizer behaves as if those estimates are exact. The result is the classic practitioner's complaint:

The optimizer gives me an "optimal" portfolio that looks extreme, unstable, and economically nonsensical.

This section introduces two workhorse methods for making optimization more robust in practice:

- **Covariance shrinkage** (especially Ledoit–Wolf) to stabilize risk estimates and correlations.
- **Resampled Efficiency** (Michaud resampling) to reduce sensitivity to small perturbations in inputs.

The goal is not to eliminate model risk. The goal is to stop the optimizer from overreacting to noise.

Why textbook mean–variance optimization produces corner solutions

Mean–variance optimization (MVO) in its canonical form selects weights w to maximize expected return for a given level of risk (or minimize risk for a given expected return). One common formulation is

$$\max_{w} w^{\top}\mu - \frac{\gamma}{2} w^{\top}\Sigma w, \quad \mathbf{1}^{\top} w = 1,$$

where μ is the expected return vector, Σ is the covariance matrix, and γ is a risk-aversion parameter.

In a perfect world where μ and Σ are known, this produces a meaningful efficient frontier. In the real world:

- **Expected returns are estimated with high error.** For most liquid assets, the signal-to-noise ratio of μ is weak at typical horizons.
- **Covariances are estimated with moderate error.** Correlations and volatilities drift, regimes change, and samples are finite.
- **The optimizer amplifies small differences.** If asset A's estimated Sharpe is slightly higher than asset B's, the optimizer may allocate vastly more to A, because it is solving an exact mathematical problem on approximate data.

This is why "optimal" portfolios often appear to *take a stand* on tiny estimated differences that are not statistically meaningful. Robust optimization techniques aim to reduce this amplification.

A useful mental model: optimization as an inverse problem

Many portfolio design problems can be understood as versions of

$$\text{Desired portfolio behavior} \Rightarrow \text{required weights.}$$

But the map from behavior to weights depends on Σ (and sometimes μ). When the map is inverted (as in MVO), small errors in Σ or μ can imply large changes in w. This is the hallmark of an ill-conditioned inverse problem.

Two practical consequences follow:

- If you must optimize, **stabilize the inputs**.
- If you cannot fully stabilize the inputs, **average over the uncertainty**.

Covariance shrinkage addresses the first point. Resampled efficiency addresses the second.

Covariance shrinkage: stabilizing Σ

The problem with the sample covariance matrix

Let R be a $T \times n$ matrix of returns (demeaned). The sample covariance is

$$S = \frac{1}{T-1} R^\top R.$$

When T is not very large relative to n (common in multi-asset, factor, or sleeve decompositions), S becomes noisy:

- off-diagonal correlations can be unstable,

- eigenvalues are distorted (typically too spread out),
- the implied inverse S^{-1} (used by many optimizers) becomes numerically unstable.

Even when $T \gg n$, regime changes mean that using long histories can reduce estimation error but increase model mismatch. Shrinkage is a practical compromise.

The shrinkage idea: trade variance for bias

Covariance shrinkage forms a convex combination of a noisy but relatively unbiased estimator and a structured, low-noise target matrix. Define the shrinkage estimator:

$$\hat{\Sigma} = \delta F + (1-\delta)S, \qquad 0 \le \delta \le 1.$$

Here, δ controls how aggressively we pull S toward the target F, and F encodes a belief like "correlations are roughly equal" or "idiosyncratic risk dominates," depending on the target choice.

This is a statistical version of a common portfolio-manager instinct: *do not trust the raw estimate too literally; blend it with a reasonable prior.*

Choosing the target F

Common shrinkage targets include:

- **Scaled identity:** $F = \bar{\sigma}^2 I$. Implies equal variance and zero correlation in the limit. This is aggressive and often too simplistic for multi-asset portfolios, but it is extremely stable.
- **Constant correlation target:** preserve each asset's variance but shrink correlations toward a common average $\bar{\rho}$. This is often a good practical target for diversified assets and sleeves.
- **Single-factor target:** $F = \beta\beta^\top \sigma_f^2 + D$, capturing a dominant factor plus idiosyncratic noise. This can be appropriate when you believe a small number of macro factors drive most co-movement.

In multi-asset allocation, constant-correlation targets are frequently useful because they stabilize off-diagonal terms without erasing economically meaningful variance differences (e.g., equities are still riskier than bonds).

Ledoit–Wolf shrinkage: selecting δ systematically

The practical question is: how much shrinkage is enough? Ledoit–Wolf shrinkage provides a data-driven estimate of δ designed to minimize mean-squared error between $\hat{\Sigma}$ and the true (unknown) covariance matrix.

From an implementation standpoint, you can treat Ledoit–Wolf as a disciplined way to answer how much you should trust your sample covariance matrix, given the sample size and the dimensionality.

Portfolio construction impact

Replacing S with $\hat{\Sigma}$ typically reduces extreme weights in MVO, produces more stable risk contributions in ERC-type constructions (because MCTR depends on Σw), and reduces turnover caused by noisy changes in estimated correlations.

Shrinkage is not only for MVO

Even if you do not run a mean–variance optimizer, any method that uses Σ benefits from shrinkage:

- risk parity / ERC (risk contributions),
- minimum variance portfolios,
- risk forecasting and stress testing,
- hedging ratios derived from covariance estimates.

In this sense, covariance shrinkage is a foundational risk-engine technique, not a niche optimization trick.

Resampled Efficiency (Michaud): averaging over estimation uncertainty

Even with shrinkage, an optimizer can still overfit. The core reason is that the optimizer is *nonlinear* in the inputs; stabilizing Σ helps, but it does not fully address uncertainty in μ and residual uncertainty in Σ.

Resampled Efficiency (often called Michaud resampling) addresses the problem by treating the efficient frontier as uncertain.

The core idea: the "efficient frontier" is not a line, it is a cloud

Textbook charts show a crisp efficient frontier. In reality, if you perturb the input estimates slightly (as would happen with a different sample window), the frontier moves. Resampled efficiency formalizes this:

- Estimate baseline parameters $(\hat{\mu}, \hat{\Sigma})$ from the historical data.
- Generate many simulated alternative histories consistent with those parameters.
- For each simulated history, re-estimate $(\mu^{(b)}, \Sigma^{(b)})$ and compute an efficient frontier (or an optimized portfolio for a given risk aversion).
- Average the resulting optimized weights across simulations to obtain a resampled portfolio.

The averaged portfolio is typically less extreme and more stable because it is not optimized to a single fragile estimate; it is optimized to the distribution of plausible estimates.

A clean mathematical framing

Let $w^\star(\mu, \Sigma)$ denote the optimizer's solution given inputs (μ, Σ). Resampling approximates

$$\bar{w} \approx \mathbb{E}\big[w^\star(\mu, \Sigma)\big],$$

where the expectation is taken over estimation uncertainty.

This is an important conceptual shift: instead of pretending there is a single "true" frontier, you average across many plausible worlds.

Implementation details that matter

The following choices typically drive outcomes.

Resampling model

Common choices include:

- multivariate normal bootstraps (simple, often a first pass),
- block bootstraps (preserve autocorrelation and volatility clustering),
- regime-based resampling (different covariance regimes).

The more your assets exhibit fat tails and regime behavior, the more careful you must be.

Constraints are not optional

Resampled portfolios still require sensible constraints (long-only, caps, turnover limits). Without constraints, averaging many extreme solutions can still produce unstable exposures.

Number of resamples

Too few resamples yields noisy averages; too many increases compute time but usually stabilizes results. The goal is convergence of weights and risk contributions.

What to average

You can average weights (most common), or optimized portfolios along the frontier for each resample and then average the frontier itself (useful for policy discussions).

What resampling accomplishes (and what it does not)

Resampled efficiency tends to reduce corner solutions, improve out-of-sample stability, and reduce turnover from small input changes.

It does not guarantee higher returns. Its promise is more modest and more realistic: it aims to produce portfolios that remain approximately diversified when the estimated frontier shifts.

Putting it together: a robust multi-asset optimization stack

A practical robust workflow often looks like this:

- **Estimate volatilities and correlations** with a thoughtful window and frequency aligned to the rebalance horizon.
- **Apply covariance shrinkage** to form $\hat{\Sigma}$ that is stable and invertible.
- **Choose a portfolio construction objective:** ERC/risk parity using $\hat{\Sigma}$ (often robust by design), or MVO using $(\hat{\mu}, \hat{\Sigma})$ if you have a credible return model.
- **If using an optimizer that depends strongly on μ (e.g., MVO), apply resampled efficiency** and average weights.
- **Enforce real constraints** such as liquidity, leverage, turnover, and concentration limits.
- **Validate with diagnostics:** check risk contributions for concentration, run stress tests to see if correlations spike, and perform scenario analysis for inflation, growth, or liquidity shocks.

How robust optimization interacts with risk parity

Risk parity is often presented as an alternative to mean–variance optimization, and in a sense it is: ERC relies only on Σ, not μ. But ERC is still sensitive to noisy correlations, especially when assets are highly correlated or when a sleeve's diversification benefit is marginal. Two practical integrations are common:

- **Shrinked covariance for ERC:** compute risk contributions using $\hat{\Sigma}$ rather than S to avoid chasing unstable correlations.
- **Resampled covariance for ERC-like portfolios:** generate multiple $\Sigma^{(b)}$ scenarios, compute the ERC portfolio under each, and average the weights. This is conceptually parallel to Michaud resampling, but applied to a risk-budgeting objective.

The unifying idea is the same: you are not optimizing for a single estimated world; you are designing for a range of plausible covariance structures.

A final caution: robustness is not conservatism, it is humility

Robust optimization should not be confused with "always lower risk" or "always closer to equal weights." A robust method can still recommend meaningful tilts if the evidence is strong. The philosophical stance is different:

When the data are weak, do not let the optimizer manufacture certainty.

In the next section, we build on this idea of disciplined humility by introducing a framework that blends a neutral baseline with explicit investor views and confidence levels: the Black–Litterman model. It is, in many ways, robust optimization expressed in the language of investment judgment.

4.5 Black–Litterman and View Integration

The previous section made a central point that every portfolio manager learns the hard way: optimization is not primarily a math problem; it is an *input uncertainty* problem. Mean–variance optimizers treat estimated parameters as truth, then amplify small errors into extreme weights. Robust techniques such as covariance shrinkage and resampling reduce the damage, but they do not address a practical reality of discretionary and semi-systematic investing:

> Most investors *do* have views—but those views are partial, uncertain, and expressed relative to a baseline.

The Black–Litterman model is a formal way to combine (i) a neutral baseline implied by the market portfolio with (ii) investor views expressed in a simple, intuitive language, while (iii) explicitly incorporating confidence. Done correctly, Black–Litterman produces allocations that are more stable than classical mean–variance optimization and more interpretable than ad hoc tilts.

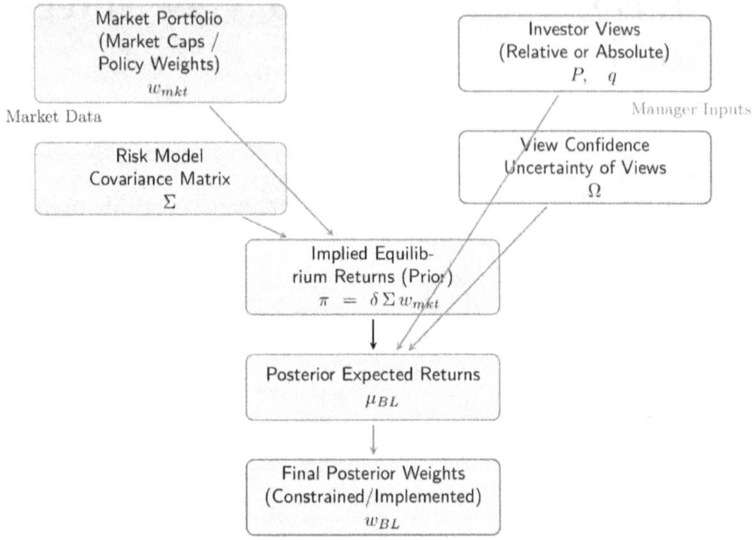

The motivation: a stable baseline plus controlled deviations

In multi-asset portfolios, a sensible default question is not "what is the optimal portfolio from scratch?" but rather:

> Given a reasonable strategic baseline, how should we tilt *and how strongly*?

The baseline can be a market-cap portfolio, a policy benchmark (e.g., a strategic allocation), or a risk-parity reference portfolio. Black–Litterman is most classically presented with the *market portfolio* as the starting point. The key insight is that the market portfolio, combined with a risk model, implies an equilibrium set of expected returns. You do not need to guess expected returns from a noisy historical mean; you can *reverse engineer* them from observed weights.

Step 1: From market weights to implied equilibrium returns

Let:

- w_{mkt} be the baseline (market-cap) weights across n assets,
- Σ be the $n \times n$ covariance matrix of returns (ideally shrinked/robust),
- δ be the risk-aversion parameter (a scalar that scales the overall level of risk premia).

In the classical Black–Litterman setup, the equilibrium expected excess returns (the **prior**) are:

$$\pi = \delta \, \Sigma \, w_{mkt}.$$

Interpretation.
This equation says: if the market portfolio is (approximately) mean–variance optimal for the representative investor, then the vector of expected returns that rationalizes those weights must be proportional to Σw_{mkt}. In other words, assets that covary more with the market portfolio must offer higher expected returns in equilibrium.

What δ does.
δ scales the overall magnitude of equilibrium premia. In practice, δ is often calibrated so that the implied portfolio Sharpe ratio matches a reasonable long-run estimate for the baseline portfolio. Importantly, small errors in δ tend to change the *level* of expected returns more than the *relative* structure of the implied premia; the structure is mostly driven by Σ and w_{mkt}.

Step 2: Expressing views in a portfolio-manager language

Black–Litterman's practical genius is how it encodes views. Rather than forcing you to forecast every asset's expected return, it lets you state a small number of views in linear form.

Define:

- P as a $k \times n$ matrix of view exposures,
- q as a $k \times 1$ vector of view returns.

Each view is:

$$P_i \mu = q_i, \quad i = 1, \dots, k,$$

where P_i is the i-th row of P.

Examples (how PMs actually think).

- **Absolute view:** "Emerging equities will return 6% (excess) over the next year."
$$P = [0 \ 1 \ 0 \ \dots \ 0], \quad q = [0.06].$$
- **Relative view:** "Investment-grade credit will outperform duration-matched government bonds by 1%." If asset 1 is gov bonds and asset 2 is IG credit:
$$P = [-1 \ 1 \ 0 \ \dots \ 0], \quad q = [0.01].$$
- **Theme view across a basket:** "Value equities will outperform growth equities by 2%." If $w^{(value)}$ and $w^{(growth)}$ are basket exposure vectors, one view is:
$$P = \left[(w^{(value)})^\top - (w^{(growth)})^\top \right], \quad q = [0.02].$$

This structure is flexible: you can encode macro views (inflation-linked vs nominal), regional tilts, factor tilts, or hedging preferences without forecasting the entire return vector.

Step 3: Confidence levels as explicit uncertainty (the Ω matrix)

Most investment mistakes are not caused by having a view. They are caused by having too much confidence in a view.

Black–Litterman forces you to quantify uncertainty via a $k \times k$ covariance matrix Ω, where (in the simplest case) Ω is diagonal and each entry ω_i is the variance of view error:

$$q = P\mu + \varepsilon, \qquad \varepsilon \sim \mathcal{N}(0, \Omega).$$

Interpretation.

- Small ω_i means high confidence: the view is treated as relatively precise.
- Large ω_i means low confidence: the view is treated as noisy and will have a small impact.

In practical terms, Ω is the dial that controls how far the posterior portfolio is allowed to move away from the baseline.

Step 4: The Black–Litterman posterior expected returns

Black–Litterman combines the prior π with the views (P, q) and their uncertainties Ω. A common formulation introduces τ, a scalar that reflects uncertainty in the prior (often small, e.g., $\tau \in [0.01, 0.10]$ in many implementations). The posterior expected returns are:

$$\mu_{BL} = \left[(\tau\Sigma)^{-1} + P^\top\Omega^{-1}P\right]^{-1}\left[(\tau\Sigma)^{-1}\pi + P^\top\Omega^{-1}q\right].$$

How to read this formula without getting lost.
Think of it as Bayesian updating in linear regression clothing:

- $(\tau\Sigma)^{-1}$ is the *precision* (inverse variance) of the prior.
- $P^\top\Omega^{-1}P$ is the precision contributed by the views.
- The posterior is a precision-weighted blend: strong, confident views pull μ_{BL} away from π; weak views barely move it.

This is the conceptual payoff: you are no longer forced to choose between "trust the optimizer" and "trust my gut." You can blend them in a controlled way.

Step 5: From posterior returns to portfolio weights (and why constraints matter)

Once you have μ_{BL}, you can compute an unconstrained mean–variance optimal portfolio:

$$w_{BL}^{\star} = \frac{1}{\delta}\Sigma^{-1}\mu_{BL}.$$

In practice, you almost never implement $w_{BL}^{\star}$ directly because real portfolios have constraints. A realistic implementation typically solves:

$$\max_{w} \; w^{\top}\mu_{BL} - \frac{\delta}{2}w^{\top}\Sigma w$$

s.t.

$$\mathbf{1}^{\top}w = 1, \;\; w \in \mathcal{C},$$

where $\mathcal{C}$ encodes long-only requirements, leverage limits, tracking-error constraints, sleeve caps, turnover limits, and liquidity rules.

A practical point that improves stability.
Many teams implement Black–Litterman not to *rebuild* the whole portfolio, but to compute *tilts* around the baseline. A common operational design is:

$$w_{impl} = w_{mkt} + \Delta w,$$

where Δw is constrained to be small, diversified, and capacity-aware. This aligns with how investment committees think: "We are mostly strategic; we want measured deviations where we have conviction."

Where Black–Litterman fits relative to ERC/risk parity

Risk parity and Black–Litterman solve different problems:

- **ERC/risk parity** is primarily a *risk allocation* framework: it designs exposures so risk contributions match a budget, usually without forecasting returns.
- **Black–Litterman** is primarily a *return-and-risk integration* framework: it produces stable expected returns by anchoring to a baseline and then incorporating views with explicit confidence.

They can also be complementary. Two common integrations are:

- **Risk parity baseline + BL tilts:** use an ERC portfolio as w_{mkt} (or as the policy weights), compute $\pi = \delta\Sigma w_{mkt}$, then apply views to generate μ_{BL} and constrained tilts. This approach preserves balanced risk as the foundation while allowing controlled alpha expressions.
- **BL returns inside a risk-budgeted optimizer:** use μ_{BL} for expected returns but impose risk-budget constraints (e.g., limit equity beta risk contribution). This prevents "alpha views" from accidentally rebuilding the portfolio into a concentrated bet.

In both cases, the philosophy is the same: *use a stable baseline, then make deliberate, risk-aware deviations.*

Common implementation mistakes (and how to avoid them)

Mistake 1: Treating Σ as a minor detail.
Black–Litterman inherits the covariance problem. If Σ is noisy, the implied equilibrium returns π are noisy, and the mapping from returns to weights will be unstable. Use shrinkage (and possibly regime-aware correlation assumptions) as discussed earlier.

Mistake 2: Encoding too many views.
The strength of Black–Litterman is that you can express a *few* high-conviction views without forecasting everything. If you encode dozens of weak, overlapping views, you are often rebuilding the same estimation error problem you were trying to avoid.

Mistake 3: Overconfidence via Ω.
If you set Ω too small (too confident), the posterior can be dominated by the views and revert to corner-solution behavior. When in doubt, err on the side of *less* confidence and let constraints and diversification do more of the work.

Mistake 4: Forgetting the economic meaning of the prior.
The prior is not "the truth"; it is the set of expected returns consistent with your chosen baseline weights under mean–variance equilibrium

logic. If your baseline is not a sensible policy portfolio (or if it embeds constraints that deviate from mean–variance optimality), interpret π as a *neutral anchor*, not as a literal forecast.

The practical payoff: stable allocations that respect judgment

Black–Litterman is best understood as a portfolio communication tool as much as a quantitative model. It forces explicit answers to questions investment committees always ask:

- What is our neutral baseline and why?
- What are our active views, stated clearly and testably?
- How confident are we, and what would change our mind?
- How does the portfolio move if we increase or decrease that confidence?

By combining equilibrium structure with explicit view uncertainty, Black–Litterman produces portfolios that are typically more diversified, less extreme, and more stable than classical optimization—while still allowing the manager to express differentiated beliefs.

4.6 Portfolio Archetypes and Reference Designs

The previous sections built a toolkit: risk decomposition (MCTR and Euler attribution), risk-balanced construction (ERC/risk parity), the operational layer (leverage and funding constraints), and robustness methods (shrinkage and resampling), culminating in Black–Litterman as a disciplined way to express views around a baseline.

This section turns that toolkit onto the portfolios many institutions actually hold. *Reference designs* are not merely convenient templates; they are *bundles of implicit bets*. Each archetype embeds assumptions about:

- which macro regimes will dominate (growth vs. recession, inflation vs. disinflation),
- whether diversification works when you need it (correlation behavior under stress),
- the availability and cost of leverage,
- liquidity, governance, and complexity constraints.

The goal is not to crown a universally best portfolio. The goal is to help you *diagnose what you already own* and to choose (or modify) a reference design that matches your objectives and your implementation reality.

A framework for comparison: translate portfolios into risks and regimes

Before discussing specific archetypes, it is helpful to standardize the evaluation. For any portfolio template, ask four questions.

1) What is the dominant risk contributor? Compute risk contributions (PRC) by sleeve. Many portfolios marketed as diversified are, in practice, dominated by a single risk:

- global equity beta,
- duration (for heavily bond-tilted portfolios),
- credit spread risk (for yield-seeking "diversified" income portfolios),
- illiquidity (for endowment-style alternatives),
- funding liquidity (for levered risk parity).

2) What does the portfolio need to go right? (the implicit macro bet) Every portfolio has a macro "comfort zone." Examples:

- 60/40 likes *disinflationary* environments where bonds hedge equities.

- Endowment-like portfolios like *stable growth* plus functioning capital markets.
- All-weather designs are meant to be robust across regimes but often rely on *diversification plus sufficient duration exposure* and/or leverage.

3) What breaks in stress? (correlations, liquidity, convexity) Diversification is not a static correlation coefficient; it is a *behavior under drawdown*. Ask:

- Which hedges are expected to rally in equity drawdowns?
- Are those hedges liquid at the moment you need them?
- Is the portfolio short volatility anywhere (explicitly or implicitly), e.g., via leverage, carry trades, private market smoothing, or liquidity transformation?

4) What are the binding constraints? Most archetypes are feasible only under certain constraints:

- Can you use derivatives? (futures, swaps)
- Can you use leverage? If yes, what are margin rules and governance tolerances?
- What is the liquidity profile required by liabilities?
- How much complexity can the organization operate (monitoring, manager selection, valuation, rebalancing cadence)?

With those questions in mind, we now analyze three widely used archetypes: 60/40, the endowment model, and all-weather/risk-parity-inspired designs.

Archetype 1: The 60/40 portfolio (and what it is really betting on)

What it is The canonical 60/40 portfolio holds roughly:

$$w_{eq} \approx 60\%, \qquad w_{bond} \approx 40\%,$$

often implemented as broad equity exposure plus intermediate-to-long duration government and/or high-quality bond exposure.

Its implicit risk budget The first section's 60/40 fallacy is the correct starting point: a balanced capital allocation is typically not a balanced risk allocation. Using risk decomposition:

$$\text{PRC}_{eq} \gg \text{PRC}_{bond}$$

in most regimes, because equity volatility is higher and equities often dominate covariance with the portfolio.

In practice, many 60/40 portfolios are *equity risk portfolios with a duration diversifier*. That is not an insult; it is simply a more accurate description.

The core macro bet: stock–bond diversification The 60/40 model's most important assumption is not "equities will outperform bonds." That is likely but not the defining feature. The defining feature is:

When equities sell off, high-quality bonds will usually rally (or at least hold up), reducing drawdowns and improving risk-adjusted returns.

Historically, this relationship has been strongest in disinflationary or deflation-scare environments, where growth shocks dominate and central banks respond by cutting rates.

Structural weaknesses Weakness 1: Inflation regime risk. In inflationary shocks, both equities and bonds can draw down together as discount rates rise and margins compress. In that regime, the stock–bond correlation can become positive, and the 40% bond sleeve may fail as a hedge precisely when it is most needed.

Weakness 2: Duration is doing "too much work." When yields are low, bonds have less cushion (lower carry and less room to rally), while still retaining downside if yields rise. A 60/40 portfolio can become a portfolio that is simultaneously long equity beta and long duration at an awkward point in the rate cycle.

Weakness 3: Concentration hidden by simplicity. 60/40 looks diversified because it has two sleeves. Risk decomposition often reveals concentration because the sleeves are effectively two macro factors:

- growth (equities),
- real rates / duration (bonds).

If your liabilities or spending needs are sensitive to inflation, that missing exposure is not a cosmetic gap; it is a structural mismatch.

When 60/40 is a good reference design 60/40 is often appropriate when:

- governance prefers simplicity and transparency,
- leverage is not permitted or not desired,
- liquidity needs are high,
- the investor's objective is a straightforward growth-plus-stability mix,
- the investor accepts that the portfolio's dominant risk will be equity beta.

A sophisticated improvement is not necessarily to abandon 60/40, but to *risk-budget it*: measure risk contributions and add diversifiers (inflation-linked bonds, commodities, trend, defensive equity quality, explicit tail hedges) based on a defined risk budget.

Archetype 2: The Endowment model (what it buys, and what it sells)

What it is The endowment archetype is typically characterized by:

- meaningful allocations to private equity, venture capital, private credit,
- real assets (real estate, infrastructure, timber, farmland),
- hedge funds or absolute return strategies,
- reduced allocations to traditional public bonds relative to 60/40.

In public discussions, the endowment model is often summarized as "diversification into alternatives." A more precise description is:

The endowment model is a portfolio that intentionally harvests illiquidity premia *and* active manager dispersion, *financed by giving up some daily liquidity and some transparency.*

Its implicit risk budget (and why it is hard to measure) Endowment portfolios frequently appear less volatile than public-market portfolios, but this can be misleading because:

- private assets are marked infrequently and often with appraisal smoothing,
- reported correlations to equities are mechanically damped,
- drawdowns can be delayed rather than eliminated.

A robust risk-budgeting approach treats private assets as having higher effective beta to public equities than naive reported data suggest, especially in stress. Practically, many institutions overlay public-market factor models to estimate economic exposures.

The core macro and structural bet: liquidity is not always scarce Endowment portfolios tend to assume that:

- capital markets will remain functional enough to fund commitments and meet spending needs,
- liquidity can be managed through pacing models and reserves,
- the investor can tolerate multi-year capital lockups and J-curve dynamics.

This is not a bet that markets will never crash; it is a bet that the institution can *survive* crashes without being forced to sell illiquid assets at distressed prices or miss capital calls.

Structural weaknesses Weakness 1: Liquidity mismatch and the denominator effect. In sharp public-market drawdowns, liquid assets fall immediately, while private valuations adjust more slowly. This can mechanically raise the portfolio's reported allocation to illiquid assets (the denominator effect), right when liquidity is most valuable. If spending needs and capital calls persist through the downturn, the portfolio can be forced to sell liquid assets at unfavorable prices, increasing concentration.

Weakness 2: Hidden equity beta and crowded risk. Many alternatives have implicit equity exposure (private equity) and/or credit exposure (private credit). In benign environments, these may look diversifying. In crises, correlations can converge upward, and the portfolio may discover that it owns a complicated expression of the same underlying risk: growth and liquidity.

Weakness 3: Governance and selection risk. The endowment model requires:

- manager selection skill (access and underwriting),
- operational due diligence,
- patience with multi-year evaluation windows,
- robust reporting and oversight.

Without those, the model can devolve into high fees plus mediocre beta.

When the endowment model is a good reference design It is often appropriate when:

- liabilities are long-dated and the investor can tolerate illiquidity,
- the organization has strong governance and manager-selection capabilities,
- the investor wants to diversify away from public-market concentration and is willing to accept complexity,
- the investor can maintain liquidity buffers and survive stress without forced liquidation.

In risk-budget language, the endowment model is viable when the investor can allocate a substantial *liquidity budget* to illiquid strategies without jeopardizing solvency or policy discipline.

Archetype 3: All-Weather / Risk-Parity-inspired designs (robustness with implementation strings attached)

What it is "All-weather" is a family of designs rather than a single portfolio. The common objective is regime robustness: a portfolio that can weather growth slowdowns, inflation surprises, and rate shocks better than a simple equity-dominant mix.

In practice, all-weather designs often combine:

- diversified growth exposure (equities),
- meaningful nominal duration exposure (government bonds),
- explicit inflation sensitivity (TIPS, commodities, real assets),
- sometimes systematic trend or defensive strategies as crisis diversifiers,
- and, in many implementations, **leverage** to bring the overall risk/return to a desired level.

Many such portfolios are built with risk-budgeting logic: equalize or target risk contributions across macro-sensitive sleeves.

Its implicit risk budget All-weather portfolios are often closer to balanced *risk* than 60/40, especially if they include inflation-sensitive and crisis-sensitive components. But their risk budget often shifts from equity beta concentration to a more nuanced set of exposures:

- duration risk (and convexity),
- inflation risk premia and commodity curve behavior,
- carry and roll effects across futures-based exposures,
- correlation regime risk,
- funding/liquidity risk if levered.

The core bet: diversification works across regimes The all-weather idea assumes that:

- different sleeves dominate in different macro environments,
- correlations are low enough (or sufficiently state-dependent in the right direction) that diversification reduces drawdowns,
- the portfolio can be held and rebalanced through regime transitions.

Structural weaknesses Weakness 1: Sensitivity to interest-rate regimes. If the portfolio uses substantial nominal duration as a recession hedge, it benefits when yields fall in growth shocks. But if inflation shocks dominate (or if yields are structurally rising), duration can become a drag rather than a hedge. A robust design typically needs inflation-sensitive components that are sufficiently large to matter *and* not prohibitively expensive to hold.

Weakness 2: Leverage and funding constraints. As discussed in the leverage section, portfolios that achieve balanced risk using low-volatility sleeves often require leverage to reach target returns. This introduces margin, liquidity, and funding risk. The portfolio may be well diversified in market risk and still be fragile in *cash-flow* terms.

Weakness 3: Complexity and model dependence. All-weather designs typically require:

- a covariance model that does not overfit,
- careful treatment of correlations in stress,
- ongoing monitoring of risk contributions,
- explicit decisions about rebalancing speed and turnover.

Without robust estimation (shrinkage/resampling) and disciplined governance, the portfolio can drift or churn.

When all-weather is a good reference design It is often appropriate when:

- the investor wants to reduce reliance on a single macro regime,
- the organization can operate a more complex rebalancing and risk-monitoring process,

- derivatives and/or leverage are permitted (or the investor accepts lower unlevered expected returns),
- the investor explicitly budgets not only volatility risk, but also liquidity and funding risk.

Comparing archetypes by their implicit bets (a summary table) A useful way to anchor the discussion is to summarize each archetype in terms of dominant risk, diversification assumption, and primary failure mode. The following table is intentionally high-level; the point is to prompt structured thinking, not to provide a one-size-fits-all prescription.

Archetype	Dominant risk (typical)	What it needs to go right	Structural weakness / failure mode
60/40	Equity beta (risk contribution often dominated by equities)	Stock–bond diversification holds in drawdowns; bonds provide ballast	Inflationary shocks; rising-rate regimes; correlation flips; limited inflation hedging
Endowment	Illiquidity + equity/credit economic beta (often masked by smoothing)	Access/skill in alternatives; ability to fund commitments; liquidity is manageable through stress	Liquidity mismatch; denominator effect; correlation convergence; governance/selection risk
All-weather / Risk parity inspired	Diversified macro sleeves; often includes material duration and inflation exposure; funding risk if levered	Diversification across regimes; rebalancing discipline; stable financing conditions if levered	Rate regime shifts; carry/roll headwinds; leverage-induced deleveraging risk; model/estimation error

Table 4.1: Archetypes as bundles of implicit bets. Robust portfolio design begins by making these bets explicit.

How to choose (or adapt) a reference design using the chapter toolkit

A reference design is a starting point. The correct question is rarely "Which archetype is best?" It is:

Given my objective function and constraints, which archetype is the least wrong baseline, and what modifications are required to align its risk budget with my true liabilities and beliefs?

A disciplined selection and adaptation process looks like this:

Step 1: Start with a baseline that matches your constraints If you cannot use leverage and need high liquidity, do not start with a levered all-weather design. If you have limited governance capacity, do not start with a manager-heavy endowment structure. Begin where implementation feasibility is high.

Step 2: Measure risk contributions and regime exposures Compute MCTR and PRC across sleeves. Then stress test correlation regimes:

- equity crash with flight-to-quality,
- equity crash with inflation shock (bonds down too),
- inflation spike with commodities up,
- liquidity shock with credit spreads widening.

The key is to observe *what actually diversifies what.*

Step 3: Make the missing risks explicit and decide how to pay for them If a 60/40 portfolio is missing inflation protection, decide whether to add it via:

- TIPS (rate + inflation mechanics),
- commodities (roll and curve risks),
- real assets (illiquidity and valuation lag),
- trend or convex hedges (explicit premium cost).

Every hedge has a carrying cost or a complexity cost. Risk budgeting is the process of deciding which costs are worth paying.

Step 4: Use robust estimation and view integration for tilts If you tilt:

- use shrinked covariance estimates to avoid unstable correlation noise,
- consider resampling if optimization is sensitive,

- use Black–Litterman if the tilt is view-driven and you need an explicit confidence mechanism.

Step 5: Treat liquidity and funding as hard constraints, not afterthoughts Particularly for endowment and levered all-weather designs, the portfolio is only as robust as its liquidity plan. Explicitly budget:

- cash buffers,
- margin usage,
- commitment pacing,
- forced-sale scenarios.

Closing perspective: archetypes are tools, not identities

A portfolio archetype should not be a brand identity. It should be a tool that helps you start from a coherent structure and then tailor it intelligently. The key lesson from modern portfolio construction is that *structure matters*:

- capital weights do not equal risk weights,
- diversification depends on correlation behavior in stress,
- leverage turns market risk into funding risk,
- optimizers require robust inputs,
- and views must be integrated with explicit confidence.

If you internalize those principles, any archetype can become a strong reference design—not because it is famous, but because you have made its implicit bets explicit and aligned them with your objectives, constraints, and governance capacity.

Chapter 5

Advanced Risk Management and Tail Control

Standard deviation measures the noise; it does not measure the silence before the earthquake. In this chapter, we abandon the comfort of Gaussian distributions to confront the harsh reality of fat tails, liquidity traps, and correlations that converge to one exactly when you need diversification most. We move beyond passive risk measurement to active risk engineering, focusing on how to construct multi-asset portfolios that can survive-and potentially capitalize on-the events that destroy careers.

5.1 VaR and Expected Shortfall: Uses and Limitations

Portfolio construction is ultimately an exercise in making trade-offs under uncertainty. In earlier parts of this book, we emphasized that (i) multi-asset portfolios are built from a small number of underlying risk drivers (growth, inflation, real rates, credit/liquidity, and volatility), and (ii) the practical goal of risk budgeting is not to eliminate risk, but to *allocate* it deliberately so that no single shock can dominate the portfolio's outcome. This chapter now turns from the *design* of diversified portfolios to the *control* of their downside, especially in markets where diversification is least reliable.

In institutional practice, the first stop on that path is almost always a pair of tail-oriented risk metrics: Value-at-Risk (VaR) and Expected Shortfall (ES). These measures sit at the intersection of governance and reality. They are heavily used in reporting, limits, and regulation because they offer standardized, communicable summaries of downside. Yet they also tempt managers into a false sense of precision-particularly when the key question is not "what is a typical bad day?" but "what could break us?"

This section builds a practical framework for using VaR and ES *as tools*, while remaining clear-eyed about their failure modes during regime shifts, liquidity shocks, and fat-tailed returns.

A plain-language definition of VaR

Value-at-Risk answers a specific question:

> Over a given horizon (e.g., 1 day, 10 days, 1 month), what loss level will we *not* exceed with a chosen confidence (e.g., 95%, 99%)?

To be precise, define the portfolio return over the horizon as R and the portfolio loss as $L = -R$. The α-VaR (with α close to 1, such as 0.99) is the α-quantile of the loss distribution:

$$\mathrm{VaR}_\alpha(L) = \inf\{\ell \in \mathbb{R} : \mathbb{P}(L \leq \ell) \geq \alpha\}.$$

Interpreting that statement carefully:

- A **99% 1-day VaR of $10 million** means: under the model and assumptions used, the portfolio is expected to lose *more* than $10 million on *about 1 out of 100 days.*
- VaR does *not* say anything about how large losses are on those worst 1% days.

That last bullet is the hinge on which most practical problems turn. VaR is a *threshold*, not a *severity* measure.

Why VaR became the lingua franca of governance

VaR remains central in investment organizations for reasons that are more operational than philosophical:

- **Comparability:** A single dollar number (or percentage) that can be compared across desks, portfolios, and time.
- **Limit-setting:** It maps naturally into governance: "Desk A has a $5MM VaR limit." Limits based on ES are possible, but VaR limits are easier to explain and to negotiate.
- **Backtesting simplicity:** VaR produces clear "exceptions." If you run a 99% VaR model for 250 trading days, you expect roughly 2–3 exceedances. That makes oversight tractable.
- **A useful first derivative:** When VaR is computed via parametric models, it links to sensitivities and factor risk, enabling decomposition and incremental risk accounting.

These are real advantages. In a multi-asset setting-where the portfolio combines equities, rates, credit, commodities, and alternatives-governance often fails not because the organization lacks intelligence, but because it lacks a shared, operational language. VaR supplies that language.

But VaR's usefulness as a governance metric does not make it a sufficient description of tail risk.

VaR's central limitation: it is silent about the tail beyond the cutoff

Consider two portfolios with identical 99% VaR. Portfolio A has mild, thin-tailed behavior: once in a while it breaches VaR by a little. Portfolio B sells crash insurance (or is structurally short volatility): it tends to look stable most days, but occasionally experiences a very large loss.

Both can show the same VaR. Yet their *economic* risk-especially their risk of impairment, forced deleveraging, or mandate breach-is radically different.

This is not a theoretical quibble. Many strategies that "manufacture" steady returns (selling options, leveraged carry trades, liquidity provision, relative-value strategies) specifically concentrate risk *past* the VaR threshold. VaR can understate the existential question for the portfolio manager: *What happens when the model is wrong in the worst way?*

Expected Shortfall (ES): measuring average severity in the worst cases

Expected Shortfall (also called **Conditional VaR**, or CVaR in many practitioner contexts) directly addresses VaR's blindness to magnitude. ES answers:

> If we are *already* in the worst $(1 - \alpha)$ fraction of outcomes, what is the *average* loss we should expect?

Formally, for loss L and confidence level α,

$$\mathrm{ES}_\alpha(L) = \mathbb{E}[\, L \mid L \geq \mathrm{VaR}_\alpha(L)\,] ,$$

when the distribution is well-behaved (more generally, ES can be defined via an integral over quantiles). The intuition is simple:

- **VaR is a cliff edge.** It tells you where the worst-case region begins.
- **ES measures the depth of the canyon.** It averages the outcomes *beyond* that cliff edge.

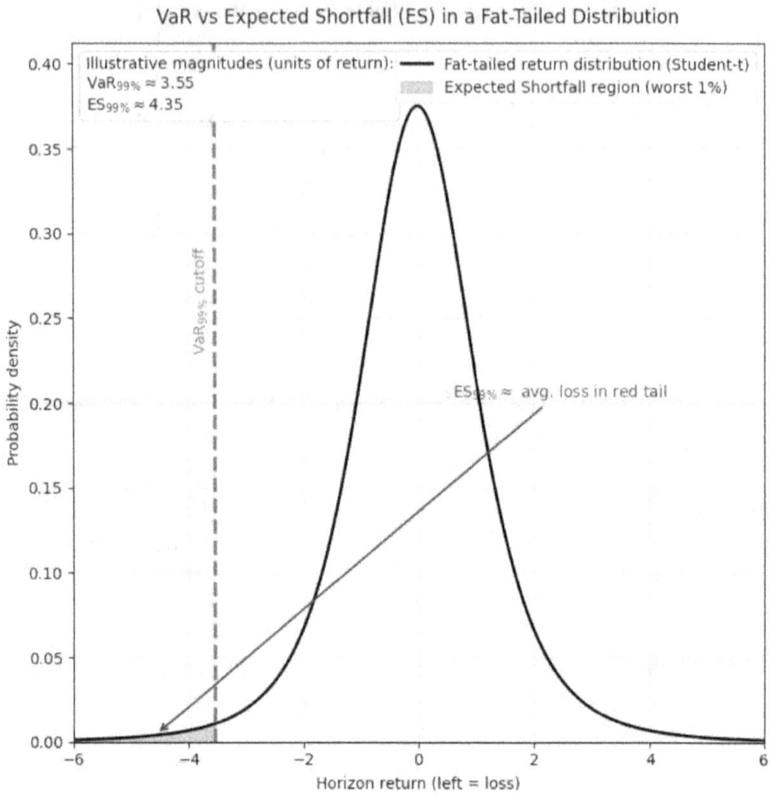

Why regulators increasingly prefer ES (and why governance still leans on VaR)

Expected Shortfall is often viewed as "better" because it incorporates tail severity and (under common technical conditions) has desirable properties for portfolio risk measurement, including improved behavior under diversification. Practically, it is harder to game: a strategy that concentrates losses in rare crashes may keep VaR low while ES rises materially.

Yet VaR persists for governance because it remains:

- easier to backtest with exception counts,
- easier to communicate as a single threshold,
- deeply embedded in risk limit infrastructure and compensation conversations.

A pragmatic stance for portfolio managers is therefore:

> Use VaR for *day-to-day limit discipline* and transparency, but use ES (and scenario tools) for *tail realism* and capital survival planning.

The three implementation families: parametric, historical, and Monte Carlo

In practice, VaR and ES are not single numbers "given by the market." They are *outputs of a modeling pipeline.* The modeling choices often matter more than the difference between VaR and ES.

Parametric (variance–covariance) VaR/ES

The parametric approach assumes portfolio returns are (approximately) normally distributed and summarizes risk using volatility and correlations. For a portfolio with return standard deviation σ_p over the horizon, a mean μ_p (often set to zero for short horizons), and standard normal quantile z_α:

$$\mathrm{VaR}_\alpha \approx -\mu_p + z_\alpha \sigma_p.$$

The appeal is speed and decomposability: you can attribute risk to factors and positions. The limitation is structural: normality underestimates fat tails, and linear approximations miss nonlinear exposures (options, mortgages, dynamic strategies, and path-dependent leverage).

For multi-asset portfolios, parametric VaR/ES can still be valuable *as a diagnostic*, provided you interpret it as "correlation-times-volatility risk under normal conditions," not as a statement about crisis behavior.

Historical simulation

Historical VaR/ES replays a window of past returns (e.g., 1,000 days) and computes quantiles and tail averages from those empirical outcomes. Its main advantages:

- no explicit distribution assumption,
- naturally incorporates some non-normal behavior if it occurred in the window.

However, historical simulation can be **dangerous during regime shifts**. The model's tail is only as bad as the sample. If the window excludes a crisis-like episode, the estimated 99% tail is likely to be far too benign. Conversely, immediately *after* a crisis, the window may be dominated by extreme observations, mechanically inflating risk estimates and potentially forcing de-risking at exactly the wrong time.

In other words, historical simulation is *pro-cyclical* unless it is supplemented by forward-looking scenarios and a regime-aware volatility model.

Monte Carlo / factor simulation

Monte Carlo methods simulate many possible future outcomes for relevant risk factors (equity index returns, yield curve changes, credit spreads, FX moves, commodity shocks, volatility changes), then map those outcomes into portfolio P&L using a pricing or approximation model.

This approach is powerful for multi-asset portfolios because it can:

- incorporate nonlinear payoffs and convexity (options, callable bonds, vol strategies),
- incorporate time-varying correlations and volatility regimes,
- stress specific factors (e.g., "real rates up" plus "credit spreads wider") in a controlled way.

The limitation is model risk: simulated tails can be *too optimistic* if the factor model understates joint extremes, omits liquidity dynamics, or assumes stable correlations.

The regime-shift problem: why tails are not stationary

The most common managerial misuse of VaR/ES is treating them as if they were physical constants. They are not. They are estimates based on assumptions about:

- the distribution of returns,
- the stability of volatility,
- the stability of correlations,
- the ability to trade (liquidity) at or near modeled prices.

Regime shifts break those assumptions simultaneously. In a stress:

- **volatility rises** (often nonlinearly),
- **correlations move toward 1** among risky assets,
- **liquidity premia widen** and market depth vanishes,
- **pricing becomes discontinuous** (gaps), so the "distribution" may have jumps.

This is the core trade-off we must navigate:

> VaR/ES are essential for standardized control in normal conditions, but the most important losses often occur in conditions that violate the assumptions used to compute VaR/ES.

A useful governance implication follows: **never attach existential decisions to a single modeled quantile.** Attach them to a *stack* of evidence: VaR, ES, factor stress tests, liquidity metrics, and exposure to crash-sensitive risk premia.

A multi-asset lens: what VaR/ES capture well (and what they miss)

In multi-asset portfolios, VaR and ES are most informative when the main risks are:

- broad beta exposures (equity, duration, credit),
- stable carry profiles with modest convexity,
- liquid instruments where marks approximate realizable prices.

They are least informative when the portfolio contains:

- **embedded short volatility** (option selling, certain relative-value trades, levered credit carry),
- **liquidity transforms** (holding less-liquid assets funded by short-liability structures),
- **hidden correlations** ("diversifiers" that correlate in crises due to forced selling),
- **model-priced assets** (where the mark can be slow, but the economic loss can be immediate).

A practical rule is to treat VaR/ES as describing *market risk under continuous trading*, not *financing risk under discontinuous markets*. The latter is often what ends careers.

How to use VaR and ES correctly in a portfolio risk budget

To make VaR and ES useful rather than decorative, connect them directly to decisions:

1) Tie horizons to the decision cycle

A 1-day VaR is aligned with daily risk monitoring, but many portfolio decisions (rebalancing, de-leveraging, hedge adjustments) operate on a multi-day cadence. If it takes 5–10 trading days to materially reduce exposure without excessive market impact, then a 10-day horizon is often more relevant for solvency planning than a 1-day horizon.

2) Use VaR for *discipline*, ES for *survival*

A clean governance split:

- **VaR limits** manage normal-to-stressed fluctuations and keep risk-taking consistent with mandate.
- **ES limits** (or ES triggers) are better aligned with tail vulnerability and should inform hedging posture, gross/net constraints, and leverage ceilings.

3) Report both, and report the gap

The difference $\text{ES}_\alpha - \text{VaR}_\alpha$ is a compact indicator of tail "fatness" under the model. If VaR is stable but ES is rising, the portfolio may be accumulating crash sensitivity (for example, through crowded carry, short vol, or liquidity exposure).

4) Decompose risk by asset class and factor-not only by position

For a multi-asset strategist, the key question is not merely "which line item drives VaR?" but:

> Which macro shocks (equity drawdown, real-rate spike, credit spread widening, dollar rally, volatility regime shift) dominate VaR and ES, and do we want that dominance?

The purpose of decomposition is to keep the risk budget aligned with intended sources of return. If a portfolio is supposed to be balanced, but ES is dominated by one factor (often equity crash beta or credit), you have discovered an allocation problem masquerading as a measurement problem.

The crucial caveat: VaR/ES are not stress tests

It is tempting to interpret "99%" as meaning "very extreme." But in daily space, the 99% quantile is not a once-in-a-career event; it is closer to a few days per year. The truly portfolio-defining outcomes-liquidity spirals, funding shocks, correlation breakdowns-often live *beyond* what a simple quantile estimate can credibly describe.

Therefore, VaR/ES should be treated as:

- **necessary** for standardized monitoring,
- **insufficient** for tail governance.

The remainder of this chapter takes the next steps. We will examine how correlations change precisely when you need diversification most, how to stress test portfolios in factor space (including reverse stress tests), how liquidity mismatch creates nonlinear loss dynamics, and when tail hedges are worth their ongoing cost.

5.2 Correlation Breakdown and Contagion

The previous section introduced a practical tension: *risk metrics that behave well in normal conditions* (VaR, and even ES) can become less informative precisely when they matter most. One major reason is that the portfolio's effective diversification is not stable. In calm markets, cross-asset correlations often look low and reasonably mean-reverting. In crises, those same relationships can compress into a small number of dominant drivers, and assets that were diversified on paper begin to move together.

This section explains why diversification often evaporates during drawdowns and, critically, how to distinguish two very different crisis patterns:

- **Flight-to-quality:** risky assets fall while high-quality government bonds (and sometimes reserve currencies) rally, providing negative correlation and true ballast.

- **Contagion:** selling pressure propagates across markets, causing correlations to spike broadly-even among assets that do not share fundamental drivers-because liquidity and funding constraints force investors to sell what they *can*, not what they *want*.

This distinction is not academic. It determines whether your portfolio's "diversifiers" are likely to work when you need them, how you should size risk premia trades, and what kind of stress testing is appropriate.

Correlation is a conditional object, not a permanent property

Investors often speak of correlation as if it were a stable characteristic of an asset pair: "stocks and Treasuries are negatively correlated" or "commodities diversify equities." A more accurate statement is:

> Correlation is conditional on the regime: volatility, liquidity, macro policy, and investor positioning.

Mathematically, for asset returns R_i and R_j,

$$\rho_{ij} = \frac{\text{Cov}(R_i, R_j)}{\sigma_i \sigma_j}.$$

In crises, all three elements can change at once:

- **Covariances rise** because a small set of common shocks dominates returns (growth scare, liquidity shock, deleveraging).
- **Volatilities rise** for most assets, but not uniformly.
- **The joint distribution changes shape:** tails become fatter and dependence strengthens in extremes.

A portfolio manager's key takeaway is operational: correlation estimates based on average conditions (monthly or weekly correlations over long samples) are not designed to describe the portfolio's behavior on the worst days. Yet those are exactly the days that determine drawdown, rebalancing feasibility, and survival under leverage or redemption pressure.

Why correlations spike in sell-offs: a factor story

A useful intuition for correlation breakdown starts with factor decomposition. In normal times, a multi-asset portfolio is exposed to several partially independent drivers:

- **Growth (risk-on/risk-off):** dominates equities and credit; can affect commodities.
- **Inflation and real rates:** dominate nominal bonds, TIPS, and rate-sensitive equities.
- **Credit and liquidity:** dominate corporate spreads, EM risk, and funding-sensitive trades.
- **Volatility:** matters for options, systematic strategies, and any position with convexity.

In a crisis, these drivers often collapse into a single dominant composite: **forced deleveraging under uncertainty**. That composite factor loads positively on many assets' losses:

- equities fall (growth risk + risk premium repricing),
- credit spreads widen (default/liquidity),
- EM sells off (dollar funding, risk aversion),
- commodities can fall (growth) even if inflation risk exists,
- alternative risk premia (carry, value, relative value) can de-risk simultaneously.

If many assets share exposure to the same "crisis factor," then diversification fails not because the math is wrong, but because the portfolio is not diversified across the *right* risks. It is diversified across labels (asset classes) while remaining concentrated in a small set of latent exposures.

Asymptotic dependence: when the tail has its own correlation

Traditional correlation is an average measure. Tail events are not average. A portfolio that appears diversified based on full-sample correlation can still be fragile if assets become more dependent in the left tail (large losses).

Practitioners describe this phenomenon informally as **correlation goes to one in a crisis**. More precisely, the portfolio experiences stronger *tail dependence*: the probability of one asset selling off severely *conditional* on another selling off severely rises dramatically in stress regimes.

An intuitive way to internalize this:

- In calm markets, small daily moves are driven by idiosyncratic news and modest factor fluctuations; dependence is limited.
- In crises, the marginal investor changes. Prices are set by risk constraints, funding limits, and liquidity needs; dependence increases.

This is one reason Expected Shortfall can be more informative than VaR: ES is directly influenced by how dependence behaves in the tail. But even ES can understate risk if it is estimated from a window that does not include severe correlation regimes or if the model assumes stable correlations.

Two crisis regimes: flight-to-quality vs contagion

A robust multi-asset framework should explicitly separate two kinds of bad environments. They feel similar emotionally (markets down, volatility up), but the portfolio mechanics are different.

Flight-to-quality: the diversifier works

In a flight-to-quality episode, investors seek safety in high-quality nominal government bonds (e.g., U.S. Treasuries) and sometimes in reserve currencies. The defining feature is **negative stock–bond correlation**:

- equities and credit sell off (growth scare),
- yields fall and high-quality bonds rally (duration hedges),
- the portfolio's ballast is delivered through *rate convexity* and the market's demand for safe collateral.

When flight-to-quality holds, a classic balanced portfolio can behave much better than a risk-parity-skeptic expects: the bond sleeve does not merely reduce volatility in the long-run; it provides *crisis-time offset* that allows rebalancing into depressed risk assets without immediate impairment.

What makes flight-to-quality more likely. While no rule is universal, flight-to-quality is more likely when:

- inflation is contained or falling,
- central banks have room to cut policy rates or ease liquidity conditions,
- the shock is primarily a negative growth shock rather than an inflation or credibility shock.

Contagion: correlation spikes because of constraints, not fundamentals

Contagion is different. Here, correlations rise not primarily because fundamentals suddenly became identical, but because market participants are forced into similar actions:

- margin calls and risk limits trigger deleveraging,
- redemptions force selling,
- dealers reduce balance sheet, widening bid–ask spreads,
- "safe" assets may be sold to raise cash (even if their fundamental outlook is strong).

In contagion, you can observe selling pressure in assets that are *supposed* to diversify:

- high-quality bonds may not rally (or may even sell off) if inflation risk dominates or if there is a broad liquidation,
- gold may fall because it is liquid and profitable to sell, even if it is a long-term hedge,
- equity factor exposures that normally diversify each other can become highly correlated as quant/risk-parity/vol-control strategies de-risk in parallel.

The hallmark is a portfolio-level experience that feels like "everything is one trade." In such a regime, portfolio resilience depends less on static diversification and more on *liquidity management, leverage control, and explicit tail convexity.*

How to diagnose which regime you are in

Portfolio managers need a practical dashboard for distinguishing flight-to-quality from contagion in real time. The goal is not prediction; it is *decision relevance.*

1) The sign and stability of the equity–rates relationship

The simplest diagnostic is: do high-quality nominal bonds rally when equities sell off?

- If yes, you are more likely in a growth-driven risk-off with flight-to-quality characteristics.
- If no (or if yields rise as equities fall), diversification is impaired; inflation/credibility or liquidation dynamics may dominate.

2) Dispersion across risky assets

In a more "fundamental" risk-off, dispersion remains: some risky assets underperform more than others. In contagion, dispersion often collapses because flows dominate fundamentals. If EM, HY, small caps, and cyclicals all gap lower together while correlations across these segments jump, you are likely seeing forced selling dynamics.

3) Liquidity and funding indicators

Contagion is fundamentally about constraints. Look for signs of:

- widening bid–ask spreads,
- deteriorating market depth,
- unusual price gaps,
- rising haircuts and tighter financing (where observable),
- stress in short-term funding or collateral channels.

Even without perfect data, the *trading experience* (ability to execute size without moving price) is itself information. When execution quality collapses, correlation estimates based on closing marks become less meaningful because the market is no longer continuous.

Portfolio design implications: building diversification that survives stress

Once you accept that correlations are regime-dependent, portfolio design becomes less about finding assets with low average correlation and more about **engineering robustness across regimes**.

Diversify across *crisis drivers*, not just asset classes

A practical checklist is to ensure the portfolio has exposures that respond differently to:

- growth shocks (equity beta, credit beta),
- inflation shocks (real assets, inflation-linked bonds, pricing power equities),
- real-rate shocks (duration exposure and rate-sensitive equities),
- liquidity shocks (cash buffers, reduced leverage, instruments that retain tradability),
- volatility shocks (explicit convexity via options or strategies with crisis convexity).

Size "diversifiers" by their crisis behavior

A diversifier that works only in normal times is not a diversifier; it is a volatility reducer. That may still be valuable, but it should be budgeted differently. In risk budgeting language:

- treat normal-regime diversifiers as tools for tracking error and smoothness,
- treat crisis diversifiers as tools for drawdown control and rebalancing optionality.

Avoid hidden concentration through leverage and crowded trades

Even well-diversified allocations can become fragile if they share the same financing or de-risking trigger. Examples include:

- volatility-targeting overlays that reduce exposure when realized vol rises,
- leveraged carry trades that unwind when funding costs rise,
- crowded relative-value positions that rely on continuous liquidity.

In such cases, the portfolio may be diversified by holdings but *not* by liquidation dynamics. During stress, those positions can become correlated because the exit door is the same.

Risk management implications: how correlation breakdown should change your process

Correlation breakdown should be treated as a *design constraint* on your risk process, not as an unpleasant surprise.

1) Stress correlations explicitly

Do not rely on a single covariance matrix. Maintain at least two:

- a **normal regime** estimate for day-to-day risk and budgeting,
- a **crisis regime** estimate (or stress correlation overlay) for drawdown and solvency analysis.

The exact methodology can vary (regime-switching models, conditional correlations, or simply a conservative stressed correlation template). What matters is institutionalizing the idea that "correlation is a scenario."

2) Connect correlation breakdown to liquidity planning

When correlations rise, losses cluster. When losses cluster, the portfolio's need to trade (rebalancing, meeting redemptions, maintaining leverage constraints) tends to rise at the same time liquidity worsens. This is why the next section's stress-testing framework must incorporate not only price shocks, but also *action constraints*: how much can you realistically sell, when, and at what cost?

3) Use tail-aware metrics, but do not outsource judgment to them

Expected Shortfall is more tail-relevant than VaR, and it will reflect some of the effect of tail dependence if the estimation window and model capture stress behavior. But correlation breakdown is often *path-dependent* and *policy-dependent* (e.g., rate cuts vs hikes, liquidity facilities vs balance-sheet contraction). That reality calls for explicit scenarios and reverse stress testing, not only refined distributional measures.

5.3 Stress Testing and Scenario Analysis

The previous sections established two uncomfortable truths. First, VaR (and even Expected Shortfall) can become less reliable exactly when the portfolio is most vulnerable, because tails are regime-dependent and the underlying joint distribution is not stable. Second, diversification itself is conditional: correlations often rise in crises, and the portfolio can shift from a multi-driver system to a single "forced deleveraging" factor.

Stress testing is the practical response. It accepts, explicitly, that the world can move in ways your historical window did not contain and your distributional assumptions do not capture. Instead of asking *"What loss corresponds to the 99th percentile under my model?"* stress testing asks:

> *If a particular adverse configuration occurs, what happens to my portfolio, and can I survive it operationally?*

This is why stress testing is sometimes called *destruction testing*. Its purpose is not to produce a single risk number. Its purpose is to identify failure modes—the specific combinations of shocks and constraints that violate your risk covenants, your liquidity capacity, or your mandate.

From probability-weighted metrics to impact-weighted questions

Quantile-based metrics (VaR/ES) summarize the loss distribution in a compact way. They are valuable for routine governance, but they remain anchored to a model. Stress testing changes the emphasis:

- **VaR/ES:** "How bad could it get *with probability* $1-\alpha$?" (Model-dependent tail description.)
- **Stress testing:** "What happens if *this* happens?" (Impact conditional on a hypothesized state.)

The shift matters because many portfolio-breaking events have two features:

1. They are **rare** relative to typical risk reports.
2. They are **path- and constraint-dependent**: the loss is amplified by margin, liquidity, forced selling, and hedging nonlinearities.

Stress testing is how a multi-asset strategist integrates market mechanics (correlation breakdown, liquidation) into risk management.

Three pillars of a usable stress-testing program

A stress-testing program becomes operationally useful when it has three distinct components:

1. **Historical scenario replay:** "What would have happened to *this* portfolio in past stress episodes?"
2. **Factor-based hypothetical scenarios:** "What if a small set of macro factors moves sharply, even if history has not shown this exact combination?"
3. **Reverse stress testing:** "What combination of factor moves would cause the portfolio to breach a specified failure threshold?" (Work backwards from failure to causes.)

The common mistake is to stop at (1), usually by replaying a single famous episode (e.g., 2008). Historical replays are necessary—but not sufficient—because the next crisis rarely arrives in the same costume.

Historical replay: a necessary baseline (with clear limits)

A historical replay takes realized market moves from a defined period and maps them to current holdings. Examples might include:

- a global risk-off event (equities down, credit wider),
- an inflation shock (rates up, duration losses),
- an FX funding squeeze (dollar up, EM down),
- a volatility shock (vol up, convexity repriced).

Why it is useful. Historical replay is good at exposing:

- directional exposures you did not realize were large (hidden beta),
- nonlinearities in options or structured products,
- concentration in a single crisis driver,
- inconsistencies between stated objectives and actual behavior under stress.

Why it is limited. Historical replay is constrained by what happened *in that sample*:

- It may **miss** a regime your portfolio is sensitive to (e.g., a sustained inflation shock if your sample is disinflationary).
- It may embed a particular policy response (rate cuts, liquidity facilities) that may not be available next time.
- It may not reflect today's **positioning and market structure** (dealer balance sheet, systematic flows, leverage).

So, historical replay should be treated as a calibration exercise: it tells you whether your portfolio behaves as expected in known crises. It does not define the full space of possible failures.

Factor-based scenario analysis: the multi-asset strategist's workhorse

For multi-asset portfolios, the most informative scenarios are not "asset A down 10%." They are **factor shocks** that propagate across asset classes. Factor-based scenarios also help reduce the dimensionality of the problem: a portfolio may hold hundreds of positions, but its crisis behavior is often dominated by a handful of macro drivers.

Step 1: Choose a factor set that matches your book

A typical factor set for a balanced multi-asset portfolio might include:

- **Equity level (beta):** global equity drawdown factor.
- **Nominal rate level:** parallel shift in the yield curve (or key-rate durations).
- **Curve shape:** steepening/flattening (important for curve trades and financials).
- **Credit spreads:** IG/HY spread widening.
- **Inflation breakevens / real rates:** distinguishes inflation vs growth shocks.
- **FX (USD):** reserve currency strength in stress.
- **Volatility:** implied vol up, skew steepening (for option-sensitive exposures).
- **Commodity shock:** energy up/down, broad commodity down in growth scare.

You do not need the perfect factor model. You need a factor set that is interpretable and maps to how risk is discussed in your investment committee.

Step 2: Translate factors into instrument shocks

Each factor shock must be translated into position-level P&L. In practice, you need a mix of:

- **Linear sensitivities** (delta, duration, spread duration, key-rate durations),
- **Convexity** (bond convexity, gamma/vega for options),
- **Cross-effects** (e.g., equity down *and* vol up, which impacts option books nonlinearly).

A simple and effective approximation for many liquid instruments is a second-order Taylor expansion:

$$\Delta V \approx \sum_k \beta_k \Delta f_k + \frac{1}{2} \sum_k \sum_\ell \Gamma_{k\ell} \Delta f_k \Delta f_\ell,$$

where Δf_k are factor shocks, β_k are first-order exposures, and $\Gamma_{k\ell}$ captures convexity and interactions. The point is not to model every nuance; it is to avoid systematically underestimating losses when convexity and cross-terms matter (as they often do in stress).

Step 3: Specify scenarios as coherent macro narratives

Good scenarios are *coherent*. They respect economic linkages and crisis mechanics, rather than shocking each variable independently. Examples that portfolio managers actually find decision-relevant include:

Scenario A: "Real rates +200 bps" (duration and valuation shock). A sustained rise in real rates can impact:

- nominal bonds (down),
- rate-sensitive equities (down via discount-rate channel),
- long-duration growth equities (down more),
- some commodities ambiguous (depends on growth and dollar),

- credit spreads wider if growth is impaired.

Scenario B: "Growth scare" (classic risk-off).

- equities down sharply,
- credit spreads wider,
- volatility up,
- Treasuries may rally (flight-to-quality) *if* inflation pressure is absent,
- commodities (especially industrial) down.

Scenario C: "Stagflation impulse" (bad diversification regime).

- equities down,
- nominal yields up (or do not rally),
- inflation breakevens up,
- commodities up (energy-led),
- credit spreads wider.

This scenario is particularly important because it directly attacks the stock–bond diversification that many balanced portfolios rely on.

Scenario D: "Liquidity shock / deleveraging."

- equities down,
- credit wider,
- volatility up,
- dollar up,
- forced selling pressure can cause even high-quality assets (and diversifiers) to gap.

This scenario connects directly to the previous section's contagion discussion: it is about constraints, not only fundamentals.

Step 4: Summarize outputs in decision-ready form

A stress test that produces dozens of pages of position-level detail but no decisions is theater. The output should explicitly answer:

- **Loss magnitude:** portfolio P&L under the scenario.
- **Attribution:** which factors and sleeves drive the loss.
- **Constraint check:** which limits are breached (drawdown, volatility, leverage, concentration, tracking error).
- **Liquidity feasibility:** can the portfolio be rebalanced or de-risked within the required time without unacceptable market impact?

To force clarity, many managers use a "stoplight" layer (green/yellow/red) on top of numerical results, tied to explicit governance thresholds.

Reverse stress testing: working backward from failure

Reverse stress testing flips the question:

> *What market move would cause my portfolio to fail a specific covenant?*

Define "failure" in concrete, governance terms

Failure must be defined in the same units the organization actually manages:

- **Drawdown failure:** e.g., -12% in a month breaches mandate.
- **Risk-limit failure:** ES limit breach triggers forced de-risking.
- **Leverage/financing failure:** margin call exceeds liquidity buffer.

- **Liquidity failure:** cannot meet redemptions without selling core assets at fire-sale levels.

The important point: failure is often not "the portfolio is down." Failure is "the portfolio is down *and* cannot act."

Solve for the break point

In its simplest form, reverse stress testing asks for the factor shock size s that makes loss equal to a threshold L^*:

$$\Delta V(s) \leq -L^*.$$

If you approximate portfolio loss as linear in a dominant stress factor (e.g., equity beta plus credit beta), you can get a first-pass break point quickly. You then refine with:

- nonlinearities (options, convexity),
- correlation regime shifts (contagion),
- liquidity haircuts (realizable prices worse than marks),
- dynamic feedback (risk control overlays that force selling).

The power of reverse stress testing is not the algebra; it is the discovery process. It reveals which factors you are implicitly *short* (e.g., short liquidity, short vol, short disinflation) and whether your risk budget is robust to that exposure.

Integrating stress testing with VaR/ES and correlation regime logic

Stress testing should not live in a separate binder. It should be integrated with the risk metrics discussed earlier:

- **Use VaR/ES for frequency; use stress tests for severity.** VaR/ES help answer "How often might we see losses of this size?" Stress tests answer "If the world looks like this, what do we lose?"

- **Condition stress tests on correlation regimes.** A "growth scare" scenario should be run at least two ways:

  1. *Flight-to-quality version:* bonds rally, correlations behave favorably.
  2. *Contagion version:* correlations spike, diversifiers weaken, liquidity haircuts apply.

  This operationalizes the previous section: you are no longer debating correlation philosophically; you are pricing the consequences of correlation breakdown.

- **Use ES as a check on tail curvature, not as a substitute for scenarios.** If ES is rising while baseline stress tests look stable, you may have an unmodeled tail linkage (often a hidden short-vol or liquidity exposure). Conversely, if ES is stable but a plausible macro scenario is catastrophic, the model is underspecified for the current regime.

Common pitfalls (and how to avoid them)

Pitfall 1: "We stressed 2008, so we are covered."

A portfolio can be resilient to 2008-style deflationary deleveraging and still be fragile to an inflation shock, a rates-driven equity drawdown, or a policy credibility event. Always include scenarios that challenge your portfolio's *core diversification belief.*

Pitfall 2: Incoherent shocks

Randomly shocking each asset class by a fixed percentage is easy, but often misleading. Scenario analysis should be factor-driven and narrative-consistent. If you cannot explain the story, you cannot govern the response.

Pitfall 3: Ignoring second-order effects

In stress, convexity and cross-terms matter:

- bond convexity changes rate sensitivity as yields move,
- equity drawdowns reprice volatility and skew,
- credit widening changes the effective beta of many strategies,
- liquidity costs and haircuts can dominate marked-to-market losses.

A stress framework that is purely linear will typically understate the speed and depth of losses.

Pitfall 4: No link to action

A stress test is only as useful as the decision it supports. For each material scenario, the risk process should specify at least one of:

- a hedge to add or reduce,
- a gross or leverage adjustment,
- a rebalance rule (what would you buy/sell if the scenario begins to unfold),
- a liquidity buffer requirement.

A disciplined way to operationalize scenarios

A practical weekly or monthly process for a multi-asset team often looks like:

1. **Maintain a small library** of core scenarios (5–12) that cover growth, inflation, rates, credit/liquidity, and volatility shocks.
2. **Update exposures** (duration, spread duration, beta, option Greeks, FX sensitivities) and re-run scenarios on current holdings.
3. **Run each scenario in at least two dependence settings:** normal vs crisis correlations (flight-to-quality vs contagion).

4. **Overlay action constraints:** maximum tradable size per day, expected bid–ask widening, and financing haircuts.

5. **Document triggers and responses:** define in advance what you will do if scenario losses cross pre-set thresholds.

The goal is not to predict crises. The goal is to reduce the number of surprises that matter.

Where this leads: from scenario losses to liquidity-aware portfolio survival

Stress testing exposes a final, structural issue: even if you correctly identify a scenario that hurts you, you still must be able to *act* under stress. If a portion of the portfolio is illiquid or mark-to-model, the portfolio can be forced to sell its most liquid assets at the worst time, creating a destabilizing feedback loop.

That is the bridge to the next section. Once we treat crises as regimes of constraint (not only price changes), **liquidity risk and gating** become central to tail control in real multi-asset portfolios.

5.4 Liquidity Risk and Gating

The prior sections made a central point: tail risk is not only about *how far prices can move*, but also about *what constraints bind while they move*. VaR and Expected Shortfall summarize losses under modeled distributions; correlation breakdown explains why diversification can disappear when deleveraging begins; stress testing asks what happens under explicit "what-if" shocks. Liquidity risk completes the picture by adding the most operational question of all:

> When markets are down and correlations are high, *can you actually do what your risk process assumes you will do?*

Liquidity risk is often described as "the risk of not being able to sell." That is incomplete. In institutional portfolios, liquidity risk is more accurately the risk that *the portfolio's liabilities and governance rules demand liquidity exactly when the assets cannot provide it cheaply*. The problem becomes acute in multi-asset portfolios that blend daily-liquid public markets with inherently illiquid alternatives such as private equity (PE), private credit, real assets, venture, and certain forms of real estate.

This section focuses on the structural mismatch between liquid redemption terms and illiquid holdings, the *denominator effect* that amplifies drawdowns, and the gating/liquidity-tier design choices that prevent a run on the fund.

Two kinds of liquidity that matter: market liquidity and funding liquidity

Liquidity risk arrives through two channels that interact:

Market liquidity ("can I trade, and at what cost?") Market liquidity is the ability to convert an asset to cash with limited price impact and tight bid–ask spreads. In stress, market liquidity can deteriorate sharply:

- spreads widen,
- depth vanishes,
- price gaps replace continuous trading,
- "marks" become less realizable.

Public equities and on-the-run government bonds typically retain better market liquidity than credit, EM, small caps, or structured products—but even these can experience severe intraday dislocations during acute deleveraging.

Funding liquidity ("will my financing or liabilities force me to sell?") Funding liquidity is the ability to meet cash demands—margin calls, collateral movements, redemptions, capital calls, and operating needs. Funding liquidity problems force selling even if the long-term fundamental case is intact.

In mixed public/private portfolios, funding liquidity is often the dominant risk driver, because illiquid assets cannot be monetized quickly, while public assets *can* be sold—and therefore *will* be sold.

The structural mismatch: liquid promises backed by illiquid assets

Many investment vehicles offer relatively frequent liquidity (monthly, quarterly, sometimes even daily) while investing a meaningful portion of capital in assets whose economic liquidation horizon is measured in *years*. Even when the legal structure permits gates or side pockets, investors often behave as if the fund is liquid until the day it is not.

This mismatch creates three recurring vulnerabilities:

- **Asymmetric liquidation:** in a downturn, the fund sells what is liquid (public assets) and keeps what is illiquid (private assets). This changes the portfolio's risk profile precisely when stability is needed.
- **Marking asymmetry:** public assets are marked-to-market continuously; private assets are often marked-to-model with a lag. Reported allocations therefore move mechanically in stress, even before any economic revaluation of private assets has been recognized.
- **Feedback loops:** redemptions and rebalancing rules force sales that further depress liquid asset prices, increasing the relative weight of illiquid holdings and tightening constraints.

These mechanisms turn what looks like diversification in steady-state into *concentration* under stress.

The denominator effect: why private assets appear to "take over" at the worst time

The **denominator effect** describes a mechanical reweighting that occurs when public markets fall faster (and are marked faster) than private assets.

Consider a portfolio with public and private assets:

$$w_{private} = \frac{V_{private}}{V_{public} + V_{private}}.$$

In a drawdown, V_{public} can drop quickly and visibly, while $V_{private}$ may not be revalued immediately. Even if the private assets are economically impaired, the reporting lag can make the private allocation look artificially high. The denominator shrinks, the private weight rises, and the portfolio appears "overallocated" to private assets.

That over-allocation is not merely cosmetic. It triggers real governance pressures:

- the investment policy may cap illiquid exposure,
- the risk committee may demand rebalancing back toward target weights,
- lenders or counterparties may tighten terms due to perceived liquidity deterioration,
- the fund must still meet cash needs (redemptions, capital calls).

But rebalancing *out of private assets* is not feasible on crisis timelines. So the portfolio rebalances the only way it can: by selling liquid assets. That action can deepen the drawdown and worsen the allocation distortion, creating a self-reinforcing spiral.

The denominator effect spiral (and why it becomes a tail event)

The dynamics are easiest to see as a causal loop. The spiral below is a common failure mode for mixed-liquidity portfolios during a market downturn.

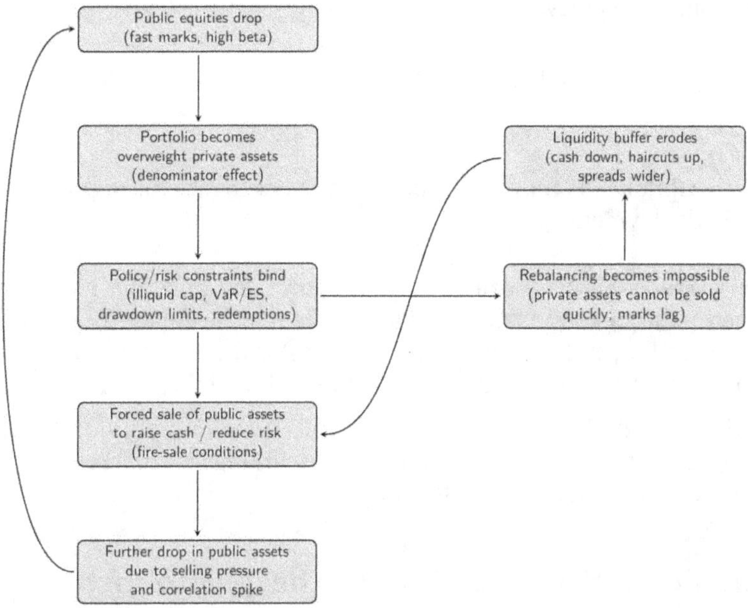

1) The spiral is governance-driven as much as market-driven. The trigger may be a market drawdown, but the amplification often comes from rules: allocation bands, illiquid caps, leverage/margin constraints, and redemption terms. In other words, the fund structure can *create* convexity: small market losses can trigger nonlinear selling pressure once constraints bind.

2) Liquidity risk converts a drawdown into a potential impairment event. A portfolio can survive a mark-to-market drawdown if it can hold risk or rebalance rationally. It becomes fragile when it must sell at stressed prices, locking in losses and raising the probability of further forced selling.

Capital calls and the "cash-demand asymmetry"

Private investments add a second cash-flow challenge: **capital calls** and delayed distributions. In benign markets, capital calls are planned and funded from portfolio cash flows. In stress, three things often happen simultaneously:

- public assets are down (denominator effect already active),
- distributions from private vehicles slow,
- capital calls may continue (or even accelerate for opportunistic deployment).

This creates **cash-demand asymmetry**: the portfolio needs cash when its liquid assets are least attractive to sell. Again, the result is forced selling of the most liquid exposures, which can increase concentration in illiquid assets and raise future vulnerability.

A disciplined allocator treats capital calls as a *liquidity liability* and budgets for them explicitly, rather than assuming that markets will provide an orderly source of cash when needed.

Liquidity tiers: designing the portfolio to meet obligations under stress

The most robust way to manage liquidity mismatch is to treat liquidity as a first-class risk budget. A practical approach is to segment the portfolio into tiers based on realizable liquidity under stress, not under normal conditions.

A simple three-tier framework

- **Tier 1 (Immediate liquidity):** cash, T-bills, highly liquid government bonds. Objective: meet redemptions/margin/calls in days without meaningful market impact.
- **Tier 2 (Contingent liquidity):** liquid public equities, large ETFs, on-the-run rates, futures. Objective: provide additional liquidity over days to weeks, acknowledging wider spreads and potential slippage.
- **Tier 3 (Illiquid / long-dated liquidity):** private assets, less-liquid credit, certain real assets. Objective: return premium over years; not a source of crisis cash.

A key discipline is to *size Tier 3* not only by return expectations, but by the maximum liquidity demands the fund could face during a drawdown. This is where stress testing from the previous section becomes operational: you stress not only prices, but also **cash needs** (redemptions, haircuts, calls).

Gates, side pockets, and redemption terms: tools and trade-offs

When a fund offers liquidity to investors, it is implicitly selling a liquidity option: investors can redeem at (or near) NAV on a schedule, while the fund may hold assets that cannot be liquidated at NAV on that schedule. Gating mechanisms are ways to manage (or reprice) that embedded option.

What gating is meant to prevent The primary purpose of gates and related tools is to prevent a **run dynamic**:

- early redeemers receive cash at relatively favorable marks,
- remaining investors are left with a more illiquid, more impaired portfolio,
- the incentive to redeem increases, accelerating the run.

Gates are therefore a form of **collective action device**: they slow withdrawals to protect remaining investors from being structurally disadvantaged by the liquidity mismatch.

Why gating can backfire if not designed and communicated well Gating is not free:

- It can **increase investor anxiety** and trigger redemptions *before* a gate is applied.
- It can create **reputational risk** and reduce future capital formation.
- It can change the investor base toward more liquidity-sensitive holders if the product is mispositioned.

The managerial implication is straightforward: liquidity terms must match the asset base *ex ante*. Gates should be treated as emergency brakes, not as the core liquidity plan.

Practical governance: making liquidity risk measurable and discussable

Because liquidity risk is partly structural and partly behavioral, it requires explicit governance. Useful practices include:

1) Liquidity-adjusted stress tests Extend scenario analysis to include:

- bid–ask widening and market impact assumptions,
- haircut increases and collateral needs,
- redemption shocks (e.g., 10% of NAV),
- delayed private marks (reporting lag),
- reduced distributions / increased calls.

The output should answer: *How many days (or weeks) of Tier 1 and Tier 2 liquidity are required to survive the scenario without selling core risk at distressed levels?*

2) A formal "liquidity budget" Just as you budget equity beta or duration, you should budget illiquidity:

- maximum percent in Tier 3,
- minimum percent in Tier 1,
- minimum unencumbered collateral buffer,
- maximum expected cash outflows over a stress horizon.

3) Rebalancing rules that respect liquidity Classic rebalancing wisdom says: "buy what is down." In mixed-liquidity portfolios, rebalancing must be made conditional:

- **If** liquid assets are down and illiquid weights have risen mechanically, naive rebalancing can force selling the liquid sleeve *into* the drawdown.
- Better is to predefine **rebalancing guardrails**: thresholds where rebalancing pauses, shifts to futures overlays, or is partially replaced by risk reduction elsewhere.

Key takeaway: liquidity terms are part of portfolio construction

Liquidity risk is not a footnote to multi-asset investing; it is a foundational design constraint. If redemption terms, leverage, and capital-call obligations are not aligned with the liquidity of the asset base, then the portfolio contains embedded convexity that appears only in stress—exactly when correlations are rising and measured tail risk is least reliable.

With this framework in place, we can now evaluate the explicit tools used to insure tails—options, volatility exposure, and convex strategies—and, just as importantly, the governance required to monetize those hedges and redeploy into risk assets during crashes.

5.5 Tail Risk Hedging and Skew Management

The prior sections built a coherent logic chain. VaR and Expected Shortfall help govern downside, but they are model-dependent and can understate tail severity. Correlations can spike in crises, undermining diversification right when it is needed. Stress testing reframes the problem as "what-if" impact, not historical frequency. Liquidity risk then reveals the hard constraint: even if your analysis is correct, you may be forced to sell at the worst moment because your liquid liabilities collide with illiquid assets.

Tail hedging is the portfolio manager's attempt to regain *optionality* under those conditions. It is explicit insurance: you pay an ongoing premium (often called the *bleed*) to obtain convex payoffs when markets gap lower, volatility spikes, correlations converge, and liquidity evaporates.

This section explains the mechanics and economics of tail hedging, how skew is priced, why many hedges disappoint in practice, and the governance required to monetize hedges in a disciplined way.

What tail hedging is (and what it is not)

A tail hedge is not a generic risk reduction. It is a position designed to have:

- **negative carry in normal times** (you pay for it),
- **convex positive payoff in bad times** (it accelerates as losses deepen),
- **reliability under correlation breakdown** (it should not require diversification to work),
- **liquidity when you need it** (ideally exchange-traded or otherwise monetizable).

In a multi-asset portfolio, tail hedging plays a specific role: it is a *liquidity and rebalancing enabler*. The goal is not merely to reduce drawdowns on paper; it is to create capital and liquidity *during the crash* so that the portfolio can:

- meet redemptions or margin calls,
- avoid forced selling of core exposures,
- rebalance into depressed risk premia when expected returns are highest.

That is the practical reason explicit convexity matters. Diversifiers can fail; cash can be finite; but convex hedges can create cash when the world is stressed.

The economics of insurance: why the bleed exists

Many investors approach tail hedging as if it should "pay for itself" over short horizons. That expectation is usually inconsistent with how insurance is priced.

A simple decomposition of hedge P&L

For option-based hedges, expected P&L over time can be decomposed into:

- **Carry (theta):** the time decay you pay to hold protection.
- **Volatility exposure (vega):** benefits if implied volatility rises (common in equity sell-offs).
- **Convexity (gamma):** benefits from large, fast moves (gaps, crashes).
- **Skew exposure:** benefits if downside options become relatively more expensive (skew steepening).

The bleed is not a bug; it is the premium for transferring tail risk to someone else. If tail hedges had positive expected carry *and* paid off in crashes, they would be arbitraged or become crowded until pricing adjusted.

Why tail hedges can still be rational

Even if the hedge has negative expected carry, it can improve the portfolio's long-run outcome by:

- reducing the probability of catastrophic impairment,
- reducing the probability of forced liquidation (liquidity spiral),
- allowing higher exposure to compensated risk premia (equity, credit, illiquidity) because the worst-case is bounded,

- improving behavioral discipline (the investor can hold risk through volatility).

Thus, the relevant evaluation criterion is not "does the hedge make money on average?" It is: *Does the hedge improve the portfolio's compounded outcome by preventing bad path dependence?*

Skew: how the market prices crash risk

Skew refers to the asymmetry in option prices across strikes. In equity indices, implied volatility is typically higher for puts (downside strikes) than for calls (upside strikes). This reflects the market's demand for downside protection and the structural tendency for equity returns to have left tails and volatility clustering.

For the tail hedger, skew has two key implications:

- **Crash insurance is expensive.** Deep out-of-the-money (OTM) puts often look "cheap" in premium dollars because their deltas are small, but their implied vol and risk premia can be high.

- **The hedge payoff is path-dependent.** In sharp drawdowns, implied volatility and skew often rise, so puts can gain value not only from the index falling (delta/gamma), but from vol repricing (vega) and skew steepening.

Skew is also not stable. In some regimes, implied volatility can be elevated even without a crash, causing hedges to be expensive at entry and vulnerable to losses if vol mean-reverts. This is one reason tail hedging must be governed as a *program*, not as opportunistic trades.

Three categories of tail risk hedges

A practical taxonomy helps clarify trade-offs.

Explicit option convexity (index puts, put spreads, collars)

These are the most direct tail hedges. Common implementations include:

- **Long index puts:** maximum convexity, straightforward crisis payoff, highest bleed.
- **Put spreads:** buy a put and sell a deeper put; reduces cost, caps protection beyond the lower strike.
- **Collars:** finance put cost by selling calls; reduces bleed, gives up upside.
- **Dynamic put rolls:** maintain a constant maturity/strike profile via systematic rolling.

Strengths.

- direct, model-light payoff in crises,
- tends to perform when correlations break down (because it is linked to the core risk asset),
- liquid and monetizable if exchange-traded.

Weaknesses.

- persistent negative carry,
- sensitive to implied volatility at entry (you can overpay),
- requires disciplined roll and sizing rules to avoid "buying high vol, selling low vol" repeatedly.

Volatility-linked hedges (VIX futures/calls, variance swaps)

Volatility often spikes during equity crashes, so a long volatility position can provide crisis convexity.

Strengths.

- can respond rapidly in shock events (vol-of-vol),
- can hedge correlation breakdown indirectly (vol rises when diversification fails),
- can be more capital-efficient in certain structures.

Weaknesses.

- term structure and roll-down costs can be severe (persistent bleed),
- basis risk: volatility may not rise as expected, or may rise after losses are already realized,
- implementation complexity (futures roll, option Greeks, convexity of the hedge itself).

A key practical point: volatility hedges often monetize best in fast, panic-style drawdowns. They may be less effective in slow-grinding bear markets where realized volatility is elevated but implied volatility does not spike dramatically relative to entry.

Crisis convexity through systematic strategies (trend following, defensive carry reduction)

Trend following and certain defensive systematic strategies can provide "crisis convexity" without paying option premium in the same way.

Strengths.

- often lower explicit carry cost than long puts,
- can benefit from sustained crisis trends across multiple asset classes (rates, FX, commodities),
- naturally diversifies across markets.

Weaknesses.

- protection can be delayed (needs trend confirmation),

- may underperform in sharp, mean-reverting crashes and recoveries,
- performance depends on model design and execution (signal speed, transaction costs).

For many multi-asset allocators, systematic convexity is a complement to, not a substitute for, explicit options. Options can respond immediately; trend can respond to persistence.

Sizing: the hedge must be large enough to matter, small enough to survive

The most common implementation failure is not instrument choice; it is sizing and persistence.

Budget the bleed explicitly

A tail hedge that is constantly being reduced after small losses is not a hedge; it is a series of regret trades. The hedge program should begin with an explicit annual (or quarterly) **premium budget**, for example:

- 25–75 bps per year for modest protection,
- 75–200 bps per year for stronger crisis convexity,

with the actual number set by the portfolio's objectives, leverage, liquidity mismatch, and drawdown tolerance.

The right framing is: *What premium am I willing to pay to reduce the probability of forced selling and deep drawdown?*

Size to a stress objective, not to a notional

A hedge should be sized to achieve a target offset under a specified stress. For example:

- "In a −20% equity drawdown with volatility up sharply, the hedge should fund one year of redemptions or cover X% of the portfolio's ES loss."

This links tail hedging directly to the stress-testing framework developed earlier and to the liquidity constraints discussed in the denominator-effect section.

Diversify the hedge itself

A single hedge structure can fail because the crisis arrives differently than expected (inflation shock vs growth shock; slow grind vs gap). A robust tail program often mixes:

- some direct equity crash convexity (puts or put spreads),
- some volatility convexity (selectively, with awareness of term structure),
- some systematic crisis convexity (trend).

The mix is a portfolio design decision: you are diversifying *crisis response mechanisms.*

Monetization governance: the difference between a good hedge and a good outcome

Buying protection is the easy part. The hard part is monetization: deciding when to realize gains and how to redeploy into risk assets. This is where many institutions fail, either by:

- holding hedges too long (watching crisis gains evaporate in the rebound), or
- monetizing too early (removing protection before the portfolio has stabilized).

Monetization is not primarily a trading skill; it is a governance problem. You need pre-committed rules that can be executed under stress.

Principle 1: Monetize to solve a constraint

A hedge should be monetized when it meaningfully relaxes the portfolio's binding constraint, such as:

- replenishing the liquidity buffer,
- reducing leverage or meeting margin calls without selling core assets,
- funding rebalancing into depressed risk premia.

This keeps the hedge program aligned with its true purpose: preventing the liquidity spiral and enabling rational re-risking.

Principle 2: Use staged monetization, not all-or-nothing

A practical approach is to predefine a **scale-out schedule** based on drawdown levels, volatility spikes, or stress indicators. For example:

- monetize 25% of the hedge when the portfolio breaches a first stress threshold,
- monetize another 25% if conditions worsen (or if the hedge reaches a target multiple),
- retain a residual hedge for "second leg down" risk.

The purpose of staging is to reduce regret in either direction. Crashes are rarely linear; they come in waves.

Principle 3: Separate hedge monetization from discretionary macro views

Under stress, it is tempting to turn hedge profits into a directional call: "This is the bottom" or "This will get worse." A stronger practice is to monetize and redeploy based on *policy and constraints*, not prediction:

- If rebalancing is part of the investment policy, hedge monetization should provide the cash to execute that policy.
- If liquidity is the binding constraint, hedge monetization should rebuild the liquidity tier.

This prevents the hedge program from being hijacked by the same emotional pressures that cause investors to buy risk late and sell risk low.

A practical checklist for tail hedge programs

To make tail hedging workable in a multi-asset portfolio, the program should answer the following questions clearly:

- **Objective:** Is the hedge meant to reduce drawdown, reduce ES, fund liquidity needs, or enable rebalancing?
- **Budget:** What annual premium (bleed) is acceptable, and under what conditions can it change?
- **Instrument mix:** How much is direct crash convexity vs volatility convexity vs systematic convexity?
- **Sizing metric:** What stress scenario must the hedge materially offset?
- **Roll rules:** How are maturities and strikes maintained? Who has authority to deviate?
- **Monetization rules:** What triggers partial or full monetization, and where does the cash go?
- **Success definition:** What does it mean for the hedge program to have "worked" over a cycle?

If these questions are not answered ex ante, the hedge will be evaluated with hindsight, and hindsight is a hostile environment for any strategy with negative carry.

Key takeaway: tail hedging is portfolio insurance plus governance

Tail risk hedging is best understood as **an institutional technology for staying solvent and liquid when the distribution breaks**. It is not free; it is not always popular; and it will often look "wrong" in calm markets. But when correlations converge, liquidity dries up, and the denominator effect forces selling, convexity can be the difference between a controlled drawdown and a forced unwind.

In the context of this chapter, tail hedging is the final layer of tail control:

- VaR/ES provide baseline governance,
- correlation regime thinking explains diversification failure,
- stress testing identifies failure modes,
- liquidity design prevents structural runs,
- tail hedges provide *crisis-time optionality* and a rulebook for monetizing it.

A multi-asset portfolio is not truly diversified until it is diversified across *states of the world*—including the state in which the portfolio must act under stress. Tail hedging, when properly governed, is one of the few tools designed specifically for that state.

Chapter 6

Derivatives, Overlays, and Alternative Strategies

Capital efficiency is the quiet engine of modern portfolio construction. While asset allocation determines the 'what,' derivatives and overlays determine the 'how'-allowing investors to separate market exposure from liquidity, collateralize diverse positions, and explicitly shape return distributions. This chapter moves beyond simple long-only exposures to examine how futures, options, and structured alternative strategies can be deployed to manage tail risk, hedge inflation, and harvest risk premia that are uncorrelated to the economic cycle.

6.1 Futures for Efficient Beta and Overlays

In the prior chapters, we treated *asset allocation* as the primary lever for portfolio outcomes: choose exposures (equity, duration, credit, commodities, etc.), size them to a risk budget, and control correlations so that the whole portfolio is more resilient than its parts. This section adds a powerful extension to that toolkit: using *futures* to obtain market exposure (beta) in a capital-efficient way, so that the portfolio can pursue *alpha* elsewhere without accidentally changing overall risk.

At a high level, futures allow you to separate two jobs that are often bundled together in a traditional portfolio:

- 1. **Owning beta:** the systematic return from broad markets (e.g., equity index exposure).
- 2. **Deploying capital:** deciding what your cash is doing while you hold that beta.

This separation is the foundation of *overlays* (derivative-based adjustments applied on top of a physical portfolio) and *portable alpha* (seeking alpha with the cash while "porting" beta via futures).

The core idea: full notional exposure, partial cash usage

A futures contract is an agreement to buy or sell an underlying asset (or index) at a future date for a price set today. In practice, most index futures are cash-settled and are rarely held to final delivery; they are typically *rolled* from one contract month to the next.

The key portfolio construction feature is that a futures position provides (approximately) the same *price exposure* as owning the underlying, but it does not require paying the full purchase price upfront. Instead, the investor posts **margin**:

- **Initial margin:** a good-faith deposit (a fraction of notional exposure).
- **Variation margin:** daily mark-to-market cash flows as the futures price changes.

As a result, you can hold close to 100% equity beta synthetically while keeping most of the cash in high-quality collateral (often T-bills). Conceptually, this turns one "lump" investment into two separable building blocks. Total return $\approx$ Collateral return + Futures excess return.

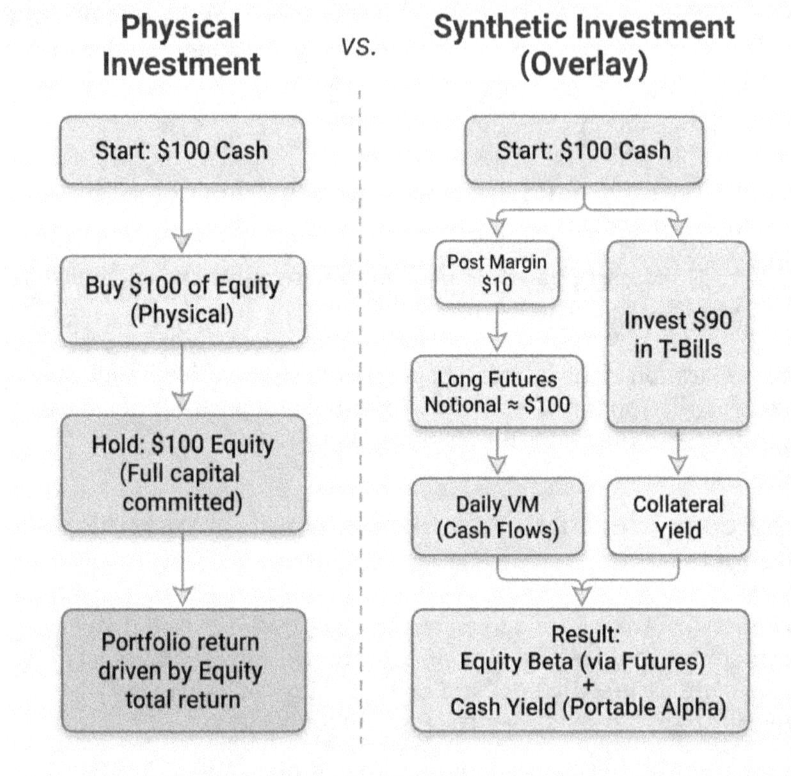

Futures as "efficient beta": what you gain, what you must manage

Why do allocators use futures overlays instead of simply buying the underlying securities?

Benefit 1: balance-sheet efficiency (capital efficiency). If an equity index futures position provides $100 of equity notional with (say) $10 of initial margin, the remaining $90 can be invested in:

- T-bills (pure collateral return, operationally simplest),
- short-duration investment-grade instruments (if permissible

and well controlled),

- or an alpha strategy that is truly independent of equity beta (the portable alpha objective).

This can increase *expected return per unit of funded capital* without mechanically increasing the portfolio's target beta.

Benefit 2: implementation speed and precision. Index futures are liquid and standardized. A CIO can raise or reduce equity beta quickly (e.g., adjusting risk after a drawdown, funding a tactical view, or managing cash flows) without trading a large number of underlying securities.

Benefit 3: clean separation of alpha and beta (conceptual clarity). Futures help the allocator measure and manage what is often blurred in physical portfolios:

- The **beta sleeve**: market exposure (e.g., S&P 500, EuroStoxx, rates duration).
- The **capital/alpha sleeve**: what the cash does while beta is held synthetically.

This separation makes it easier to enforce a risk budget. You can ask two different questions, each with its own constraints:

- 1. Are we holding the *right* betas at the *right size*?
- 2. Is our remaining capital being used in a way that diversifies and adds value net of costs?

Primary obligation: do not confuse notional with funded capital. The same feature that makes futures attractive also introduces the most common institutional mistake: confusing the low cash outlay (margin) with low risk. Futures deliver *full notional price exposure.* A $100 notional equity futures position will gain/lose roughly what $100 of equities gains/loses, even if only $10 was posted as margin.

A robust overlay process therefore tracks exposures in at least two parallel ways:

- **Notional exposure** (drives market sensitivity: beta, duration, etc.),
- **Liquidity and funding** (drives the ability to meet variation margin and avoid forced unwinds).

Mechanics: the futures return decomposition

For an allocator, the most useful mental model is that a futures-based exposure behaves like: Synthetic equity total return $\approx$ Collateral return + Futures price return − implementation frictions. The frictions are not a footnote; they are where many overlays succeed or fail. The big three are:

- transaction costs and bid/ask,
- financing/collateral drag (if collateral is held inefficiently),
- **roll yield** (the systematic gain/loss from maintaining exposure through contract rolls).

In many index futures, the futures price embeds financing and dividends (for equity) or carry economics (for commodities and some rate/-credit futures). Over time, the difference between holding the physical and holding the futures is often dominated by collateral return management and roll mechanics.

Equitizing cash: turning idle cash into market exposure

Institutions frequently hold cash for operational reasons: inflows/outflows, rebalancing windows, pending manager transitions, or risk reduction mandates. Left alone, that cash creates an unintended *beta shortfall*: the portfolio underparticipates when markets rally.

Equitizing cash means using futures to keep strategic market exposure intact while holding cash temporarily. A simple example:

- Policy target: 60% equities / 40% bonds.

- A large contribution arrives and sits in cash for 30 days.
- Without action, the portfolio is underweight equities and bonds relative to policy.
- Solution: buy equity index futures (and possibly bond futures) against the cash so that market exposure stays near policy until the cash is physically invested.

Equitization is not about leverage; it is about maintaining intended beta while operations catch up.

Overlay arithmetic: controlling beta without disturbing the underlying portfolio

A futures overlay is best viewed as a top-layer adjustment: $\beta_{total} \approx \beta_{physical} + \beta_{overlay}$. This is deceptively simple and extremely powerful. Suppose a portfolio already holds a collection of active equity managers (physical holdings), but the CIO wants to temporarily reduce equity beta by 0.10 (e.g., from 1.00 to 0.90) without forcing managers to sell positions (which may trigger taxes, transaction costs, or mandate violations). The CIO can:

- short index futures to remove a chosen amount of equity beta,
- leave the managers' security selection intact,
- later remove the hedge when conditions change.

In this way, overlays allow macro risk control while preserving micro sources of alpha.

Roll cost is not a nuisance; it is a structural return component

Because futures contracts expire, maintaining a long-term exposure requires periodically *rolling* from the near contract into a later contract. The price relationship between those contracts determines **roll yield**.

Contango vs. backwardation (intuition). Let F_1 be the price of the expiring (front) contract and F_2 the price of the next contract you roll into.

- **Contango:** $F_2 > F_1$. A long investor effectively sells lower and buys higher when rolling, creating a *negative* roll yield (a headwind).
- **Backwardation:** $F_2 < F_1$. A long investor sells higher and buys lower when rolling, creating a *positive* roll yield (a tailwind).

This effect is most visible in commodities, but the broader point generalizes: the term structure matters. Even in equity index futures, where pricing is tightly linked to financing and dividends, roll economics and implied financing can still affect realized performance versus a physical index holding (especially once collateral and cash management are included).

A practical definition of roll yield (allocator-friendly). Over a roll event, a simple approximation for the roll "drag" on a long position is: Roll yield over roll window $\approx \frac{F_1 - F_2}{F_1}$, where the position is moved from F_1 to F_2. This is not a full futures pricing model; it is a decision aid. It forces the allocator to treat the roll as a recurring P&L component, not an operational afterthought.

Why roll costs deserve governance attention. If a strategy's holding period is measured in years, but its instrument requires monthly or quarterly rolls, then implementation becomes part of the strategy. Over time:

- a persistent contango can turn "neutral" exposure into a meaningful performance drag,
- roll timing and execution quality can add or subtract basis points every cycle,
- the choice of which contract month to hold (front vs. second vs. deferred) can change both liquidity and roll profile.

A well-run overlay program treats roll policy as an investment decision with explicit objectives (liquidity, tracking, cost control), not as a back-office routine.

Avoiding inadvertent leverage: a risk-budgeting checklist

Futures create the *capacity* for leverage. Whether leverage is actually taken is a matter of policy and controls. The most common failure mode is not "using futures," but using them without recognizing that:

- Notional exposure drives market risk.
- Margin drives liquidity risk.
- Collateral choices drive funding stability and return.

A practical overlay checklist for portfolio managers:

- 1. **Define the target exposure in risk terms.** Specify the desired beta, duration, or factor exposure, not a dollar amount alone.
- 2. **Translate exposure to notional carefully.** Use contract multipliers and index levels; confirm with independent systems.
- 3. **Set a collateral policy.** Decide eligible collateral, haircuts, concentration limits, and minimum liquidity buffers.
- 4. **Stress variation margin.** Model adverse moves (e.g., equity down 5% in a day) and ensure liquidity sources are credible.
- 5. **Govern the roll process.** Predefine roll windows, execution methods, and monitoring of roll slippage.
- 6. **Monitor basis and tracking.** Track futures vs. underlying performance; investigate persistent deviations.

Portable alpha: separating "what you own" from "what you fund it with"

Portable alpha is frequently misrepresented as "getting something for nothing." In reality, it is a disciplined statement about portfolio architecture:

Hold the desired beta exposure synthetically and use the remaining funded capital for a return stream intended to be independent.

If successful, the portfolio can achieve:

$$\text{Portfolio return} \approx \text{Beta return} + \text{Alpha return} - \text{Costs}.$$

But two conditions are non-negotiable:

- The alpha engine must be genuinely diversifying (low correlation to the beta held via futures), *especially* in stress.
- The overlay must be funded and governed so that margin calls do not force liquidation of the alpha sleeve at the worst time.

In other words, portable alpha is not primarily a derivatives trick; it is a **risk-budgeting and liquidity-management discipline** enabled by derivatives.

What "success" looks like for a futures overlay

A well-executed futures overlay should deliver three outcomes:

- **Exposure accuracy:** the portfolio's realized beta stays close to the intended target.
- **Cost control:** roll costs, transaction costs, and collateral drag are minimized and predictable.
- **Operational resilience:** liquidity buffers and margin governance prevent forced deleveraging.

The rest of this chapter will build on these mechanics. Once you are comfortable with futures as efficient beta, the natural next step is to confront the practical reality that determines whether overlays remain theoretical or become durable: **cash management and collateral governance**, including how these decisions interact with currency exposure when portfolios invest globally.

6.2 Cash Management and FX Overlays

The previous section introduced futures as an efficient way to hold market beta with limited funded capital. That efficiency, however, is not "free." It shifts the portfolio's engineering problem from *raising capital to buy assets* to *managing collateral, liquidity, and cash flows* so the overlay can survive real market stress. In parallel, once you invest globally, foreign exchange (FX) becomes a second overlay layer that can either be a source of uncompensated volatility (if unmanaged) or a deliberate design choice (if hedged systematically).

This section focuses on two operationally inseparable questions:

- **Collateral and cash management:** How do we fund margin requirements and maintain overlays without forced deleveraging?
- **FX overlay design:** How much currency risk should we hedge, and how do we implement it cleanly?

Why cash management becomes a first-class investment decision

Derivative overlays convert market risk into *daily cash settlement risk*. Futures and many cleared derivatives are marked to market every day, creating cash inflows/outflows through **variation margin**. A portfolio that is "solvent" in a long-term sense can still fail operationally if it cannot meet margin calls promptly.

Variation margin is not optional. If an equity futures overlay loses money on a down day, the clearinghouse requires cash the same day (or next morning, depending on the venue). If the cash is not available, positions may be reduced or liquidated at precisely the wrong time. In practice, this is how overlays turn into unintended *path-dependent leverage*:

- Markets fall → overlay loses → margin call arrives.
- To raise cash, the investor sells liquid assets (often the same assets falling).

- Exposure is reduced at low prices, then re-added later at higher prices (a buy-high/sell-low dynamic).

Cash is a buffer, not a return engine—but it still has a return. Collateral is typically invested in very short-duration, high-quality instruments. The return on this collateral (e.g., T-bills or overnight repo) is part of the overlay's realized performance. Good collateral management therefore balances two competing goals:

- **Liquidity certainty:** cash must be available for variation margin under stress.
- **Minimizing drag:** avoid holding excessive idle cash that reduces expected portfolio return.

Collateral hierarchy: what "good collateral" really means

Not all "safe" assets behave as good collateral on the day you need cash. The question is not merely credit quality; it is *convertibility to cash under time pressure and adverse markets.*

A practical collateral hierarchy for institutional overlays looks like this:

- **Tier 1: Cash and cash equivalents** (cash, central bank reserves for eligible entities, overnight repo).
- **Tier 2: Short-term government bills** (high liquidity, low duration, predictable haircuts).
- **Tier 3: High-quality short-duration government notes** (more duration risk; can decline in price when yields rise).
- **Tier 4: Investment-grade credit and other spread products** (liquidity can gap in stress; spreads widen when risk is rising).
- **Tier 5: Equities and alternatives** (often unacceptable as margin collateral and unreliable as a liquidity source in drawdowns).

Two implementation concepts matter here.

Haircuts and the difference between "market value" and "collateral value." Even when securities are accepted as collateral, they are typically subject to a **haircut**. If a bond is worth $100, it might receive only $95 of collateral value. Haircuts can increase in stress, so portfolios that rely on borderline collateral can experience a sudden *effective leverage increase.*

Liquidity under stress beats yield in normal times. A 20–40 bps pickup from reaching for yield in the collateral pool is rarely worth the risk of a forced unwind when the overlay is losing. Collateral policy is a risk policy.

Designing the liquidity buffer: sizing for the margin call you have not seen yet

An overlay program should define a **liquidity buffer** explicitly: a pool of assets intended to be convertible to cash quickly with minimal price impact. The sizing process is not complicated conceptually, but it must be formal.

Step 1: Identify the primary drivers of margin volatility

Margin calls are driven by the volatility of the underlying exposures and the size of the overlay notional. For example:

- Equity index futures: large one-day moves are plausible, and gap risk exists.
- Rates futures: moves can be sharp during inflation shocks or policy surprises.
- Commodity futures: can exhibit both high volatility and strong trend moves.

Step 2: Stress test in dollars, not percentages

A functional buffer is defined in currency units:

$$\text{Potential margin call (USD)} \approx \text{Notional exposure} \times \text{Stress move}.$$

If the portfolio holds $200 million notional in equity futures, a -4% one-day stress implies an $8 million cash outflow. The buffer must be able to fund that amount *without selling the wrong assets*. The purpose is not to predict the exact worst day; it is to avoid being *fragile* to ordinary stress.

Step 3: Decide where the cash comes from (the funding waterfall)

A robust overlay specifies a **funding waterfall**—the sequence of liquidity sources used to meet margin calls. A typical hierarchy might be:

- Use cash on hand / overnight liquidity sleeve.
- Sell or repo T-bills.
- Sell short-duration government notes.
- Only then consider selling risk assets (equities/credit), because doing so embeds procyclicality.

This is governance as much as it is portfolio management: the portfolio team should not be improvising under pressure.

Common implementation pitfalls in collateral management

Three recurring problems appear in institutional overlay programs.

Pitfall 1: "We have plenty of assets" (but not cash). A portfolio can have ample market value and still fail liquidity demands if assets cannot be monetized quickly or are subject to operational constraints (custody settlement cycles, mandates, gating, or internal approvals).

Pitfall 2: Collateral pool is too duration-heavy. Holding longer-duration bonds as "safe collateral" can backfire in rising-rate regimes. When yields rise, bond prices fall at the same time the overlay may also be losing (e.g., an equity drawdown coinciding with a rates shock). Collateral should be designed to be *stable in value and liquid,* not simply "high quality."

Pitfall 3: Forgetting correlation in stress. Collateral assets that look diversified in normal times can become highly correlated in stress. This is particularly true for credit-like instruments, which tend to fall when risk assets fall, precisely when margin calls increase.

From collateral to currency: why FX overlays exist

Once a portfolio invests abroad, returns arrive in two layers:

$$\text{Return in home currency} \approx \text{Local asset return} + \text{Currency return} + \text{Interaction term}.$$

For practical purposes, the interaction term is usually small relative to the first two, but the key idea stands: **unhedged foreign assets embed an FX position.**

For a U.S.-based investor, owning unhedged Japanese equities means:

- long Japanese equities,
- *and* long JPY versus USD.

If the objective is global equity beta (companies), the currency layer may be an unwanted source of volatility. If the objective includes currency exposure as a diversifier, leaving it unhedged may be intentional. Either way, not deciding is itself a decision.

Static FX hedging: reducing uncompensated volatility

The simplest FX overlay is a **static hedge ratio**: hedge a fixed percentage of foreign currency exposure using FX forwards (or futures where liquid).

Mechanics of a forward hedge

If you own foreign assets denominated in currency C and your base currency is B, then:

- unhedged: you are long C (implicitly).
- hedged: you sell C forward and buy B forward.

A "100% hedge" aims to neutralize FX moves so that your performance largely reflects the *local* asset return translated at forward rates.

The forward rate is not a free lunch

The payoff to an FX hedge includes a **carry** component embedded in the forward price. In simplified terms, FX forward pricing reflects interest rate differentials between the two currencies (covered interest parity conditions under typical market functioning). Practically, this means:

- Hedging can add or subtract return depending on relative short-term rates.
- The hedge decision is therefore not purely about volatility reduction; it also changes expected return through carry.

For allocators, the right framing is: *hedging converts uncertain spot FX return into a more predictable return profile that includes forward carry*. The "cost" (or benefit) should be measured, not assumed.

Choosing a hedge ratio: the allocator's trade-off

A hedge ratio h (from 0 to 1) represents the fraction of currency exposure hedged.

Risk lens: hedge what you are not paid to hold. If you believe the long-run expected return to taking FX risk is small relative to its volatility (a common view for developed market currencies), then a higher hedge ratio may improve risk-adjusted returns.

Diversification lens: currencies can diversify, but not reliably. FX sometimes diversifies equity risk, but the relationship is regime-dependent:

- "Safe haven" currencies may appreciate in global risk-off periods, cushioning drawdowns.
- Other currencies may behave like risk assets (or be linked to commodity cycles), amplifying volatility.

Therefore, hedge ratio policy is best set by *risk budgeting*: what fraction of total portfolio volatility are you willing to allocate to currency fluctuations?

A practical hedge ratio formula (minimum-variance intuition)

Let:

- R_A be the local-currency return of the foreign asset,
- R_{FX} be the currency return (foreign currency vs. base),
- hedged return $\approx R_A + (1-h)R_{FX}$ (i.e., hedging removes fraction h of FX exposure).

A common intuition is to choose h to reduce variance:

$$h^* \approx 1 - \frac{\text{Cov}(R_A, R_{FX})}{\text{Var}(R_{FX})}.$$

Interpretation:

- If FX moves are *uncorrelated* with the asset (Cov ≈ 0), then $h^* \approx 1$: hedge most FX risk to remove uncompensated volatility.
- If FX tends to *offset* asset risk (negative covariance), then h^* can be less than 1: leave some FX exposure unhedged because it provides diversification.

In practice, allocators cap h to a feasible range (e.g., 0%–100%) and use robust estimates rather than brittle point estimates. The formula is a guide to thinking, not a commandment.

Dynamic FX overlays: when hedging becomes an active strategy

Some institutions treat currency management as a potential return source (an "alpha overlay"). This can include:

- value signals (purchasing power parity deviations),
- carry strategies (systematically holding high-rate currencies),
- trend signals (time-series momentum in FX).

The caution for multi-asset allocators is structural: active FX strategies can behave like risk-on exposures or can crash in crowded regimes. If implemented, they should be budgeted as an explicit risk sleeve with clear drawdown expectations and stop-loss/liquidity governance.

Integrating FX overlays with collateral management: one balance sheet, two overlays

Futures overlays and FX hedges meet on the same balance sheet:

- Both generate cash flows (variation margin for futures; settlement and roll cash flows for forwards/futures).
- Both require collateral and liquidity buffers.
- Both can increase operational complexity through roll schedules and settlement cycles.

A common institutional mistake is to manage them in separate silos—equities team controls futures, treasury team controls cash, and currency hedging sits elsewhere. The portfolio then discovers, in stress, that all overlays demand liquidity at once.

A coherent governance model ties them together:

- **One liquidity budget** for all overlays, sized by scenario analysis.

- **One collateral policy** defining eligible assets, haircuts, and concentration limits.
- **One roll calendar** to avoid bunching (e.g., rolling futures and FX hedges on the same days without planning).

What to measure: the overlay "dashboard"

To keep overlay programs robust, portfolio managers should monitor a small set of metrics continuously:

- **Notional exposures** (beta and FX) versus policy targets.
- **Liquidity coverage** (how many stress days of margin can the buffer fund?).
- **Collateral composition** (tiers, duration, credit exposure, and concentration).
- **Overlay P&L attribution** (market move vs. roll vs. financing/-carry vs. trading slippage).
- **Tracking and basis** (are derivatives behaving as expected versus physical benchmarks?).

The objective is not to eliminate day-to-day noise, but to prevent small implementation leaks from compounding into structural underperformance or operational fragility.

Bridge to the next section: from nominal exposure to real purchasing power

Futures and FX overlays are tools for shaping *nominal* exposures efficiently and managing the currency translation of global assets. The next step in building a resilient multi-asset portfolio is to address a different dimension of risk that can dominate long horizons: **inflation and real rates**. We now turn to inflation-linked bonds and the hedging of real purchasing power.

6.3 Inflation-Linked Bonds and Real Rate Hedging

The previous sections emphasized that overlays are ultimately *balance-sheet and risk-budget* problems: futures overlays require disciplined collateral and liquidity governance, and FX overlays require explicit decisions about what risks you intend to own. Inflation protection fits naturally into the same framework. It is another place where the allocator must decide, with precision, which *risk* is being hedged.

Nominal bonds hedge many things well (especially in disinflationary or recessionary shocks), but they do not directly hedge the risk most relevant to long-horizon liabilities: **real purchasing power**. Inflation-linked bonds (TIPS in the U.S.; "linkers" elsewhere) and inflation swaps are the primary instruments for that job. They allow you to:

- separate **nominal duration** risk from **real duration** risk,
- hedge **inflation surprises** more directly,
- and design portfolios whose long-horizon outcomes are less hostage to the path of prices.

A clean starting point: nominal returns vs. real returns

A portfolio manager can tolerate nominal volatility if long-term purchasing power is stable; conversely, a smooth nominal path is not very helpful if inflation erodes real wealth. The relevant identity is:

$$1 + R_{real} \approx \frac{1 + R_{nominal}}{1 + \pi},$$

where π is realized inflation over the period. For small changes, a useful approximation is:

$$R_{real} \approx R_{nominal} - \pi.$$

This is the core motivation for inflation-linked instruments: they reduce the sensitivity of your wealth to π.

What TIPS (and other linkers) are—and what they are not

Treasury Inflation-Protected Securities (TIPS) are U.S. government bonds whose principal is adjusted by the Consumer Price Index (CPI). Many other sovereign issuers offer similar instruments linked to their domestic inflation indices.

Mechanics: inflation-adjusted principal and coupons

Let:

- P_0 be original principal (par),
- I_t be the inflation index ratio at time t,
- $P_t = P_0 \cdot I_t$ be inflation-adjusted principal.

The coupon rate is fixed at issuance, but the coupon payment at time t is proportional to the coupon rate times P_t. If inflation rises, I_t rises, the principal grows, and the coupon payments grow in dollar terms. At maturity, TIPS repay the greater of inflation-adjusted principal and original par (a principal floor at par), providing some protection in deflationary outcomes.

Interpretation: TIPS deliver a real yield plus realized inflation

Conceptually, a linker can be viewed as a combination of three components: a real yield component, a realized inflation component, and price effects from changes in real yields. That is,

$$\text{TIPS return} \approx \text{Real yield component} + \text{Realized inflation component}$$
$$+\text{Price effects from changes in real yields.}$$

The last term is crucial: **TIPS are still duration instruments**. They are less sensitive to *inflation* than nominal bonds, but they remain sensitive to *real rates*. When real yields rise, TIPS prices fall; when real yields fall, TIPS prices rise. Therefore, owning TIPS is not the same as owning "inflation insurance with no mark-to-market risk."

Decomposing nominal yields: real yields and breakeven inflation

A practical allocator needs a mental model that links three objects:

1. the yield on a nominal Treasury of a given maturity,
2. the yield on a TIPS of similar maturity (a real yield),
3. and the market-implied inflation compensation (breakeven inflation).

A common decomposition is:

$$y_{nominal} \approx y_{real} + \pi_{breakeven} + \text{inflation risk premium} - \text{liquidity effects.}$$

In the simplest classroom version (ignoring risk premia and liquidity), you often see:

$$y_{nominal} \approx y_{real} + \pi_{breakeven}.$$

Even when you take the simple identity seriously, you must interpret it carefully:

- **Breakeven inflation** is not a pure forecast; it is a price that includes risk premia and liquidity conditions.
- **Real yields** can move independently of inflation expectations, especially when monetary policy, growth expectations, and risk appetite shift.

Allocator intuition: what breakeven inflation means for performance. Breakeven inflation is the realized inflation rate over the bond's horizon at which an investor would be indifferent (in total return terms, roughly) between holding the nominal Treasury and the TIPS, all else equal. If realized inflation is higher than breakeven, TIPS tend to outperform nominal Treasuries; if lower, nominal Treasuries tend to outperform.

This is not a trading rule; it is a way to clarify what risk you are taking:

- Buying TIPS over nominals increases exposure to inflation outcomes relative to the market-implied breakeven.

- Buying nominals over TIPS implicitly bets that inflation will be lower than what is priced (or that inflation risk premia will compress in your favor).

Nominal duration vs. real duration: what are you hedging?

A central practical decision is whether your portfolio problem is primarily:

1. **Nominal duration hedging** (sensitivity to changes in nominal yields), or

2. **Real rate hedging** (sensitivity to changes in real yields and inflation-adjusted discounting).

When nominal bonds hedge well

Nominal Treasuries often hedge equity drawdowns in classic growth scares and disinflationary recessions. In those regimes:

- inflation is stable or falling,

- central banks cut rates,

- nominal yields fall and bond prices rise,

- bonds diversify equity risk effectively.

In this environment, TIPS may behave more like duration instruments with less of the "flight-to-quality" benefit (because real yields can behave differently from nominal yields).

When linkers are the right tool

Inflation-linked instruments are designed for a different hedge objective: unexpected inflation that erodes the real value of nominal cash flows. They are particularly relevant when:

- liabilities are real (pensions indexed to inflation, endowment spending rules, real consumption targets),
- the portfolio is heavily exposed to long nominal duration (which is harmed by inflation surprises),
- inflation volatility is elevated, or inflation credibility is in question.

Key point: linkers hedge inflation, not necessarily inflation regimes with rising real yields. In inflation shocks, both inflation expectations and real yields can rise. TIPS protect the inflation-linked principal, but their price can still fall if real yields rise enough. Therefore, "inflation protection" is not synonymous with "no drawdowns in an inflation shock." It is protection of *real purchasing power* over the life of the instrument, subject to interim mark-to-market.

Liquidity premia and stress behavior: why linkers can disappoint in the short run

TIPS and other linkers can trade with a **liquidity premium** relative to nominal Treasuries. In stressed markets:

- investors may sell what they can sell (not what they want to sell),
- liquidity conditions can deteriorate unevenly,
- breakevens can move sharply due to technical flows, not purely macro information.

This has two implications for allocators:

1. Do not interpret every move in breakevens as a clean signal of inflation expectations.

2. If linkers are a strategic hedge, size them with the expectation that they may be temporarily painful in liquidity-driven episodes.

This is the same lesson as with derivatives collateral: *a hedge that fails operationally in stress is not a hedge.* For linkers, operational failure is not margin calls, but forced selling into illiquidity.

Inflation swaps: targeted inflation exposure without owning the bond

Inflation swaps allow a portfolio to exchange a fixed inflation rate for realized inflation over a specified horizon. They are useful when you want inflation exposure but do not want to commit balance sheet to a bond position (or when you want a cleaner hedge of a specific inflation measure).

Basic structure: fixed vs. realized inflation

In a plain-vanilla (zero-coupon) inflation swap:

- One side pays a **fixed** rate K (the swap's fixed inflation rate).
- The other side pays **realized inflation** over the period (linked to CPI index changes).

At maturity, the net payment is based on the difference between realized inflation and the fixed rate, applied to a notional.

Interpretation for hedgers. If you pay fixed and receive realized inflation, you benefit when realized inflation exceeds K. This position can hedge an investor whose liabilities rise with inflation.

Why swaps can be cleaner than TIPS (and why they can be harder)

Inflation swaps can be attractive because they:

- target inflation directly (less embedded duration than a linker bond),
- can be customized by maturity and index,
- can be scaled precisely to liability sensitivities.

However, they introduce classic derivative realities:

- collateral and margin requirements (especially if cleared),
- counterparty and legal documentation considerations (if uncleared),
- roll and liquidity considerations if hedges are maintained over time.

Thus, inflation swaps should be governed with the same discipline as futures overlays: collateral policy, liquidity buffers, stress testing of cash flows, and clear ownership of operational processes.

Putting it together: a practical real-rate hedging toolkit

A useful way to structure the decision set is to separate **exposures** from **instruments**.

Exposure menu

- **Nominal duration exposure:** sensitivity to nominal yields.
- **Real duration exposure:** sensitivity to real yields.
- **Inflation exposure:** sensitivity to realized inflation and changes in inflation expectations.

Instrument mapping

- **Nominal Treasuries:** nominal duration; diversifier in disinflationary shocks.
- **TIPS/Linkers:** real duration plus realized inflation; strategic purchasing-power hedge.
- **Inflation swaps:** more direct inflation exposure; requires collateral governance.

The portfolio manager's job is to choose a combination that fits the portfolio's objectives and constraints:

1. **Objective:** hedge real spending power, stabilize funded status, reduce left-tail inflation risk.
2. **Constraints:** liquidity needs, ability to manage derivatives collateral, permissible instruments.
3. **Risk budget:** how much tracking error versus traditional 60/40 benchmarks can be tolerated, especially in disinflationary regimes when linkers may lag.

Implementation guidance: sizing, rebalancing, and monitoring

Three practical points help keep inflation hedges effective rather than merely well-intentioned.

1) Size to a risk objective, not a narrative. If the goal is to hedge a fraction of real liabilities, size TIPS and/or inflation swaps relative to that liability sensitivity. If the goal is to reduce portfolio sensitivity to inflation surprises, size relative to the contribution of inflation shocks to portfolio variance in stress tests.

2) Rebalance with a policy, not discretion. Inflation protection can be whipsawed by shifts in real yields and breakevens. A rules-based rebalancing band (for allocation weights or risk contribution) reduces the temptation to abandon the hedge after short-term underperformance.

3) Monitor the right drivers. For linkers, monitor:

- real yield changes (dominant driver of price),
- breakeven movements (market inflation compensation),
- liquidity conditions and technicals (especially in stress).

For inflation swaps, monitor:

- collateral requirements and potential cash flow timing,
- counterparty exposures and documentation,
- hedge effectiveness versus the specific liability index.

Bridge to the next section: from linear hedges to convexity

Inflation-linked bonds and inflation swaps primarily reshape *linear* exposures: they change the slope of portfolio outcomes with respect to inflation and real rates. The next logical step is to address a different problem: portfolio losses that are not well managed by linear hedges alone. Options introduce **convexity**—the ability to alter the *shape* of the return distribution, particularly by truncating left-tail risk. We now turn to options foundations for allocators.

6.4 Options Foundations for Allocators

The previous sections focused on largely *linear* tools: futures, FX forwards, linkers, and inflation swaps. These instruments change exposures by changing slopes—more equity beta, less currency risk, more real-rate sensitivity, and so on. Options add something different and strategically valuable: they change the *shape* of the return distribution.

For allocators, the correct question is rarely "Should we trade options?" It is:

Where do we want convexity in the portfolio, and what are we willing to pay (or give up) to get it?

Convexity is the property that portfolio behavior improves *nonlinearly* in certain states of the world, typically the states that matter most for risk management (large drawdowns, crashes, liquidity spirals). Options are the primary standardized instrument for buying or selling convexity.

The allocator's mental model: options reshape outcomes, not forecasts

An option is a contract with a nonlinear payoff:

- A **call** gives the right (not the obligation) to buy an underlying at a strike price K.
- A **put** gives the right (not the obligation) to sell an underlying at a strike price K.

You pay a premium upfront (or equivalently accept an expected carry cost) to obtain the right to participate differently when markets move sharply.

This is the allocator's advantage: options allow you to express *preferences about tail outcomes* without needing a precise point forecast. Instead of predicting the exact next 3% move, you can design the portfolio to behave better if the next -30% happens.

Payoff fundamentals: linear vs. nonlinear exposure

Consider an equity index level at maturity S_T. The simplest payoffs are:

$$\text{Call payoff} = \max(S_T - K, 0), \qquad \text{Put payoff} = \max(K - S_T, 0).$$

These shapes are the building blocks of portfolio convexity:

- A **long put** limits downside below the strike—a *floor*.
- A **long call** limits upside cost (premium) while keeping upside participation—useful for *replacement* of a funded equity position.

The key contrast is with linear exposures (stocks, futures, bonds), whose payoff changes one-for-one with the underlying. Linear instruments are excellent for strategic beta and duration, but they do not *cap* losses.

Three allocator-relevant profiles: baseline, put-protected, and call replacement

Portfolio managers often compare option strategies by their payoff profiles. The goal is not to show a perfect replication of real-world multiperiod returns, but to build intuition about distribution shaping.

We will compare three stylized strategies over a single horizon:

- **Baseline 60/40:** a traditional balanced portfolio with linear exposure.
- **60/40 with put protection:** baseline plus a protective put overlay (pay premium to buy a floor).
- **Call replacement:** hold bonds plus a call to obtain equity upside with limited downside (in exchange for less participation and/or an upfront premium).

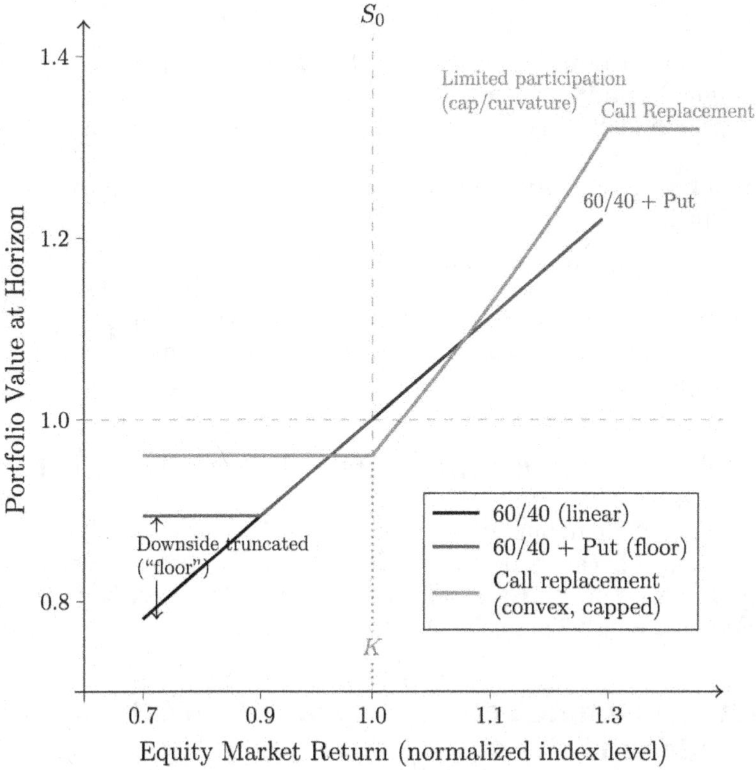

How to read the diagram (allocator interpretation)

Baseline 60/40. The baseline line is approximately linear in equity outcomes: when the equity market does poorly, the portfolio declines; when the market does well, the portfolio rises. Diversification from bonds reduces slope, but it does not prevent large drawdowns if equities fall sharply or if bonds fail to hedge.

60/40 with put protection. The protected portfolio behaves like baseline in normal and up markets (minus the option premium), but in sufficiently negative outcomes the payoff flattens: the put begins to pay, establishing a **floor**. This is the most direct way to purchase crash convexity.

Call replacement. Call replacement seeks equity upside while limiting funded equity exposure. The portfolio holds more in bonds/cash-like assets and buys a call for upside participation. The payoff has:

- a **bond-like floor** (though still subject to bond price risk over the horizon),
- **convexity** after the strike,
- but typically **less upside** than full equity ownership once premiums and realistic sizing are considered (and sometimes explicit caps if structured).

Greeks for allocators: the few that matter most

Options are often taught through a long list of sensitivities (the "Greeks"). Allocators do not need to become options traders, but they do need enough Greek intuition to govern the risk-budget and understand why hedges behave the way they do.

Delta: how much equity exposure does the option provide today?

Delta is the sensitivity of the option price to small changes in the underlying:

$$\Delta \approx \frac{\partial V}{\partial S}.$$

For allocators:

- A call's delta is between 0 and 1; it behaves like a *partial* equity position.
- A put's delta is between -1 and 0; it behaves like a *short* equity position.

Delta matters because it tells you how the option contributes to the portfolio's immediate beta.

Gamma: the source of convexity

Gamma is the sensitivity of delta itself:

$$\Gamma \approx \frac{\partial^2 V}{\partial S^2}.$$

A long option has positive gamma: as markets move, the option's delta changes in a way that is favorable to the holder:

- In a selloff, a long put becomes more negative delta (more hedge when you need it most).
- In a rally, a long call becomes more positive delta (more participation as the upside grows).

Gamma is the *engineering definition* of convexity.

Vega: sensitivity to volatility (the hidden driver in stress)

Vega measures sensitivity to implied volatility:

$$\text{Vega} \approx \frac{\partial V}{\partial \sigma}.$$

In equity stress, implied volatility often rises sharply. Long options tend to benefit (positive vega). This is one reason protective puts can hedge drawdowns more effectively than their delta alone suggests: the option can increase in value because volatility reprices upward.

Volatility as an "asset class": the carry vs. convexity trade

Many allocators discover an uncomfortable truth quickly: systematic put buying often has a negative expected carry in calm markets. The premium paid is a drag when crashes do not occur.

This is not a flaw; it is the economic essence of insurance:

- You pay a **premium** for a payout in adverse states.
- The premium shows up as a **cost of carry** (bleed) when adverse states do not happen.

Therefore, buying convexity should be treated like any other allocation decision:

- **What risk is it reducing?** (left-tail, liquidity spiral risk, sequence-of-returns risk)
- **What is the budgeted cost?** (annual premium, negative carry, tracking error)
- **When does it pay off?** (mild drawdowns vs. crash regimes; volatility spikes; gap moves)

Two canonical allocator use cases

Use case 1: protective puts as tail-risk insurance

A protective put overlay is best framed as buying a **floor** under an otherwise strategic equity allocation. The allocator chooses:

- **Tenor** (e.g., 1–3 months vs. 6–12 months): shorter tenors often have higher roll intensity; longer tenors can be more stable but costlier in dollar terms.
- **Moneyness** (ATM vs. OTM): deeper OTM puts are cheaper but pay off mainly in severe crashes.
- **Budgeting approach:** constant notional, constant premium spend, or conditional hedging bands.

The right choice depends on what drawdown the portfolio cannot tolerate and how much ongoing drag can be accepted.

Use case 2: call replacement to limit funded equity exposure

Call replacement is often used when the allocator wants equity upside but must control drawdowns or manage capital constraints. A stylized structure:

- Hold high-quality bonds (or cash-like collateral).
- Buy calls on an equity index for upside participation.

This can reduce left-tail risk relative to fully funded equities, but it introduces important trade-offs:

- **Path dependency:** if equities grind higher with low volatility, calls may underperform full equity due to time decay and premium costs.
- **Volatility regime dependence:** call prices rise when implied volatility is high; replacement is more expensive exactly when fear is elevated.

In allocator terms, call replacement is not "free equity exposure." It is *paying premium to transform linear exposure into convex exposure.*

Governance and implementation: the allocator's checklist

Options overlays fail most often not because options are misunderstood, but because they are governed like a tactical trade rather than a structural risk sleeve. A disciplined process includes:

1) Define the objective in distribution terms. Examples:

- reduce expected maximum drawdown by $X\%$,
- limit one-year loss beyond a specified percentile (e.g., 95% VaR / expected shortfall),
- reduce equity crash sensitivity in specific stress scenarios.

2) Budget premium explicitly. Premium is an ongoing expense. Treat it like an insurance budget (e.g., 50–150 bps/year), not like an incidental trading cost. If you do not budget it, you will abandon the hedge after a benign period—exactly when it becomes psychologically easiest to cut.

3) Integrate with the liquidity plan. Options are generally premium-paid instruments (unlike futures with daily variation margin), but they still require operational discipline:

- cash planning for premiums and potential re-hedging,
- understanding collateral/margin requirements for any option spreads or overwriting programs,
- clear authority for rolling and re-striking hedges.

4) Monitor the Greeks at the portfolio level. You do not need perfect precision, but you do need to know:

- portfolio delta (how much beta you actually hold today),
- portfolio gamma (how the hedge strengthens in a drawdown),
- portfolio vega (sensitivity to volatility spikes).

6.5 Hedge Fund Styles and Alternative Risk Premia

The previous section introduced options as a way to reshape portfolio outcomes by buying or selling convexity. That same idea provides a useful bridge into hedge funds. Many hedge fund strategies are not mysterious collections of security selections; they are *portfolios of exposures*—often nonlinear—to a small number of systematic drivers such as equity beta, credit spreads, carry, volatility, and liquidity. The allocator's job is to separate:

- 1) **Alternative risk premia ("alt beta"):** systematic, repeatable return sources that can often be replicated (at least approximately) with transparent rules and liquid instruments.

- 2) **Idiosyncratic alpha:** manager skill that persists after controlling for these systematic exposures, net of fees and trading costs.

This decomposition is not an academic exercise. It changes real portfolio decisions:

- It clarifies what you are *actually* buying when you allocate to a hedge fund.
- It prevents paying "2 and 20" for exposures that could be accessed more cheaply.
- It improves risk budgeting by revealing hidden leverage, hidden tail risk, and crowded exposures.

A simple return model: hedge funds as exposure stacks

A practical allocator framework starts with a "return stack" identity:

$$R_{HF} \approx \alpha + \sum_i \beta_i F_i - \text{costs},$$

where F_i are systematic factors (equity market, value, momentum, carry, volatility, credit spreads, term, etc.), and "costs" include fees, financing, and implementation frictions.

In this view:

- $\sum_i \beta_i F_i$ is **alternative beta** if the factors represent compensated premia and are accessible systematically.
- α is **true alpha** only if it remains after controlling for those factor exposures *and* is robust across regimes.

The allocator's key insight is that many hedge fund categories cluster around a few familiar building blocks:

- **Carry:** earning a premium for providing financing or insurance (often short volatility).

- **Value and convergence:** earning a premium when mispricings mean-revert (often liquidity-sensitive).
- **Trend:** earning a premium from persistent price moves (often long convexity-like behavior).
- **Quality security selection:** genuine skill in forecasting relative returns (harder to replicate).

What counts as "alternative risk premia"?

Alternative risk premia are systematic strategies that:

- 1) have an economically interpretable source of return (risk bearing, liquidity provision, behavioral bias),
- 2) can be expressed with transparent rules (at least in principle),
- 3) and tend to persist across time because they are *structural* rather than purely informational.

Common examples include:

- **Equity factors:** value, momentum, quality, low volatility (often accessible in long/short form).
- **Credit premia:** spread carry and roll-down (bearing default-/liquidity risk).
- **Volatility risk premium:** systematically earning premium by selling insurance (short options).
- **Merger arbitrage spread:** bearing deal break risk and financing/liquidity risk.
- **Term and curve premia:** exposures to yield curve slope/shape.
- **FX carry:** interest rate differentials (crash-prone in risk-off regimes).

Two cautions matter for allocators:

- **Premia can be real and still unpleasant.** Many premia pay most of the time and then suffer sharp drawdowns (carry and short-volatility are the canonical examples).
- **Replicable does not mean easy.** Replication requires robust implementation, financing, risk limits, and governance. A low-fee product can still deliver poor outcomes if it is structurally short liquidity.

A taxonomy of hedge fund styles (through the alt-beta lens)

Traditional hedge fund labels ("macro," "relative value," "event-driven") become more useful when translated into exposure language.

Long/Short Equity: beta management plus factor tilts

Long/short equity portfolios typically combine:

- a **long book** (often higher quality/growth or favored sectors),
- a **short book** (often lower quality/overvalued or challenged businesses),
- and **net exposure management** (controlling market beta, sometimes dynamically).

The replicable components often include:

- residual equity beta (sometimes hidden),
- factor exposures (value, momentum, quality),
- and sometimes implicit volatility selling (e.g., running concentrated books or harvesting crowded shorts).

True alpha in this category is difficult and tends to come from:

- superior security selection,
- disciplined risk control (avoiding blow-ups on the short side),
- and robust portfolio construction (position sizing and factor neutrality).

Global Macro: diversified bets on growth, inflation, and policy

Macro strategies trade across rates, FX, equity indices, and commodities. The systematic components often show up as:

- carry (rates/FX),
- trend (time-series momentum),
- volatility positioning (long or short depending on style),
- and crisis behavior that can resemble a convex hedge if risk is managed conservatively.

Macro can produce genuine alpha when managers exploit:

- policy reaction functions,
- cross-market relative value (e.g., curve dislocations),
- and regime shifts that are difficult to capture with static factor models.

But allocators should be alert to "macro" that is essentially:

- levered bond carry,
- or levered equity risk expressed via derivatives.

Merger Arbitrage (Event-Driven): carry with crash risk

Merger arbitrage typically involves:

- buying the target company after a deal announcement,
- sometimes shorting the acquirer in stock-for-stock deals,
- earning the spread between the current price and the deal price.

The spread is often interpreted as compensation for:

- deal break risk,
- time to completion,
- financing conditions and liquidity risk.

From an exposure standpoint, merger arb often behaves like:

- a **carry strategy** that earns small gains most months,
- with episodic sharp drawdowns when deals break or financing conditions tighten.

This is a classic example of a premia strategy that looks "low volatility" until it is not. It should be sized like a risk asset with *tail risk*, not like cash plus.

Relative Value (Fixed Income/Convertible/Stat Arb): convergence and funding sensitivity

Relative value strategies seek small mispricings between closely related instruments (on-the-run/off-the-run Treasuries, swap spreads, yield curve butterflies, convertibles versus equity/vol). Common structural features:

- **Low expected spread per trade → need for leverage** to make returns meaningful.

- **Convergence assumptions** → vulnerability to widening spreads before convergence.
- **Funding dependence** → sensitivity to margin/haircuts and liquidity conditions.

In the allocator's language, these strategies are often:

- **short liquidity** (they suffer when liquidity evaporates),
- and sometimes **short volatility** (if forced deleveraging occurs during volatility spikes).

They can be valuable diversifiers *if* sized appropriately and if the overall portfolio already has liquidity buffers, but they can also amplify stress if combined with other short-liquidity sleeves.

Replication: what it can and cannot do

The goal of replication is not to copy a manager's monthly returns perfectly. It is to answer: *How much of this return stream is explained by systematic exposures that could be obtained more cheaply and transparently?*

What replication tends to capture well

Replication is often effective at approximating:

- broad equity beta and factor tilts,
- carry and roll-down exposures in liquid rates/FX,
- simple trend-following components,
- and persistent short-volatility profiles (where present).

What replication tends to miss

Replication typically struggles with:

- complex or fast-changing trades (true discretionary macro),
- security-level information advantage (deep fundamental work),
- capacity-constrained niches,
- and path-dependent risk management decisions that are central to the strategy (e.g., when to cut, when to re-risk).

Allocator implication: replication is a diagnostic tool. Even when you choose not to invest in an "alt beta" product, thinking in alt-beta terms improves manager selection:

- If a manager's returns are largely explained by simple factors, fees should be lower.
- If a manager claims market neutrality but shows persistent equity beta, portfolio hedging should reflect reality, not marketing.

The fee test: are you paying for beta, alternative beta, or alpha?

A disciplined allocator asks three sequential questions:

1) What is the strategy's core exposure? Is it primarily:

- equity risk with some hedging,
- credit carry,
- convergence/leverage,
- or something closer to crisis convexity?

2) Is that exposure cheap to access elsewhere? If yes, then:

- require a clear justification for paying hedge fund fees,

- or consider allocating to a lower-fee alternative beta implementation.

3) If we believe alpha exists, is it robust and scalable? Robust alpha should show:

- persistence after adjusting for factors,
- a credible investment edge (information, structure, execution),
- and risk controls that prevent catastrophic loss.

Hidden risks: leverage, liquidity, and short convexity

The most important allocator contribution is often not return enhancement but *risk clarification.* Hedge funds frequently embed risks that do not show up in simple volatility statistics.

Leverage

Leverage is not inherently bad—it can be a rational way to monetize low-volatility spreads. But it must be governed:

- leverage can rise endogenously when volatility falls (risk models permit larger positions),
- and deleveraging can be forced when volatility rises or haircuts increase.

These dynamics can create **nonlinear losses**—options-like behavior—even when the underlying positions are linear securities.

Liquidity mismatch

Strategies that promise frequent liquidity while holding less liquid assets (or crowded trades) can experience:

- gated redemptions,
- adverse pricing on exits,
- and performance decay during stress.

From a portfolio construction perspective, liquidity is a *shared resource*. If multiple sleeves are short liquidity, the whole portfolio becomes fragile.

Short convexity (implicit option selling)

Many premia strategies are effectively:

- short volatility,
- short tail risk,
- or short correlation (they suffer when correlations spike toward 1).

This is not necessarily undesirable; insurance selling can be profitable. But it must be sized as a **risk premium strategy**, not mistaken for diversification.

A practical allocator framework: mapping hedge funds into the multi-asset risk budget

To integrate hedge funds cleanly into a multi-asset portfolio, treat each allocation as an exposure bundle and map it into your risk budget:

- 1) **Identify exposures:** estimate equity beta, duration, credit beta, FX beta, and volatility sensitivity (delta/vega-like behavior).
- 2) **Classify the return source:** market beta vs. alternative premia vs. residual alpha.
- 3) **Stress test the strategy:** ask how it behaves in (i) equity crash, (ii) rates up sharply, (iii) liquidity shock, (iv) inflation shock.

- 4) **Size to drawdown tolerance:** especially if the strategy is carry-like or convergence-like.
- 5) **Decide the fee level you will pay:** align fees with the portion you believe is true alpha.

This discipline also improves diversification: instead of owning five different funds that are all short liquidity in disguise, you can intentionally combine:

- some carry/convergence exposure (if desired and sized),
- some structural diversifiers (e.g., trend, defensive macro),
- and a limited number of high-conviction true-alpha managers.

Bridge to the next section: systematic trend as a crisis overlay

One of the most allocator-relevant alternative styles is systematic trend following (often implemented through managed futures). Unlike many carry and convergence strategies that are short liquidity, trend has historically displayed a more *convex* profile in prolonged stress: it can profit from sustained bear markets and inflation shocks when traditional diversification fails. The next section examines trend following as a **crisis overlay** and how to size it within a multi-asset risk budget.

6.6 Systematic Trend Following as a Crisis Overlay

The previous section decomposed hedge fund returns into (i) replicable alternative risk premia and (ii) residual alpha. That framework is especially helpful for understanding managed futures and systematic trend following. Unlike many "convergence" and "carry" strategies that earn small premia most of the time but can suffer in liquidity shocks, trend following is often positioned as a *crisis overlay*: a diversifying sleeve designed to help when traditional diversification fails.

This section explains what trend following is, why it can diversify a multi-asset portfolio, and how to size it sensibly given that it is volatile, can underperform in choppy markets, and requires patience.

What managed futures and CTAs actually do

A **Commodity Trading Advisor (CTA)** is a manager that trades futures and forwards (and sometimes options) across many markets. In institutional practice, "managed futures" typically refers to diversified, systematic CTAs whose core signal is **time-series momentum**:

> *Go long assets that have been going up; go short assets that have been going down, across equities, rates, FX, and commodities.*

Two structural features matter for allocators:

1) Futures provide capital-efficient, multi-asset access. Trend programs are implemented primarily with futures, so they share the mechanical advantages introduced earlier in this chapter:

- broad and scalable market access,
- the ability to be both long and short efficiently,
- collateral held in high-quality cash instruments.

2) Position sizing is usually volatility-targeted. Most systematic programs scale positions so that each market contributes a controlled amount of risk. This makes managed futures less about "commodity speculation" and more about **risk-balanced directional exposure** across a global opportunity set.

Time-series momentum: the simplest signal that works

Time-series momentum (trend) is conceptually simple: compare an asset's current price to its past price (or compare its recent return to zero). A basic monthly signal can be written as:

$$\text{Signal}_t = \text{sign}(R_{t-L,t}),$$

where $R_{t-L,t}$ is the return over a lookback window L (e.g., 3, 6, or 12 months). The position is then:

$$w_t \propto \text{Signal}_t \times \frac{1}{\sigma_t},$$

where σ_t is a volatility estimate used to scale risk.

This is not presented as the "best" model; it is presented because it captures the core allocator intuition:

- Trend does not require forecasting fundamentals precisely.
- It reacts to realized price information.
- It can adapt when regimes shift, because the signal updates systematically.

Why trend following can diversify: it is long *directional persistence*

A multi-asset allocator cares about diversification in *stress*. Trend's diversification potential comes from two properties:

1) It can go short risk assets during prolonged drawdowns Traditional portfolios are structurally long growth-sensitive assets (equities, credit) and may also be long duration. In an extended equity bear market, a trend program can:

- reduce or reverse equity exposure (go short equity futures),
- potentially profit as the downtrend persists,
- and allocate risk to other markets where trends may be positive (for example, long duration in a disinflationary recession, or long commodities in an inflation shock).

2) It can exploit large macro regimes across many markets Crisis periods are often periods of strong, persistent moves:

- sharp and sustained equity declines,
- persistent rate hiking or cutting cycles,
- extended currency trends (risk-off USD strength, EM devaluations),
- commodity spikes or collapses.

Trend is designed to monetize *persistence*, wherever it appears. This is why it is often categorized as "crisis alpha": not because it always profits in crises, but because it is structurally equipped to benefit from extended, directional stress regimes.

What trend is *not*: a free hedge or a constant crash put

It is essential to set correct expectations. Trend following is not the same as owning puts.

Trend is typically slow relative to sudden crashes. If markets gap down sharply and then mean-revert quickly, trend systems may:

- take losses before the signal flips,
- reduce exposure only after some of the move has occurred,
- and potentially give back profits if the rebound is fast and violent.

Trend tends to struggle in range-bound, mean-reverting markets. When prices oscillate without a sustained direction, trend systems can experience "whipsaw":

- signals flip back and forth,
- trading costs rise,
- performance can be flat or negative despite significant risk taken.

Therefore, the allocator should treat trend as:

> *A diversifying, liquid, systematic strategy that is most valuable when markets move persistently.*

Trend as "crisis overlay": portfolio role and implementation

To use trend following as a crisis overlay, be explicit about its job in the portfolio. Common roles include:

Role 1: Diversifier to equities and credit Trend has historically exhibited lower correlation to equities than many alternative strategies, especially over full cycles. In risk budgeting terms, it can provide an additional independent return stream, improving diversification beyond the stock/bond mix.

Role 2: A defensive sleeve in inflation and rate shock regimes In inflation shocks, traditional stock/bond diversification can fail because:

- equities fall as discount rates rise,
- bonds fall as yields rise,
- correlations can turn positive.

Trend programs can adapt by:

- being short duration (if rates are trending up),
- potentially being long commodities (if commodity inflation is trending up),
- and being short equities (if equities trend down).

This is not guaranteed, but it explains why allocators often view trend as a candidate hedge when the stock/bond relationship is unstable.

Role 3: A liquid alternative to "short-liquidity" hedge fund sleeves As discussed in the hedge fund section, many relative value and carry strategies are short liquidity and can delever in stress. Trend, implemented with liquid futures and systematic risk controls, is often more *operationally resilient*. That does not mean it cannot lose; it means it is less likely to be trapped by illiquidity or forced gating.

Sizing: trend is volatile, so size by risk contribution

Trend following is often high volatility. A small capital allocation can contribute a meaningful fraction of portfolio risk. As with all overlays discussed in this chapter, sizing should be done through a risk-budget lens rather than a nominal-weight lens.

A practical approach:

- **Choose a target role:** diversification, crisis overlay, or return enhancement.
- **Estimate volatility and correlations** in a conservative way (do not rely on one benign sample).
- **Size to risk contribution:** allocate so that trend contributes an intentional share of portfolio volatility (often modest, but meaningful).
- **Stress test:** include scenarios where trend underperforms during equity rebounds and choppy markets.

If the portfolio is already heavy in other alternatives that are short volatility or short liquidity, a trend allocation can be particularly valuable as a counterweight. Conversely, if the portfolio already holds substantial explicit option protection, trend may still diversify, but its incremental benefit should be evaluated honestly.

The "smile" intuition: trend can do well in large up *and* down equity regimes

A useful way to build intuition is to compare trend performance to equity performance across many periods. The stylized pattern often discussed is a "smile" (or U-shape):

- When equities are strongly up, trend can often be long equities and other risk-on assets, producing positive returns.
- When equities are strongly down *and the decline is persistent,* trend can often flip short and profit.

- In the middle—mild moves, choppy markets—trend may struggle.

The point is not that the relationship is mechanically U-shaped at all times. The point is that trend is not a simple "risk-off" strategy; it is a **directional persistence** strategy. Big moves, in either direction, are the raw material.

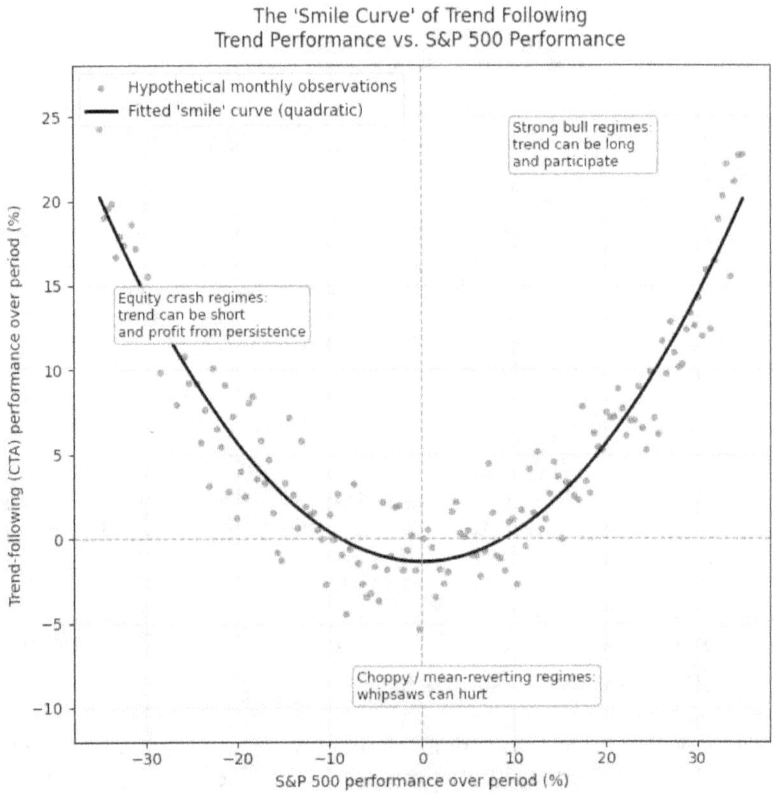

Operational considerations: trend is an overlay business

Because trend is typically implemented via futures:

- **Collateral management** matters (as in earlier sections): cash buffers, variation margin readiness, and a well-defined funding waterfall.
- **Leverage awareness** matters: notional exposures can be large relative to capital, even if risk is volatility-targeted.
- **Transaction costs and roll costs** matter: diversified programs trade and roll many contracts; execution quality and roll governance affect realized returns.

In other words, trend is not just an "allocation." It is a strategy whose success requires the same institutional discipline as any derivative overlay program.

Practical expectations and allocator discipline

A trend allocation is most effective when the allocator commits to three disciplines:

1) Evaluate across full cycles, not short windows. Trend can underperform for extended periods in range-bound markets. Selling after underperformance often means abandoning the diversifier before the next stress regime.

2) Treat it as a diversifier, not a benchmark race. The objective is portfolio resilience and improved risk-adjusted outcomes, not beating equities in equity bull markets.

3) Size so you can hold through volatility. A crisis overlay that is too large will be cut at the wrong time. A smaller, well-budgeted allocation that is held consistently is typically more valuable than a large, tactical allocation that is mistimed.

Chapter integration: how trend fits with futures, options, and alternative premia

Trend following completes the chapter's progression:

- **Futures overlays** showed how to implement exposures efficiently.

- **Cash and FX overlays** showed how to keep the balance sheet functional.
- **Linkers and inflation swaps** showed how to protect real purchasing power.
- **Options** showed how to buy explicit convexity.
- **Alternative risk premia** showed that many hedge fund returns are exposure stacks with hidden nonlinearities.
- **Trend** offers a systematic, liquid diversifier that can exhibit crisis resilience in persistent stress regimes.

For the multi-asset strategist, the central message is not that trend is always profitable. It is that *portfolio resilience is engineered*, and trend following is one of the more scalable tools available for adding a distinct, disciplined return stream that can behave differently from stocks and bonds when regimes shift.

Chapter 7

Performance, Governance, and Lifecycle Management

A strategic asset allocation is only as good as its execution. While the design phase relies on theoretical models and historical data, the lifecycle phase confronts the messy reality of market mechanics, friction, and human psychology. This chapter provides the operational handbook for the strategy: how to maintain the portfolio's harmony through disciplined rebalancing, how to navigate the drag of taxes, how to rigorously dissect returns beyond simple benchmarks, and-perhaps most critically-how to erect governance guardrails that protect the strategy from its greatest threat: the investor's own behavioral biases.

7.1 Rebalancing Design and Trading Rules

A strategic asset allocation is a long-term statement of intent: a set of target weights meant to express the portfolio's risk budget and economic exposures. Yet the market continuously pushes the realized portfolio away from those targets. Left unattended, this drift can quietly change the portfolio's risk profile: the portfolio may become more equity-heavy after a bull market, more duration-heavy after a bond rally, or more concentrated in a single factor that happened to perform well.

Rebalancing is the discipline that converts a static policy portfolio into a living portfolio. It is also one of the few investment actions that is (i) repeatable, (ii) scalable across multi-asset mandates, and (iii) largely independent of manager forecasting skill. The central design problem is not whether to rebalance, but *how* to rebalance: choosing rules that control two competing costs:

- **Tracking error to the policy benchmark:** letting weights drift increases deviations from the intended exposures.
- **Transaction costs and market impact:** trading too frequently (or in size) turns discipline into drag.

This section compares **time-based (calendar)** rebalancing against **state-based (threshold)** rebalancing, and then builds a practical framework for writing rebalancing rules that are robust enough to survive real-world trading constraints.

The mechanics: weights drift because returns compound

Consider a portfolio with N assets and target weights $w_1^\star, \ldots, w_N^\star$ such that $\sum_i w_i^\star = 1$. If the portfolio starts exactly on target at time $t = 0$, then after a period of realized returns r_i, the pre-rebalance weights become

$$\tilde{w}_i = \frac{w_i^\star(1 + r_i)}{\sum_{j=1}^{N} w_j^\star(1 + r_j)}.$$

Assets that outperform mechanically gain weight; underperformers lose weight. In a multi-asset portfolio, this drift can be substantial even over modest horizons because (i) equities can move quickly, (ii) durations can amplify bond price moves, and (iii) alternatives can have episodic jumps (and limited liquidity) that complicate "clean" rebalancing.

Two implications matter for design:

1. **Drift is endogenous to volatility and correlation.** Higher volatility assets drift faster. Lower correlations also increase dispersion in relative returns, accelerating drift.
2. **Rebalancing is inherently contrarian.** The trades are typically "sell winners, buy losers," which often feels uncomfortable in real time.

Why rebalance at all? Risk control first, return effects second

Rebalancing is often sold as a way to "buy low and sell high." That may occur, but the primary reason to rebalance in institutional practice is **risk governance**:

- Keeping the portfolio close to its intended **risk budget** (equity risk, duration risk, credit risk, inflation sensitivity, and so on).
- Preventing regime-dependent **risk concentration** (e.g., equity weight creeps up during extended rallies, setting the portfolio up for large drawdowns).

The return effect is best treated as a *secondary* outcome: sometimes favorable (often called a *rebalancing premium* or *contrarian rebalancing bonus*), sometimes neutral, and sometimes negative (notably during strong, persistent trends).

A useful way to teach the intuition is to separate two forces:

1. **Volatility harvesting (beneficial in mean-reverting relative returns):** when assets oscillate, periodically selling relative strength and buying relative weakness can create a small systematic tailwind.
2. **Trend drag (harmful in persistent trends):** if one asset persistently outperforms, repeatedly trimming it can reduce returns versus a drifting portfolio.

This duality is why rebalancing must be designed as a **risk and cost** problem, not as a guaranteed alpha source.

Two families of rules: calendar vs. threshold

Rebalancing rules are governance rules: they must be precise enough to implement, auditable, and stable through stress.

Calendar (time-based) rebalancing

Definition. Rebalance at predetermined dates (e.g., monthly, quarterly, annually), restoring weights to targets (or partially toward targets).

Strengths.

- **Simple and predictable.** Trading calendars are easy to operationalize and explain to committees.
- **Budget-friendly operations.** The team can plan staffing, cash flows, and execution windows.

Weaknesses.

- **Insensitive to market state.** You may trade aggressively after small drifts (wasting costs), yet do nothing during large intraperiod drifts (accepting unintended risk).
- **Cost clustering.** If many institutions rebalance at month/quarter ends, liquidity may be worse and market impact higher.

Calendar rebalancing is often reasonable for small portfolios with low transaction costs, or where governance simplicity dominates. But in multi-asset mandates with meaningful costs (especially alternatives, credit, EM, small caps), calendar rules can be blunt instruments.

Threshold (state-based) rebalancing

Definition. Rebalance when deviations from target weights exceed pre-specified tolerances. These tolerances are often called **bands, corridors**, or **no-trade regions**.

Strengths.

- **Trades only when needed.** The portfolio is allowed to "breathe" inside corridors, reducing turnover.
- **More directly manages risk drift.** Large drifts trigger action even if they occur quickly.

Weaknesses.

- **More design work.** Bands must be calibrated and periodically reviewed.
- **More monitoring.** The team needs drift measurement, alerts, and execution protocols.

In practice, many sophisticated investors use a **hybrid**: thresholds as the primary trigger, plus a periodic "maintenance" rebalance (e.g., annual) to clean up smaller drifts, incorporate strategic changes, and handle assets with infrequent pricing.

Designing threshold corridors: from intuition to implementable rules

A corridor is a formal statement of when drift becomes *material enough* to justify trading costs. The simplest corridor is an **absolute weight band**:

Rebalance asset i if

$$|\tilde{w}_i - w_i^\star| > b_i,$$

where b_i is a fixed number such as 2% (200 bps) or 5%.

Absolute bands are easy, but they treat all assets as equally "drift-prone," which is rarely true. A more realistic approach is to tie bands to the asset's volatility and its role in portfolio risk.

Volatility-aware bands (risk-scaled corridors)

If asset i has higher volatility, it will drift more quickly and will require either:

- a *wider* band (to avoid excessive turnover), or
- more frequent trading (if risk control demands tight exposures).

A pragmatic compromise is to scale the band with volatility:

$$b_i \;=\; k \cdot \sigma_i \cdot \sqrt{\Delta t},$$

where σ_i is an annualized volatility estimate, Δt is the monitoring interval expressed in years (e.g., daily monitoring $\Delta t \approx 1/252$), and k is a governance parameter controlling how "tolerant" the investor is of drift.

Interpretation. This makes the band roughly proportional to a typical short-horizon move. If k is larger, the no-trade region is wider, turnover falls, and tracking error rises. If k is smaller, the portfolio stays close to target, but turnover and costs rise.

Correlation matters: drift in one asset is rarely isolated

In multi-asset portfolios, correlations determine how quickly relative returns diverge. When correlations are high, assets often move together and weights drift less. When correlations are low (or unstable), dispersion rises and drift accelerates.

A simple governance-friendly implication is:

When cross-asset correlations are lower and volatility is higher, bands should generally be wider unless the policy benchmark demands tight exposures.

This statement is not a law; it is a *design posture*. The final choice must also reflect transaction costs, liquidity, and the investor's tolerance for unintended bets.

Two-dimensional corridors: absolute + relative bands

Many committees prefer rules that are stable across portfolio sizes and market levels. A common institutional specification combines:

- an **absolute** band in percentage points (controls operational noise), and
- a **relative** band as a percentage of the target weight (scales with allocation size).

One implementable rule is

$$|\tilde{w}_i - w_i^\star| \; > \; \max\left(b_i^{abs},\; b_i^{rel} \cdot w_i^\star\right).$$

This avoids pathological behavior such as extremely small target allocations triggering frequent trades (absolute floor), while still providing proportionate control for large core exposures (relative scaling).

Partial rebalancing: trading toward target, not necessarily to target

Full rebalancing restores weights exactly to $w^\star$. But with costs and market impact, it can be superior to rebalance *partially*. A simple partial rule is

$$w_i^{post} \;=\; \tilde{w}_i + \lambda\,(w_i^\star - \tilde{w}_i), \quad \text{with } 0 < \lambda \leq 1.$$

Here, $\lambda = 1$ is full rebalance; $\lambda = 0.5$ moves halfway back. Partial rebalancing is especially useful when:

- the asset is illiquid (credit, small caps, some alternatives),
- trading costs are nonlinear (impact rises rapidly with size),
- the portfolio is managing multiple constraints simultaneously (tax, leverage, cash flow needs).

Trading costs: the often-mispriced side of the trade-off

The key economic decision is not "tracking error versus turnover," but "benefit of risk control versus total trading cost." Trading cost is broader than commissions:

- **Bid–ask spread** (paying the spread when crossing).
- **Market impact** (moving the price against yourself), which increases with trade size and decreases with liquidity.
- **Opportunity cost** (not getting filled, or delaying trades in fast markets).
- **Implementation shortfall** relative to the decision price.

Rebalancing rules that ignore costs tend to overtrade precisely when it is least attractive: after volatility spikes, when spreads widen and liquidity thins. This is one reason threshold rebalancing can be more cost-efficient: it avoids frequent "cosmetic" trades and concentrates activity on material drifts.

A practical framework: writing rebalancing rules that survive committees and markets

An effective rebalancing policy reads like a small operating manual. It should specify:

1) Targets and measurement.

- Targets are defined at the **asset-class sleeve** level (e.g., US equity, ex-US equity, nominal duration, inflation-linked, diversifiers/alternatives).
- Drift is measured using **market values** (with stated conventions for stale-priced assets).

2) Trigger logic (calendar, threshold, or hybrid).

- Threshold triggers based on absolute and/or relative bands.
- A calendar "maintenance rebalance" frequency (e.g., annually) even if thresholds are not hit.

3) Priority and funding order. When multiple assets breach bands simultaneously, the policy must state whether trades are:

- proportional across all breaches, or
- prioritized (e.g., first correct the largest contribution to risk, then smaller issues).

This is where risk budgeting becomes operational: you are not just moving weights; you are reducing unintended risk concentrations.

4) Practical constraints.

- Minimum trade sizes and lot constraints.
- Liquidity gates for certain funds/alternatives.
- Leverage or margin limits.
- Cash buffers (especially for portfolios with distributions or capital calls).

5) Execution protocol.

- Allowed instruments (spot, futures/overlays, ETFs).
- Trading windows (avoid predictable "crowded" times when possible).
- Escalation steps during stress (e.g., widen bands temporarily if liquidity collapses).

Interpreting the trade-off: tracking error versus turnover as an efficiency frontier

To compare methodologies, it helps to map them onto a two-axis trade-off:

- **Tracking Error** (vertical axis): deviation from the policy benchmark.
- **Annual Turnover** (horizontal axis): how much trading the rule generates.

Calendar rebalancing typically produces a set of points determined by frequency (annual, quarterly, monthly). Threshold rebalancing produces a set of points determined by band width (tight, moderate, wide). Empirically and intuitively, threshold approaches often trace a more efficient curve: for the same tracking error, they can deliver lower turnover because they avoid unnecessary trades when drift is small.

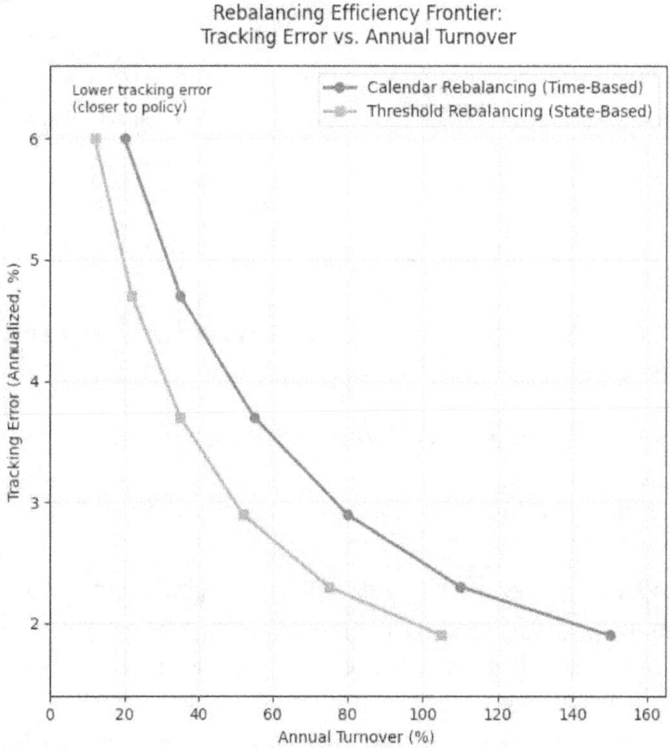

Putting numbers to the rule: a committee-ready calibration checklist

Band setting is often where theory meets governance. The goal is not a perfect formula; it is a **defensible calibration** that aligns with cost, liquidity, and risk tolerance.

Calibration Input	How it should influence bands and rules
Asset volatility (σ)	Higher volatility generally implies faster drift. Use wider bands (or partial rebalancing) to avoid chronic overtrading, unless exposures must be tightly controlled.
Cross-asset correlation	Lower correlations typically increase dispersion in relative returns, raising drift frequency. Consider wider bands or less aggressive "to-target" trading.
Liquidity and impact	Illiquid assets justify wider bands, higher minimum trade sizes, and partial rebalancing. Consider using liquid overlays (futures) to manage exposures when cash markets are costly.
Transaction cost estimates	Higher expected costs call for wider bands and/or less frequent maintenance rebalances. Costs should be stress-tested under crisis liquidity assumptions.
Risk budget sensitivity	If an asset dominates portfolio risk (e.g., equities), tighter bands may be warranted even if it increases turnover. If risk contribution is small, bands can be wider.
Operational constraints	Stale prices, fund dealing schedules, and cash flow timing often force hybrid designs (threshold triggers with periodic clean-up).

Common implementation patterns (and their failure modes)

Pattern A: quarterly full rebalance.

Works when: costs are low, liquidity is high, governance is simple.
Fails when: volatility spikes inside the quarter; the portfolio carries unintended risk until the next date.

Pattern B: $\pm 2\%$ absolute bands with full rebalance.

Works when: allocations are moderate and fairly stable.
Fails when: small sleeves trigger frequent noise trades, or high-volatility sleeves trigger repeated trading that is mostly cost.

Pattern C: hybrid threshold + annual maintenance, with partial rebalancing.

Works when: multi-asset complexity and cost matter; it reduces "unnecessary" turnover while still enforcing discipline.
Fails when: monitoring and governance are weak (missed triggers), or band logic becomes too complex to explain and audit.

Takeaway: rebalancing is a control system

A well-designed rebalancing policy behaves like a control system with three ingredients:

1. **A target** (the strategic weights and risk budget).
2. **A sensor** (drift measurement and monitoring cadence).
3. **An actuator** (a trading rule that accounts for costs and liquidity).

Calendar rebalancing is the simplest control system: it acts on a schedule, whether or not the system needs it. Threshold rebalancing is state-aware: it acts when deviations become meaningful, often producing a better balance of tracking error and turnover. For multi-asset portfolios—where correlations shift, liquidity is heterogeneous, and transaction costs are real—threshold or hybrid designs tend to produce more resilient, committee-survivable outcomes.

7.2 Tax Efficiency and Structural Constraints

The previous section treated rebalancing as a *control system*: you choose targets, define corridors, and trade only when the economic benefit (risk control, sometimes a rebalancing bonus) exceeds the cost (spreads, impact, commissions). In taxable portfolios there is a second cost channel that is often larger than explicit transaction costs and more persistent than market impact: **tax drag**.

Tax drag is the gap between a strategy's *pre-tax* compound return and its *after-tax* compound return. It comes from three recurring frictions:

- **Taxation of ongoing income** (coupons, dividends, non-qualified distributions).
- **Taxation of realized capital gains** (often triggered by rebalancing or fund distributions).
- **Structural limits** (account types, product wrappers, and rules such as wash sales) that restrict what trades you can do and when.

For a multi-asset strategist, the objective is not to "avoid taxes" (impossible) but to **spend the tax budget intelligently**: realize gains deliberately, defer when deferral is valuable, and place the most tax-inefficient exposures in the accounts and vehicles where they do the least harm.

Tax drag as a compounding problem

Because taxes reduce the capital that remains invested, their effect compounds. A simple way to see it is to compare two portfolios with identical pre-tax return r but different effective tax drag d (expressed as an annual percentage reduction in return due to taxes and tax-induced frictions). The after-tax compound growth rate is approximately $r - d$, so over T years the wealth ratio is

$$\frac{(1 + r - d)^T}{(1 + r)^T}$$

Even a modest-seeming drag can matter greatly over long horizons.

A useful mental model: "tax drag is a fee you don't see." Investment committees rigorously negotiate explicit fees because they are visible. Tax drag is often larger, but it is less visible because it is embedded in distributions, realized gains, and year-by-year filings. Treat it with the same seriousness as an ongoing expense ratio.

Two levers: asset location and vehicle selection

Tax efficiency is achieved primarily through two design decisions that sit *above* security selection:

- **Asset location:** which assets go in which account types.
- **Vehicle selection:** which wrappers you use to hold those assets (ETF vs. mutual fund vs. SMA, and related structures).

These decisions interact with rebalancing design. In a taxable setting, the "best" rebalancing rule is rarely the one that is best pre-tax.

Asset location: placing exposures where their tax profile fits

Asset location means placing different assets in different account types to minimize taxes *without changing* the total portfolio's strategic exposures. Conceptually, you still manage one total portfolio; you simply distribute holdings across account "containers" more intelligently.

Account types and why they matter

While the precise details depend on jurisdiction and investor type, most U.S. investors face some combination of:

- **Taxable accounts:** ongoing income and realized gains typically create current-year tax liabilities.
- **Tax-deferred accounts:** taxes are generally deferred until withdrawal; turnover inside the account does not create current-year tax bills.
- **Tax-exempt accounts:** taxes may be largely avoided if rules are satisfied (often with constraints on withdrawals and contributions).

For portfolio design, the key distinction is whether **realizations matter today**. In tax-deferred/exempt accounts, rebalancing resembles the pre-tax textbook case: trade to manage risk and costs. In taxable accounts, rebalancing is constrained by the embedded tax liability in unrealized gains.

Classifying assets by tax profile

A committee-ready framework is to classify exposures along two axes:

- **Tax efficiency:** how much of the expected return arrives as currently taxable income or short-term realizations versus deferred capital gains.
- **Return/yield character:** whether the asset's expected return is dominated by yield-like cash flows (coupons, distributions) or by price appreciation.

Examples (stylized, but operationally useful):

- **Tax-inefficient, yield-heavy:** taxable bonds, many credit strategies, some income-oriented alternatives.
- **Tax-inefficient, realization-prone:** high-turnover active strategies, some multi-strategy funds that distribute gains.
- **More tax-efficient, appreciation-heavy:** broad equity index exposures held via low-turnover vehicles.
- **Special cases:** municipal bonds (often designed to be tax-advantaged in taxable accounts), tax-managed equity strategies, and certain commodity/derivative structures whose tax treatment can differ materially by product.

Location heuristics (what to put where)

A practical starting point is:

Use tax-advantaged space for tax-inefficient return streams.

- Place **taxable bond** exposure (especially higher-yielding credit) preferentially in tax-deferred or tax-exempt accounts when possible.
- Place **high-turnover strategies** (that realize gains frequently) in tax-advantaged accounts when feasible.

Reserve taxable accounts for exposures that can "compound quietly."

- Favor **low-turnover equity exposures** held in tax-efficient vehicles.
- Favor strategies that can realize gains **selectively** (e.g., via tax-loss harvesting in SMAs) rather than distributing gains on a schedule.

Use muni bonds as a deliberate taxable-account tool (when appropriate). Municipal bonds exist largely to deliver after-tax income efficiency in taxable accounts. The decision is not "munis are good" but rather "do munis deliver a better *after-tax* risk-adjusted return for this investor's bracket and objectives than taxable bonds placed elsewhere?"

Asset location meets rebalancing: where you trade matters

In the prior section, threshold corridors reduced turnover. In taxable portfolios, turnover has a second cost: it can *force* capital gains realization.

A useful operational rule is the following:
When the total portfolio needs to rebalance, try to do the highest-turnover portion of the rebalance in tax-advantaged accounts first, and use taxable accounts as the "last resort."
This is not about hiding risk; it is about choosing the least expensive place (after tax) to do the necessary risk-control trade.

Vehicle selection: ETF vs. mutual fund vs. SMA (and why structure dominates)

Once you know *what* you want to own and *where* you want to hold it, vehicle selection determines *how* returns are delivered (income vs. gains, distributed vs. deferred), and therefore how large the tax drag will be.

Mutual funds: convenient, but distributions can create uncontrolled realizations

In a pooled mutual fund, the investor's tax outcome depends partly on the fund's trading and shareholder flows. When the fund realizes gains and distributes them, taxable shareholders may owe taxes even if they personally did not sell.

Two structural implications matter:

- **You cannot fully control the timing of realizations.** Even long-term holders can receive taxable capital gains distributions.
- **Rebalancing at the total-portfolio level may be dominated by fund-level activity.** You can design a low-turnover policy, yet still face distributions.

Mutual funds can still be appropriate (liquidity, access to managers, operational simplicity), but in taxable accounts they require explicit monitoring of distribution behavior.

ETFs: typically more tax-efficient for broad beta exposures

ETFs often exhibit strong tax efficiency for index-like exposures because of structural mechanisms that can reduce the need to distribute capital gains. Practically, for many investors, ETFs are a common default for tax-efficient equity beta in taxable accounts.

However, do not treat "ETF" as synonymous with "tax-efficient" in all cases:

- Some ETFs follow higher-turnover strategies.
- Certain exposures rely on derivatives or commodity-linked structures whose tax treatment may differ from plain equities.

The principle is to evaluate the **expected distribution profile** and **turnover** of the specific vehicle, not the label.

Separately Managed Accounts (SMAs): customization and tax control, at a price

An SMA holds the underlying securities directly in the investor's account. The investor typically has more control over realizations:

- **Tax-loss harvesting (TLH):** realizing losses to offset gains, potentially reducing current taxes while maintaining similar exposures (subject to constraints).
- **Gain deferral:** choosing which lots to sell (specific identification) and avoiding unnecessary sales of large embedded gains.
- **Restriction management:** excluding securities for policy reasons without abandoning the strategy.

Trade-offs:

- **Operational complexity:** lot tracking, wash-sale monitoring, and customization require robust systems.
- **Capacity and implementation costs:** smaller accounts may face higher relative trading costs; some strategies are difficult to implement efficiently as SMAs.

Wash-sale constraints: why tax rules reshape buy-the-dip discipline

Tax-aware management must respect **wash-sale** rules, which (in general terms) can disallow a tax loss if you sell a security at a loss and repurchase the same or a "substantially identical" security within a specified window.

For multi-asset strategists, wash-sale constraints matter because rebalancing and tax-loss harvesting can conflict:

- A threshold rule may signal "buy the loser," but if the investor recently harvested a loss in that exposure, immediate repurchase may jeopardize the loss.

- Even if the trade is economically sensible, the tax outcome may be worse than waiting, using a proxy, or rebalancing elsewhere in the portfolio.

Practical responses used by professionals.

- **Use correlated substitutes (not substantially identical) to maintain exposure.** For example, switch between similar (but not identical) broad exposures where permitted.
- **Shift the rebalance burden across accounts.** If taxable lots are constrained, rebalance using tax-advantaged accounts or overlays.
- **Coordinate TLH and rebalancing calendars.** Treat them as one integrated process, not two separate playbooks.

The key governance message: **in taxable portfolios, rebalancing is not only a trading problem; it is also a compliance-and-tax-lot problem.**

Tax-aware rebalancing: a disciplined modification of the prior section's rules

Tax-aware rebalancing does *not* abandon risk control. It changes the order of operations and the definition of "cost."

Step 1: Compute drift at the total portfolio level

You still begin with the policy targets and compute current weights $\tilde{w}_i$. Threshold corridors remain useful because they reduce unnecessary turnover.

Step 2: Identify the least-tax-cost funding sources

When an asset class is overweight and must be sold, rank sale candidates by:

- **Tax-advantaged accounts first** (no current tax from realizations).
- **Taxable lots with losses** (realizing losses can offset gains).
- **Taxable lots with small gains or long-held gains** (depending on the investor's situation and constraints).
- **Taxable lots with large embedded gains last** (these represent a deferred tax liability; selling converts it into a current tax bill).

Step 3: Prefer cash flow rebalancing when possible

One of the cleanest ways to reduce tax drag is to rebalance using external and internal cash flows:

- Direct new contributions toward underweights.
- Fund withdrawals from overweights.
- Use income distributions (coupons/dividends) as a natural funding source to correct drift.

This often delivers meaningful drift control with minimal forced realizations.

Step 4: Consider overlays for temporary precision

When you need fast exposure control but want to avoid taxable sales (or the cash markets are illiquid), overlays such as futures can be used to adjust net exposure while deferring cash sales. This is not "free"-it introduces basis risk, roll costs, and operational requirements-but it can be a tax-efficient bridge when used deliberately.

Structural constraints that shape the feasible set

Even an elegant tax-aware plan can fail if it ignores structural realities. Common constraints include:

- **Account segmentation:** targets may need to be met across multiple accounts with different rules, custodians, or legal restrictions.
- **Minimum holding periods / redemption terms:** especially for certain funds and alternatives.
- **Stale pricing and valuation frequency:** private assets may not provide daily marks, complicating drift measurement and corridor triggers.
- **Contribution and withdrawal timing:** real investors have cash flow needs; rebalancing must be designed around them.

The correct response is governance, not improvisation: define in advance how the portfolio will behave when constraints bind.

A practical tax efficiency checklist for multi-asset portfolios

Tax efficiency is best institutionalized as a repeatable checklist that sits next to the rebalancing policy:

- **Classify each sleeve** by expected yield/distribution profile and turnover (tax efficiency).
- **Assign a preferred account type** for each sleeve (taxable vs. tax-advantaged), recognizing real-world capacity limits.
- **Choose the default vehicle** (ETF, mutual fund, SMA) based on expected distributions, customization needs, and operational cost.
- **Write tax-aware rebalancing funding rules:** rebalance in tax-advantaged accounts first; use cash flows; sell losses before gains; avoid large embedded-gain sales unless risk requires it.
- **Define exception protocols:** what triggers an override (e.g., risk limit breach), who approves it, and how it is documented.

Key takeaway: after-tax portfolio design is still portfolio design

Tax efficiency is not a bolt-on optimization; it is part of the core multi-asset process. The same logic that justified threshold rebalancing-trading only when the benefit exceeds the cost-becomes even more important once taxes are included. The best practitioners treat taxes as a real, compounding expense, and they manage it with the same discipline applied to fees, tracking error, and liquidity.

This sets up the next task in lifecycle management: once we have sensible rules for trading and taxes, we need the right **performance metrics** to evaluate what the portfolio is actually delivering-across regimes, in drawdowns, and after all the frictions that make real portfolios different from backtests.

7.3 Performance Metrics and Risk-Adjusted Evaluation

The prior two sections treated portfolio management as an exercise in *implementation realism*. Rebalancing rules convert policy weights into tradable actions while respecting transaction costs. Tax-aware design recognizes that *after-tax compounding* is what investors actually experience, and that the timing and character of returns matter as much as their magnitude.

This section completes the loop: once we have a portfolio that can be implemented and governed, we need to evaluate whether it is succeeding. The central mistake in performance review is to default to a single metric-most commonly the Sharpe ratio-and then reverse-engineer narratives around it. Multi-asset portfolios live through multiple regimes (inflation shocks, growth scares, liquidity crises), and each regime stresses a different dimension of risk. A robust evaluation framework uses a **small set of complementary metrics**, each aligned to a specific objective and failure mode.

Start with the right question: "What problem is the portfolio hired to solve?"

Before choosing metrics, define the portfolio's **job description**. Multi-asset mandates typically fall somewhere on a spectrum:

- **Growth-oriented** (maximize long-run real wealth with tolerable drawdowns),
- **Balanced** (earn equity-like returns with shallower drawdowns),
- **Capital preservation / liability-aware** (minimize large losses and maintain funding stability).

Metrics are only meaningful relative to a stated objective. For example:

- A defensive portfolio with low volatility but occasional deep drawdowns is *not* defensive in the way clients mean it.
- A return-seeking portfolio that avoids drawdowns by holding excessive cash may fail its growth objective even if its Sharpe looks good.

The Sharpe ratio: useful, but easy to misuse

Definition and interpretation

Let R_p be the portfolio return, R_f the risk-free rate, and define excess return $R_p - R_f$. The Sharpe ratio is

$$\text{Sharpe} = \frac{\mathbb{E}[R_p - R_f]}{\sigma(R_p - R_f)}.$$

Interpretation: *excess return per unit of total volatility.* It is a sensible starting point for comparing diversified strategies when returns are approximately symmetric and when volatility is a meaningful proxy for pain.

Why Sharpe is often insufficient in multi-asset portfolios

Three issues are especially important for multi-asset evaluation:

1) Volatility treats upside and downside symmetrically. Many investors do not mind upside volatility; they mind drawdowns and downside surprises. A strategy that occasionally experiences severe losses but is otherwise stable may have an acceptable Sharpe while still being unacceptable in practice.

2) Sharpe can reward "volatility suppression." Strategies that sell convexity (for example, certain carry or short-volatility profiles) can exhibit smooth returns most of the time and a high Sharpe, until a regime shift produces a large drawdown. Multi-asset portfolios that lean heavily on short-vol-like premia may look superior in calm periods and then fail precisely when diversification is most needed.

3) Non-normality and time-varying correlations distort interpretation. Multi-asset returns are often skewed and fat-tailed. Correlations can jump in crises, changing the distribution of outcomes. In such settings, volatility alone is a weak summary of risk.

Sharpe in practice: make it harder to fool yourself

If you use Sharpe (you should), make it *regime-aware* and *implementation-aware*:

- Compute Sharpe on **net-of-fee** returns, and where possible **after-tax** for taxable investors.

- Review Sharpe over multiple windows (e.g., 1-year, 3-year, 5-year, full sample) and compare the stability of the estimate.

- Pair Sharpe with a tail metric (e.g., maximum drawdown) so that "smoothness" is not confused with robustness.

Sortino ratio: focus on downside volatility

Definition

The Sortino ratio modifies Sharpe by penalizing only downside variability relative to a minimum acceptable return (MAR), often set to 0, inflation, or the risk-free rate. Define downside deviation:

$$\sigma_D = \sqrt{\mathbb{E}\left[\min(0, R_p - MAR)^2\right]}.$$

Then:

$$\text{Sortino} = \frac{\mathbb{E}[R_p - MAR]}{\sigma_D}.$$

When Sortino is the right tool

Sortino is especially relevant when:

- the investor's utility is **asymmetric** (downside matters much more than upside),
- the portfolio includes assets with **option-like convexity** (trend, protective overlays) where upside volatility is not "bad,"
- the mandate is framed as **loss control** or **smooth compounding**.

What Sortino can miss

Sortino improves on Sharpe, but it still reduces risk to a single dispersion statistic. Two portfolios can have identical downside deviation while having very different **drawdown paths** (one experiences frequent small losses; the other experiences rare but catastrophic losses). For that, we need drawdown-based measures.

Calmar ratio: reward per unit of drawdown

Definition

The Calmar ratio is typically defined as:

$$\text{Calmar} = \frac{\text{CAGR}}{|\text{Max Drawdown}|},$$

where CAGR is the compound annual growth rate over the measurement window, and Max Drawdown is the maximum peak-to-trough loss over that window (as a positive number in the denominator).

Why Calmar matters for multi-asset investors

In real governance, drawdowns are where strategy abandonment happens:

- Risk committees tighten limits.
- Clients redeem.
- The IPS gets "reinterpreted" under stress.

A portfolio that looks good on Sharpe but suffers deep drawdowns may be uninvestable for the very stakeholders it is meant to serve. Calmar forces the evaluation to acknowledge the **worst observed path**, not just average variability.

Practical cautions

Calmar is path-dependent and sample-dependent:

- Max drawdown depends heavily on the chosen time window; a longer window has more chances to experience a severe drawdown.
- A strategy that has not yet experienced its "bad regime" can look artificially strong.

For this reason, Calmar should be paired with stress testing and scenario analysis (covered elsewhere in a risk-management workflow), not used as a standalone truth.

A minimal multi-metric dashboard (and why each metric earns its place)

For most multi-asset mandates, a compact dashboard is more effective than a long list. A practical set is:

Return and implementation reality.

- **CAGR (net)**: measures realized compounding after fees (and, where relevant, after taxes).
- **Turnover and estimated trading cost**: connects performance back to the rebalancing design of the prior sections.

Dispersion-based risk.

- **Sharpe**: broad efficiency under "normal" conditions.
- **Sortino**: efficiency when downside volatility is the primary concern.

Path-based risk.

- **Max Drawdown** and **time-to-recover**: capture behavioral and governance stress.
- **Calmar**: integrates compounding and drawdown into a single ratio.

This set creates a useful tension: if a portfolio looks strong on Sharpe but weak on Calmar, you have learned something important about its regime behavior.

Matching metrics to regimes: what changes when the market environment changes

Multi-asset portfolios face regimes that alter which risks dominate:

Risk-on growth regimes

Equities tend to lead; correlations across risky assets often rise. In such periods:

- Sharpe may look strong for equity-heavy portfolios.
- The evaluation question becomes: *Are we being paid for extra equity risk, or for true diversification?*

Inflation and rate-shock regimes

Nominal bonds may fail as diversifiers; duration becomes a source of risk rather than ballast. In such periods:

- A portfolio's historical Sharpe can break down because covariance structure changes.
- Downside measures and drawdowns become more informative than long-horizon volatility estimates.

Liquidity and crisis regimes

Correlations can jump toward one across risk assets; bid–ask spreads widen; forced selling pressure appears. In such periods:

- Max drawdown and recovery time become central governance metrics.
- Turnover and trading-cost estimates matter because implementation friction increases exactly when risk is highest.

The meta-lesson is that performance evaluation must be **conditional**: the "right" metric is the one that captures the portfolio's most relevant failure mode in the regime you care about.

Benchmarking: a metric without a reference point is incomplete

Risk-adjusted ratios are not substitutes for a benchmark; they are *complements*. In multi-asset settings, a benchmark might be:

- a policy mix (e.g., 60/40 or a custom strategic allocation),
- a risk-based reference (e.g., risk-parity-like benchmark),
- a liability proxy (for institutions with explicit liabilities).

Two practical points:

- **1. Benchmark selection determines what counts as skill.** If the benchmark embeds the same exposures the portfolio holds, outperformance must come from timing, selection, or implementation advantages.
- **2. Net-of-fee and tax-aware benchmarking is not optional.** A portfolio that "beats" gross benchmarks while delivering inferior net outcomes is failing the investor's actual objective.

A disciplined evaluation sequence for investment committees

To make the discussion repeatable (and less narrative-driven), committees can adopt a standard sequence:

- **1. Confirm objective and constraints** (growth vs. preservation; taxable vs. tax-advantaged; liquidity needs).
- **2. Measure net outcomes** (net-of-fee, and after-tax when relevant): CAGR, tracking error vs. policy benchmark.
- **3. Evaluate dispersion risk** (Sharpe, Sortino) and test stability across windows.
- **4. Evaluate path risk** (max drawdown, recovery time, Calmar).

- **5. Connect results back to process** (turnover, realized tax impacts, rebalancing rule behavior during stress).

This sequence forces the right kind of accountability: if the portfolio underperforms, you can locate whether the failure is due to (i) wrong exposures, (ii) poor implementation and excessive frictions, or (iii) a mismatch between the chosen metrics and the mandate's real objective.

Key takeaway: use multiple metrics, but keep them purpose-built

Moving beyond the Sharpe ratio does not mean abandoning simplicity; it means adopting a small set of metrics that are each tied to a specific investor concern:

- Sharpe for general efficiency,
- Sortino for downside-focused efficiency,
- Calmar (and drawdown measures) for governance reality and regime survival,
- plus net compounding measures that incorporate the frictions emphasized in the previous sections.

With these tools, the next step is to explain *why* results differed from the benchmark-translating outcomes into allocation and selection narratives. That is the role of multi-asset attribution.

7.4 Multi-Asset Attribution

The previous sections established two pillars of real-world portfolio management: (i) you must implement the policy portfolio with disciplined trading rules (rebalancing) while controlling transaction costs and taxes, and (ii) you must evaluate results with metrics that reflect multiple regimes and failure modes, not only volatility.

Attribution is the bridge between those two. Performance metrics tell you *what* happened; attribution aims to explain *why*. A credible attribution framework turns a confusing set of returns into a governance-ready narrative:

> *Did we outperform because we held the right asset classes (allocation), because we selected better instruments within each sleeve (selection), because timing and sizing interacted favorably (interaction), or because implementation frictions (fees, taxes, trading costs) overwhelmed the gross edge?*

This section adapts the classic Brinson-Fachler attribution model to the multi-asset context and highlights practical choices that make the output decision-useful for portfolio managers and stakeholders.

The attribution problem: turning a single number into a story

Suppose the portfolio return over a period is R_P and the benchmark return is R_B. The **active return** (excess return versus benchmark) is

$$R_A = R_P - R_B.$$

Attribution decomposes R_A into components that map onto controllable decisions.

For a multi-asset portfolio, those decisions typically occur at two levels:

- **Top-down allocation:** deviations from benchmark weights across asset classes (equities, nominal rates, credit, inflation-linked, diversifiers, alternatives).
- **Within-sleeve implementation:** instrument and manager selection, and how efficiently exposures are obtained (ETFs, futures, active managers, SMAs, factor tilts).

A well-built attribution system respects this hierarchy; it does not mix "policy decisions" with "implementation noise."

The multi-asset Brinson-Fachler framework

Notation

Partition the portfolio and benchmark into N sleeves (asset classes or policy buckets). For sleeve i:

- $w_{P,i}$: portfolio weight in sleeve i (beginning of period or average weight; choose one convention and stick to it).
- $w_{B,i}$: benchmark weight in sleeve i.
- $r_{P,i}$: portfolio return within sleeve i (as implemented).
- $r_{B,i}$: benchmark return for sleeve i (the sleeve index return).
- R_B: total benchmark return.

Then

$$R_P = \sum_{i=1}^{N} w_{P,i}\, r_{P,i}, \qquad R_B = \sum_{i=1}^{N} w_{B,i}\, r_{B,i}.$$

Brinson-Fachler decomposition

A common Brinson-Fachler form decomposes active return into:

- **Allocation effect** (asset-class timing / overweight-underweight decisions),
- **Selection effect** (security/manager selection within sleeves),
- **Interaction effect** (how allocation and selection combine),

using R_B as a reference level for allocation (the "Fachler" adjustment). One standard set of definitions is:

$$\begin{aligned} Allocation_i &= (w_{P,i} - w_{B,i})\,(r_{B,i} - R_B), \\ Selection_i &= w_{B,i}\,(r_{P,i} - r_{B,i}), \\ Interaction_i &= (w_{P,i} - w_{B,i})\,(r_{P,i} - r_{B,i}). \end{aligned}$$

Summing across sleeves,

$$R_A = \sum_{i=1}^{N} \left(Allocation_i + Selection_i + Interaction_i\right).$$

Intuition (why these terms make sense).

- Allocation compares the sleeve benchmark return $r_{B,i}$ to the total benchmark return R_B. Overweighting a sleeve only helps if that sleeve outperforms the overall benchmark.
- Selection measures how well you implemented within the sleeve, assuming benchmark weights.
- Interaction captures the "cross term": you were overweight (or underweight) and also had positive (or negative) selection within that sleeve.

What changes in a multi-asset setting (versus equities-only attribution)

Classic attribution examples often assume an equity benchmark partitioned into sectors. Multi-asset portfolios introduce additional complications; ignoring them can produce misleading attribution.

1) You must define sleeves that match governance decisions

Sleeves should map to decisions the committee actually controls. For example:

- **Equities:** US, ex-US developed, EM (or a single global equity sleeve if that is how decisions are made).
- **Rates:** nominal duration sleeve (or separate sleeves for US duration vs global hedged).
- **Credit:** IG, HY, EM debt.

- **Inflation:** TIPS, real assets.
- **Diversifiers/alternatives:** trend, macro, defensive overlays, illiquid alternatives (often with special handling).

If the IPS defines policy at a coarse level (say, Equity / Fixed Income / Diversifiers), an attribution done at a finer level (say, 15 sub-sleeves) can create a false sense of precision and invite overreaction.

2) Currency and hedging must be treated consistently

If the benchmark is currency-hedged but the portfolio is not (or vice versa), the attribution will misclassify currency outcomes as allocation or selection. Decide explicitly:

- Is currency exposure a separate sleeve (a deliberate active decision)?
- Or is currency embedded inside each sleeve benchmark (a structural choice)?

Either can work, but inconsistency guarantees confusion.

3) Derivatives and overlays complicate weights and returns

Futures, swaps, and overlay programs can create exposures without large market value. Simple market-value weights may understate true risk exposure.

Two practical approaches:

- **Notional or delta-adjusted weights** for overlay sleeves (more exposure-faithful).
- **Keep overlay as its own sleeve** with explicit benchmark (e.g., "zero return" benchmark for an overlay mandate) so its contribution is not hidden inside other sleeves.

The correct choice depends on the portfolio's design. The non-negotiable requirement is that the method is documented and stable.

4) Alternatives and stale pricing require governance language

Illiquid alternatives often report smoothed returns. Attribution will then show "low volatility and steady selection alpha," which can be an artifact of appraisal smoothing rather than true economic behavior.

A practical governance fix is to:

- attribute alternatives at a **higher level** (one sleeve),
- emphasize **longer horizons** for evaluation,
- supplement attribution with **cash-flow-based measures** (e.g., PME-style comparisons) when relevant.

From gross to net: including fees and implementation frictions

Brinson attribution is typically performed on gross-of-fee sleeve returns, and then fees are handled separately. For real-world lifecycle management, stakeholders care about net outcomes, so you should explicitly show the drag.

$$R_P^{net} = R_B + (Allocation + Selection + Interaction) - Fees - Implementation_{D}$$

In many institutions, "Implementation Drag" is hard to measure precisely. That is not an excuse to omit it; instead:

- show explicit fees exactly,
- estimate trading costs via implementation shortfall,
- treat taxes (in taxable mandates) as a separate, reported line item when possible.

What you want to avoid is a situation where committees debate allocation and selection while the dominant performance driver is an unreported friction.

A manager's reading of the three effects

To make attribution actionable, each term should point to a different remedial action:

Allocation effect is about policy tilts and timing. If allocation drives underperformance, ask:

- Were we deliberately overweight the wrong sleeve (a forecast error)?
- Or did drift/rebalancing rules cause unintended overweights (a process error)?
- Did correlations shift so that our "diversifier" did not diversify in this regime (a structural assumption error)?

Selection effect is about implementation quality within sleeves. If selection is negative:

- Was the chosen manager/instrument structurally disadvantaged (fees, constraints)?
- Was the sleeve benchmark appropriate, or was it mismatched to the mandate?
- Did tax-aware constraints force suboptimal trades or prevent efficient rebalancing?

Interaction effect is about sizing skill (or lack thereof). Positive interaction often means you overweighted the sleeves where you also had good selection. Negative interaction can signal "adding to the wrong implementation." It is frequently the most revealing term because it indicates whether active risk was concentrated where you were actually skillful.

A waterfall narrative: the committee-friendly way to present attribution

Attribution becomes governance-ready when it is presented as a reconciliation from benchmark return to portfolio return. A waterfall chart is ideal because it forces additivity and prevents storytelling that does not tie to arithmetic.

The recommended order is:

- Start with **Benchmark Return**.
- Add **Allocation Effect**.
- Add **Selection Effect**.
- Add **Interaction Effect**.
- Subtract **Fees** (and optionally a separate line for other implementation drag if available).
- End at **Portfolio Return**.

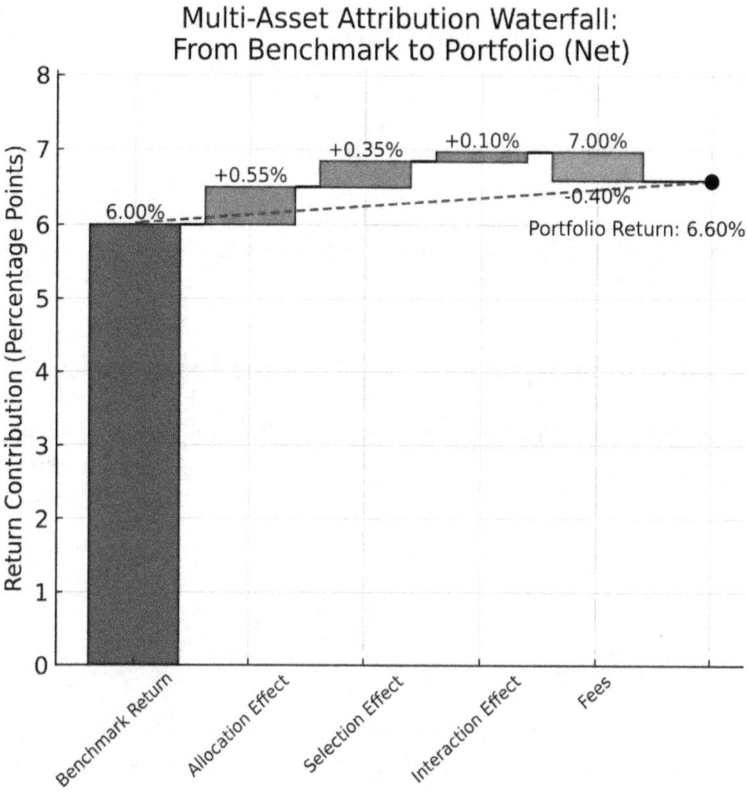

Practical implementation choices (and their consequences)

Attribution is arithmetic, but the inputs are policy choices. Two teams can compute different attributions from the same portfolio if they make different conventions. To keep attribution credible:

Use a clear weight convention

For each period, decide whether $w_{P,i}$ and $w_{B,i}$ are:

- beginning-of-period weights (simple, but can misstate decisions if large intra-period flows occur),
- average weights (often more representative),
- or a more frequent linking approach (more accurate, more complex).

The best practice is to match the convention to governance needs and data availability, then keep it consistent across time.

Linking across periods matters for long horizons

Attribution over many periods requires linking single-period effects. Additive linking is intuitive but can drift from the geometric reality of compounding. Geometric linking respects compounding but is less intuitive.

A practical governance approach:

- Use single-period (monthly/quarterly) attribution for decision accountability.
- Report long-horizon attribution with a clearly stated linking method, and emphasize that it is an approximation to a compounded reality.

Separate "beta timing" from "alpha selection" when possible

In multi-asset portfolios, "selection" can be contaminated by factor tilts. For example, selecting a value-tilted equity manager may outperform the broad equity benchmark due to factor exposure, not security selection skill.

If the organization's governance distinguishes factor tilts from manager skill, consider a two-stage framework:

- Attribute at the sleeve level (allocation/selection/interaction).

- Within sleeves, further decompose selection into factor exposures versus residual alpha (where feasible).

This is not always necessary, but it prevents misunderstanding of what the portfolio is truly being paid for.

Key takeaway: attribution is performance governance

Multi-asset attribution is not an academic exercise; it is a governance tool that:

- makes performance explanations additive and auditable,
- separates policy-level decisions from implementation outcomes,
- highlights whether active risk was taken in the right places,
- forces fees and frictions to be acknowledged explicitly.

When used consistently, attribution also reinforces process discipline: if the portfolio's allocation effect repeatedly drives outcomes, your edge is top-down (or your errors are top-down). If selection dominates, manager and vehicle choice are the primary levers. And if fees and implementation drag consistently erase gross skill, the lifecycle management problem is not forecasting-it is structure.

The remaining challenge is human: even the best-designed process can be undermined by behavior under stress. That is the focus of the final section on behavioral pitfalls and process discipline.

7.5 Behavioral Pitfalls and Process Discipline

The earlier sections treated the portfolio as a system that can be engineered: rebalancing rules translate targets into trades; tax-aware design minimizes avoidable leakage; metrics and attribution turn results into interpretable diagnostics. None of those tools matter, however, if the human operators abandon the system at the worst possible time.

This final section addresses the **behavioral and governance layer** of multi-asset investing. The core claim is simple:

> *Most long-horizon portfolio failure is not caused by a lack of intelligence, but by a lack of pre-commitment.*

Process discipline is how you convert a good strategy into a strategy that survives. It does not eliminate judgment; it *constrains* judgment so that decisions are made consistently, with documentation, and with a bias toward rules that were agreed upon in calm markets rather than invented in panic.

Why multi-asset portfolios are behaviorally hard to run

Multi-asset investing is uniquely vulnerable to behavioral errors because it combines:

- **Competing narratives.** In any regime, at least one sleeve looks "obviously wrong" in hindsight (e.g., holding duration during a rate shock, holding diversifiers during an equity melt-up).
- **Delayed feedback.** Diversifiers and risk-control overlays can underperform for long periods before paying off, making them psychologically difficult to hold.
- **Implementation frictions.** Transaction costs and taxes make it harder to "just fix it," increasing regret and second-guessing.
- **Committee dynamics.** Multi-asset portfolios are often governed by groups, amplifying social and career incentives.

The result is a predictable pattern: portfolios are redesigned (or de-risked) *after* losses, and diversified sleeves are sold *after* they disappoint-often shortly before they are needed again.

The main behavioral pitfalls (and how they show up operationally)

Behavioral finance becomes useful when it is translated into observable failure modes. The following pitfalls are common in real investment organizations:

Loss aversion and the asymmetry of pain

Losses hurt more than gains feel good. Operationally, this can cause:

- **Premature de-risking** after a drawdown (selling equities or credit into weakness).
- **Overweighting "comfort assets"** (cash, short duration) at precisely the wrong time.
- **Refusal to rebalance** into losers even when corridors trigger, because the trade feels like "adding to the mistake."

Recency bias and performance chasing

Recent returns dominate beliefs about the future. Operationally:

- Strategies are hired after strong multi-year runs and fired after inevitable mean reversion.
- Diversifiers are cut after they "haven't worked lately," typically during the late stages of a trend.

Action bias and the need to "do something"

In volatile markets, stakeholders demand action. Operationally:

- Trading increases *because* volatility increases, even though spreads and impact are worst then.
- Committees deviate from policy weights without a coherent replacement framework.

Confirmation bias and narrative lock-in

Teams seek information that supports prior decisions. Operationally:

- Attribution is used as a storytelling tool rather than a diagnostic tool.
- Data is filtered to emphasize the regime where the current portfolio looks best.

Career risk and institutional herding

The institutional version of "fear of looking stupid alone." Operationally:

- Portfolios drift toward consensus exposures near peaks ("everyone owns it") and away from unpopular hedges.
- Decisions are optimized for minimizing short-term regret rather than maximizing long-term expected utility.

The Investment Policy Statement (IPS) as a binding contract

The most effective behavioral tool in institutional investing is not a forecast model; it is a document: the **Investment Policy Statement (IPS)**. Properly written, an IPS serves as a **pre-commitment device**-a contract between the investor and their future, stressed self.

A strong IPS has three properties:

- 1. **Clarity:** it states what the portfolio is designed to do and what it is *not* designed to do.
- 2. **Actionability:** it translates beliefs into specific rules (rebalancing corridors, risk limits, liquidity buffers).
- 3. **Enforceability:** it defines who can act, under what conditions, and with what documentation.

What an IPS must specify (to prevent emotional drift)

At minimum, a multi-asset IPS should include:

Objective and horizon.

- Return objective stated in real terms where relevant (e.g., inflation + spread).
- Primary risk objective (e.g., maximum tolerable drawdown, funding ratio volatility, or volatility target).

Strategic allocation and risk budget.

- Target weights (or ranges) for each sleeve.
- A statement of the portfolio's intended diversifiers and why they are held (so they are not treated as "dead weight" during calm regimes).

Rebalancing rules.

- Calendar and/or threshold-based triggers.
- Priority rules (which accounts and sleeves are used to fund trades first).
- Conditions under which bands may be temporarily widened (and who approves it).

Tax and structural constraints.

- Asset location policy (what belongs in taxable vs tax-advantaged accounts).
- Vehicle constraints (acceptable wrappers, liquidity terms).

Risk controls and escalation.

- Explicit risk limits (e.g., maximum equity exposure, maximum duration, maximum leverage).

- Stress triggers and what happens when they are hit (monitoring steps, meeting cadence, permissible actions).

Performance evaluation and attribution standards.

- Benchmarks for each sleeve and for the total portfolio.
- Attribution method and reporting frequency.

The IPS is the place where the logic of this chapter becomes enforceable: rebalancing, tax awareness, evaluation, and attribution are not optional behaviors-they are the agreed operating system.

Governance structures: turning process into behavior

An IPS without governance is a wish. Governance provides enforcement, documentation, and accountability. The core components are:

Investment committee design

Effective committees are engineered, not improvised. Key elements:

- **Defined roles:** decision makers, advisors, implementers, and risk monitors are not the same function.
- **Voting rules and quorum:** decisions in a crisis should not depend on who happens to be available.
- **Decision rights:** what can staff do autonomously (e.g., routine rebalancing), and what requires committee approval (e.g., changing targets)?

Two-speed decision making: routine vs extraordinary actions

Most failures occur when extraordinary actions are taken with routine authority. A robust system uses two speeds:

- **Routine actions (rules-based):** rebalancing within the IPS, cash-flow rebalancing, tax-loss harvesting within constraints.
- **Extraordinary actions (deliberative):** changing strategic weights, changing benchmarks, terminating managers, adding leverage, suspending rebalancing.

This prevents "strategy drift" disguised as "implementation."

Pre-mortems and scenario playbooks

A pre-mortem asks: *If this portfolio fails, how will it fail?* Common failure narratives include:

- Diversifiers fail in the next crisis because they were implemented incorrectly or sized too small.
- The portfolio is forced to sell risk assets due to liquidity needs.
- Taxes and turnover silently destroy after-tax performance.

The output should be a short playbook: what data will we look at, who meets, what actions are permitted, and what actions are forbidden absent IPS revision.

The "Ulysses pact" approach to drawdowns

A classic governance idea is the **Ulysses pact**: you bind yourself in advance so that, under stress, you cannot take impulsive actions that your calm self would reject.

In investing, an effective Ulysses pact typically includes:

- **Explicit drawdown checkpoints** (e.g., at −10%, −15%, −20%) that trigger a predefined process, not a predefined trade.
- **A forced sequence of questions** before any de-risking: 1. Is the portfolio still within risk limits and rebalancing bands?
  2. Is the drawdown explainable by known risk exposures (as designed), or is there a structural break?

3. What does attribution say: allocation, selection, interaction, fees?
4. Are liquidity and cash needs covered?

- **A default action bias toward the policy:** if constraints are not breached and the thesis is intact, the default is to follow the pre-committed rebalancing rule, not to improvise.

This structure matters because the worst time to redesign a portfolio is when volatility is high, narratives are extreme, and stakeholders are emotionally overloaded.

Process discipline as an "implementation alpha"

Process is not merely defensive; it can be a source of edge because it prevents value-destructive behavior. The "alpha" comes from:

- **Buying when it is hardest to buy** (rebalancing into drawdowns within corridors).
- **Selling when it is hardest to sell** (trimming euphoric overweights).
- **Avoiding cost explosions** (not trading aggressively in illiquid conditions without a strong reason).
- **Avoiding tax mistakes** (not realizing large gains impulsively when other funding sources exist).

In this sense, the behavioral layer connects back to the chapter's earlier engineering layer: discipline is what allows the rebalancing rules and tax-aware structure to actually operate as intended.

A practical discipline checklist for portfolio managers

To make discipline operational, many teams use a checklist that must be completed before making discretionary changes:

- 1. **State the decision in one sentence.** (What are we changing, exactly?)
- 2. **Cite the IPS clause.** (Is this action authorized as routine, or does it require an IPS revision?)
- 3. **Quantify the trade-off.** (Expected tracking error change, turnover, tax impact, liquidity impact.)
- 4. **Consult attribution.** (Is underperformance allocation, selection, interaction, or friction?)
- 5. **Run a reversal test.** (If markets mean-revert tomorrow, will we regret this decision?)
- 6. **Document the counterargument.** (What would prove this decision was wrong?)
- 7. **Define the review date and exit criteria.** (When do we revisit, and what data changes our mind?)

This checklist does not eliminate discretion; it forces discretion to be accountable.

Key takeaway: governance is the portfolio's immune system

A multi-asset portfolio is not only a set of exposures; it is a **governed process** operating through time. Rebalancing design controls drift, tax-aware structure protects compounding, metrics and attribution provide diagnostic feedback, and governance prevents the human tendency to override the system at exactly the wrong moment.

The most successful multi-asset investors therefore treat process discipline as a first-class design variable. In calm markets, they write rules. In stressed markets, they follow them.

www.ingramcontent.com/pod-product-compliance
Lightning Source LLC
LaVergne TN
LVHW010916300926
849194LV00025B/249